Reading Like a Historian

Teaching Literacy in Middle and High School History Classrooms

Sam Wineburg, Daisy Martin,
and Chauncey Monte-Sano

Teachers College, Columbia University
New York and London

To Rachel Lotan

for her support, for her imagination

Published by Teachers College Press, 1234 Amsterdam Avenue, New York, NY 10027

Library of Congress Cataloging-in-Publication Data

Wineburg, Samuel S.
Reading like a historian : teaching literacy in middle and high school history classrooms / Sam Wineburg, Daisy Martin, and Chauncey Monte-Sano.
p. cm.
Includes bibliographical references and index.
ISBN 978-0-8077-5213-5 (pbk. : alk. paper)
1. Reading (Middle school)–United States. 2. Reading (Secondary)–United States. 3. Middle school teaching–United States. 4. High school teaching–United States. I. Martin, Daisy. II. Monte-Sano, Chauncey. III. Title.
LB1632.W565 2011
428.4071'2–dc22 2011005108

ISBN 978-0-8077-5213-5 (paper)

Printed on acid-free paper
Manufactured in the United States of America

18 17 16 15 14 13 12 11 8 7 6 5 4 3

Contents

Introduction

Born in the glorious year of 1776, Gabriel Prosser died an inglorious death. Prosser fomented a slave revolt in Richmond, Virginia, but was apprehended before he could carry it out. On October 31, 1800, his body dangled from Richmond's gallows.

Benjamin Gitlow, born in 1891, edited a newsletter called *The Revolutionary Age* and wrote a book called *The Left Wing Manifesto.* In February 1920 Gitlow was convicted under New York's Criminal Anarchy Law for "advocating the overthrow of the government."[1] He appealed his case to the Supreme Court. He lost.

Unless you have a special interest in foiled slave revolts or socialists of the 1920s, odds are that you've heard of neither Gabriel Prosser nor Benjamin Gitlow–even if you teach history. Yet both figures appear among the names, dates, and themes jammed into the 2006 National Assessment of Educational Progress ("The Nation's Report Card"), a test designed to measure the history deemed "essential" to all Americans.[2]

For too many of our students, history has become an endless procession of Prossers and Gitlows. Is it any wonder that faced with a term like "historical thinking," many scratch their heads, stumped by an alleged connection between "history" and "thinking"? And teachers, staggering under standards documents thicker than the Los Angeles phone book, find themselves as frustrated trying to teach all of this information as their students are trying to retain it.

The book you are holding offers an alternative to the vicious cycle of teaching students facts that will soon evaporate into thin air. Facts are crucial to historical understanding, but there's only one way for them to take root in memory: Facts are mastered by engaging students in historical questions that spark their curiosity and make them passionate about seeking answers. Did 10-year-old Matoaka, known to the rest of the world as Pocahontas, save Captain John Smith from mortal danger, or was this a figment of Smith's supple imagination, a spicy tale designed to boost book sales for his 1624 *Generall Historie of Virginia, New England & the Summer Isles* (Chapter 1)? Was Abraham Lincoln a racist? Depends. Is racism an ethereal quality unaffected by time and place, or are all historical judgments, particularly moral ones, conditioned by circumstance and conventional wisdom (Chapter 3)? Did Federal policy lead to the Dust Bowl crisis? Or was the real crisis caused by arrogance, the belief that armed with new technologies, human beings were immune to the fluctuations of Mother Nature (Chapter 6)? Each question sends us back to the original sources to formulate arguments that admit no easy answer. Each question requires us to marshal facts to argue our case. But facts isolated from the questions that give them meaning no more constitute historical understanding than bands of roving teenagers with AK-47s slung around their necks constitute an army.

In an age where "I found it on the Internet" masquerades as knowledge, history serves as a vital counterweight to intellectual sloppiness. When a video uploaded from a cell phone in Tehran reaches San Francisco in half a second, history reminds us to start with basic questions: Who sent it? Can it be trusted? What angle did the Flip video miss? In the era of the blogosphere, there's no shortage of forces telling students what to think. Gasping for air beneath mounds of information, today's students have never been in greater need of ways to make sense of it all. This is where *Reading Like a Historian* comes in.

Reading Like a Historian might first seem like a frill when so few students actually go on to become professional historians. But that's precisely the point. Because so few students pursue historical study beyond high school, it is crucial that they learn to read like historians in their middle and high school social studies classes. Historians have developed powerful ways of reading that allow them to see patterns, make sense of contradictions, and formulate reasoned interpretations when others get lost in the forest of detail and throw up their hands in frustration. Researchers of historical thinking have distilled these ways of knowing into practices that can be taught to students at all levels. We're not talking here about some esoteric procedure for working in an archive. Rather, the practices historians have developed can be used to make sense of the conflicting voices that confront us every time we turn on Fox News or MSNBC. Put simply, the skills cultivated by *Reading Like a Historian* provide essential tools for citizenship.

Consider the differences between how historians and high school students approach primary source documents. Many students, even some of our best readers, start with the first word at the top of a page and end their reading with the last. The attribution at the document's end receives scant attention or is ignored altogether. Historians, on the other hand, begin a document at the end, by *sourcing* it. They glance at the first couple of words to get their bearings, but then dart immediately to the document's bottom, zooming in on its attribution. Who wrote this source and when? Is it a diary entry? A memo obtained through the Freedom of Information Act? A leaked e-mail? Is the author in a position to know firsthand, or is this account based on hearsay? Even before approaching a document's substance, historians have formed a list of questions that create a mental framework to hang the details that follow. Most important, sourcing transforms the act of reading from passive reception to an engaged and passionate interrogation. For historians, the act of reading is not about gathering lifeless information to repeat on a test, but engaging a human source in spirited conversation.

Consider a second pillar of *Reading Like a Historian*: the practice of *contextualization*–the notion that events must be located in place and time to be properly understood. Faced with Abraham Lincoln's statement that he had "no purpose to introduce political and social equality between the white and black races" (Chapter 3), many students shudder in disbelief or conclude that what they've been taught about the 16th president belongs in the trash with the other lies their teachers told them.

But historians–even those who know little about the Civil War–start from a different place. Instead of issuing conclusions, they begin with questions. What was the context for Lincoln's words? (A debate with Stephen A. Douglas for a fiercely contested senatorial seat.) When and where were these words uttered? (On September 22, 1858, in Ottawa, Illinois, a hotbed of anti-Black sentiment.) What kind of people made up the audience? (Those largely supportive of Douglas and suspicious of Lincoln.) Just as students in Language Arts class are taught about similes and alliteration, so history students must be taught to *source* historical authors and to *contextualize* historical documents. When they leave our classes, students get to practice these skills every time they open their browsers to read the daily news.

Sourcing and contextualization are central to *Reading Like a Historian* and are what reading specialists mean when they refer to *discipline-specific literacy*. Each of our chapters shows you how to apply these and other ways of *Reading Like a Historian* in your classroom. We organize each of our eight chapters around a historical question in American history, beginning with Exploration and Colonization and the events at Jamestown and ending with the Cuban Missile Crisis (see Table I.1). Obviously a book of this length can't cover every topic in the curriculum. But what we can do is give you practice in using this approach with key events and provide you with models for extending these practices to other topics. Each chapter stands on its own. But you will also notice that the core concepts we introduce at the beginning build on one another as we go along. For many students, *Reading Like a Historian* will be a departure from working with textbooks and worksheets. Students will need repeated practice across topics and time periods to benefit most from this approach.

We begin each chapter with an introductory essay that sets the stage. The goal of these essays is not to supply content for content's sake, but to give you the historical background necessary for teaching these topics to middle and high school students. We weave into our discussions insights gleaned from using these documents with students in our research studies.

Following each essay are all the materials you'll need to teach this topic to your students–primary documents, charts, graphic organizers, visual images, and political cartoons–as well as suggestions for where to find additional resources on the Internet. Rather than providing scripted lesson plans, we lay out flexible scenarios for using these materials in different ways. These scenarios are written to stimulate your imagination, for no two teaching situations are the same and you will need to adapt these scenarios to fit your own classroom. Similarly, we provide ideas for ways to make students' thinking visible, so that you can better engage their underlying conceptions and beliefs. With each chapter we also provide ideas for assessing students' understanding of core historical ideas. Assessment ideas appear in **bold** in the text and are highlighted with an icon in the margin of each teaching scenario, as shown here.

In our professional development workshops with teachers, we sometimes encounter the view that original sources and open historical questions are best suited to our top students and are less appropriate for students reading below grade level. *We hold the opposite position.* We believe that it is our struggling readers who *most* need instruction in learning how to read like a historian.

Research has shown over and over that a key to adolescent literacy is exposing students to a rich diet of texts that mix genre and style "at a variety of difficulty levels and on a variety of topics."[3] It is precisely those students who find reading a textbook challenging and have never encountered sources in their other classes who most need to be exposed to historical questions and the documents that address them. Adolescents become fluent readers when their horizons are broadened. The

Table I.1. Overview of the Book

Chapter	U.S. History Unit	Core Question(s)	Key Historical Thinking Concept	Teaching Strategy
1. Pocahontas	Exploration & Colonization	Did Pocahontas rescue John Smith?	What is history vs. myth?	Inquiry lesson
2. Lexington Green	American Revolution	What happened at Lexington Green?	Questioning sources–*Sourcing*	Image analysis; explicit instruction in sourcing
3. Abraham Lincoln	Civil War	Was Lincoln a racist? How should we judge the past?	Questioning sources–*Contextualization*	Structured Academic Controversy (SAC); explicit instruction in contextualizing
4. Columbus	Immigration (late 19th c.)	Which date matters most: 1492 or 1892?	Questioning sources–*Contextualization*	Political cartoon analysis; lesson in establishing context
5. Edison & Technology	1920s	Electricity and women's work: Who really benefited, and when?	Questioning sources–*Corroboration & Making Generalizations*	Internet-based lesson; lesson in corroboration
6. Dust Bowl	1930s/ Great Depression	What caused the Dust Bowl? What story gets told?	Narrative–considering multiple stories and causes	Opening Up the Textbook (OUT) lesson
7. Rosa Parks	Civil Rights Movement	Where did Rosa Parks sit? Why did the Montgomery Bus Boycott succeed?	Narrative–Questioning accounts	Analysis of student writing and legal documents
8. Cuban Missile Crisis	Cold War	Was WW III prevented because "the other guy blinked"?	Narrative–textbooks, evidence, & changing stories	OUT & comparison of different textbook stories

documentary record, a treasury of letters, diaries, secret communiqués, official promulgations, public speeches, and the like, confronts a reader with varied styles and textures of language that push the bounds of literacy. It is this rich diet, not the thin gruel of textbooks, that our students most need.

"But wait a second," you might be thinking. "How in the world are students reading below grade level or for whom English is a second language supposed to deal with primary documents filled with odd terms and obscure vocabulary?" We provide three strategies for dealing with this very real problem.

First, we've selected our documents with precision and trimmed them to the point where they convey the essence of a historical problem. Sources provide students with an opportunity for close reading. But remember, the ability to maintain concentration with a difficult text is inversely proportional to its length. Primary sources are the place to teach students to slow down and read closely, to think deeply about word choice and subtext.

Second, to better focus students' attention, we've *modified* documents with the strategic use of ellipses. In cases where certain vocabulary and turns of phrases still pose challenges, we include a Word Bank with key definitions at the bottom of the document. For some sources, we include a head note ("Note") to help orient students to what follows.

Third, in cases where the original language of a source poses a barrier to most students, we have *adapted* primary documents, conventionalizing spelling, simplifying syntax, and occasionally introducing changes in vocabulary–all the while trying to retain as much of their original texture and feel as we can. Alongside most adapted documents we've included the original or listed an easy-to-locate web address for finding it.

Although our three names appear on the cover, many others have generously contributed to this book and the ideas it contains. Jacob Douglas wrote the first draft of the essay accompanying Chapter 2. Jack Schneider was the author of Chapters 4 and 8. The ideas in this book were put to the test in classrooms between 1998 and 2000 in a National Science Foundation project, *Promoting Argumentation Through History and Science* (PATHS), conducted at the University of Washington with colleagues Reed Stevens, Leslie Herrenkohl, and Philip Bell.[4] Wendy Ewbank, a Washington State "Golden Apple" Award-winning teacher, played an important role in PATHS, as did our program officer at the National Science Foundation, Elizabeth VanderPutten.

It was at Stanford that the *Reading Like a Historian* approach gained momentum. Our training ground was a course for future history teachers in the Stanford Teacher Education Program (STEP). Abby Reisman, Brad Fogo, and Eric Shed contributed substantially to this effort. And it was Abby who took these ideas and brought them to an entirely different level in an ambitious field study in five San Francisco high schools. Over the years we've been blessed with the unflagging support of Rachel Lotan, STEP's intrepid director, who encouraged us with her enthusiasm and inspired us with her tireless dedication. The writing of this book was supported by a grant from the Teachers for a New Era Project of the Carnegie Corporation of New York, and that support is gratefully acknowledged.

Finally, we should state what we hope is obvious: This book is no substitute for your textbook, nor does it try to be. What it can do is give you ideas for how to use your textbook creatively and how to compensate for its shortcomings. The exercises in this book will help your students understand that their textbook did not come shrink-wrapped along with the tablets that Moses received on Mount Sinai. We hope that students will come to see their textbook for what it is: another source, sometimes useful, sometimes flawed, often shaped more by the whims of adoption committees and prevailing political winds than anything in the documentary record.[5] Few teachers have the liberty to jettison their state curriculum and go off merrily on their own. But even within the constraints of state standards, 50-minute periods, and an endless regimen of testing, there's room to do good and creative work. This book provides ideas for how to do so.

We are very much interested in your feedback and experience in using this approach. Write to us at readinglikeahistorian@gmail.com, and be sure to check out the additional resources on our websites: the Historical Thinking Matters Project, http://historicalthinkingmatters.org/, and the home page for the Stanford History Education Group, http://sheg.stanford.edu.

CHAPTER 1

Did Pocahontas Rescue John Smith?

Simon van de Passe, Pocahontas, 1616, engraving, 6¾ x 4¾ in., published in John Smith's *Generall Historie*, 1624, Virginia Historical Society, available at http://www.indiana.edu/~wfh/images/pocahontas/pages/aapocengrav1616_jpg.htm

Pocahontas has captured our imaginations for centuries. Daughter of a great Indian chief, eventual bride of an English captain, and the talk of 17th-century London, she has been memorialized through poetry, art, and storytelling by generations. She and John Smith are lodged at the center of our stories about our country's origins: Her rescue of Smith may be the best-known part of the history of the original English Jamestown colony of 1607 and 1608. In 2006, a year before the 400th anniversary of the supposed rescue, new volumes about Pocahontas and John Smith filled the bookstores. You could choose from books written for children or adults, scholars, or leisurely readers. But even after 4 centuries, these new books did not agree on the story to be told. What really happened between Pocahontas and John Smith?

The Walt Disney Company is responsible for the version that many of our students know best. In the 1995 movie, we learned that Pocahontas, a svelte, free-spirited 19-year-old, and John Smith, a dashing hunk of a colonist, fell in love, flouting orders that there should be no contact between the Indians and colonists. In the movie's dramatic climax, Pocahontas prevented Powhatan, her father and chief of the tribe, from cudgeling Smith to death. Her act of courage and compassion led to both sides laying down arms, and ushered in a new era of tolerance between two warring cultures. It is a tidy story, complete with drama, romance, and a moral lesson. But people, societies, and their histories are rarely this tidy (let alone so attractive and musical). Did this rescue really happen?

Historiographical Debate

Read contemporary works and you will not find a straightforward answer. In journalist David Price's book, *Love and Hate in Jamestown: John Smith, Pocahontas, and the Heart of a New Nation*, you will find what the title suggests: a romantic tale of Smith and Pocahontas where she is attracted to the older traveler and saves him from death.[1] Price calls the rescue (a title of one chapter) the "most famous and controversial journey of Smith's career" and asserts that the evidence indicates the rescue did happen.[2] He then relegates a discussion of the controversy to the margins of his book so it doesn't divert the reader from his main story. Historian Camilla Townsend's book, *Pocahontas and the Powhatan Dilemma*, published just a year after Price's, unequivocally states that the rescue did *not* happen.[3] Both authors agree that controversy surrounds the story of Pocahontas's rescue of John Smith, both use the same historical evidence to make their case, but each comes to opposite conclusions. We have a historical problem: Did Pocahontas rescue John Smith?

The story of the rescue is not new. Generations of Americans have grown up hearing it. So how do we know whether it happened? Where did the story come from if its authenticity is debatable?

The answer is, from John Smith himself. The only eyewitness to the supposed event who left a paper trail was Smith, but his accounts of the event are riddled with inconsistencies. The first, written in 1608, the year the rescue supposedly occurred, makes no mention of the threat or rescue, and uses words like "friendship" and "kindness" to describe meeting Powhatan (see Source 1.1; all Sources are located at the end of each chapter). "Hee kindly welcomed me with good wordes and great platters of sundrie Victuals, assuring mee his friendship, and my libertie within foure days."[4] On the other hand, another account, written 16 years afterward, uses words like "barbarous" and "fearful" to describe the meeting with Powhatan, and this is where we first hear the famous claim that the chief's daughter, Pocahontas, "laid her owne [head] upon his to save him from death" (see Source 1.2).[5] The entire passage reads:

> Having feasted him after their best barbarous manner they could, a long consultation was held, but the conclusion was, two great stones were brought before Powhatan: then, as many as could layd hands on him, dragged him to them, and thereon laid his head, and being ready with their clubs, to beate out his brains, Pocahontas the King's dearest daughter, when no intreaty could prevaile, got his head in her armes, and laid her owne upon his to save him from death; whereat the Emperour was contented he should live.

Why is the rescue mentioned in one account and not the other? Was Smith scared of being berated as less of a man if the truth about an Indian girl rescuing him came to light? Was he merely trying to describe this new land and unfamiliar peoples in the first account, choosing to omit personal stories? And in the second account, was he capitalizing on Pocahontas's fame following her 1616 voyage to London as Indian princess and wife of John Rolfe, thus casting himself as a character in her early life now that she was dead and unable to respond? (Pocahontas succumbed to smallpox aboard a ship taking her back to Virginia in 1617.) Were his words designed to represent Pocahontas as exceptional, a sympathetic and peaceful Indian who converted to Christianity and differed radically from the rest of the Powhatan peoples who had become fierce enemies of the British in the intervening years?[6]

What do historians make of the contrast between Smith's two accounts? The first historian to publish an attack on John Smith's honesty was Henry Adams, great-grandson of President John Adams. Henry Adams claimed that no thinking person could believe the rescue story, given both Smith's initial silence and the inconsistencies in tone and detail between the two accounts (see Source 1.3).[7] While Adams's argument is reasonable, the year that he penned this critique, 1867, is also telling. Later historians would read Adams's personal letters and find his skepticism politically motivated: attacking Virginia's favorite son, a hero responsible for Jamestown's survival in the early, brutal days of colonization, was in effect a swipe at this state that had been on the wrong side in the Civil War. It would not be the last time that the rescue story was used to send a message that had little to do with the event itself.

Nevertheless, Adams surfaced the historical problem and later historians would continue to try to solve it. Historian Paul Lewis, in *The Great Rogue: A Biography of John Smith*, agreed with Adams about the improbability of a rescue (see Source 1.5).[8] He asked questions about corroborating sources and challenged Smith on what he claimed were embellishments and inconsistencies within his separate accounts. Lewis pointed out that Smith's rescue story first appeared just as Pocahontas was becoming the darling of the *London Gazette* and basking in royal attention.

Other historians took Smith at his word but, even while accepting that this event may have happened, claimed that Smith missed the point. Scholar J. A. Leo Lemay in *The American Dream of Captain John Smith* argued that Smith was a trustworthy author who wrote different accounts for different purposes: to describe the new land in the first account, to promote colonization of it in the second (see Source 1.4).[9] Lemay included another piece of primary evidence to make his case: a letter Smith wrote to Queen Anne in 1616 describing the rescue. Lemay claimed that there was no doubt that the event happened, but that Smith misunderstood its meaning: It was less a rescue than an elaborate native ritual. Historian Philip Barbour agreed, claiming that the event was actually a Native American rite meant to signify death and rebirth, symbolizing Smith's assumption of a new tribal identity under Powhatan's patronage (see Source 1.6).[10] Something obviously happened, but its import was misunderstood by the actor at its center.

To take stock, what exactly *are* the facts of the story? What do these facts mean? While there are no easy answers to these questions, asking them puts us at the heart of the *Reading Like a Historian* approach.

Pocahontas and John Smith are the stuff of American myth. A single paragraph in a 400-year-old account written by an adventurer whom one contemporary called "ambityous unworthy and vaynglorious"[11] spawned a story of which Americans never tire. Our story of Pocahontas, America's favorite Indian princess, usually starts with Smith's rescue, an event that shows her bravery and independence when faced with an evil deed. In fact, the representations we have of these historical figures and of the rescue story have become legitimate objects of study themselves, as they reflect the historical time and place in which they were created.[12]

Henry Adams and the Disney Company are not the only authors to narrate this story to their advantage. Consider John Chapman's painting, *Baptism of Pocahontas at Jamestown, Virginia,* hung in the Capitol Rotunda in 1840 a few years before journalist John O'Sullivan coined the term "manifest destiny," and the work of westward conquest was gaining steam. The painting glorifies Pocahontas's conversion to Christianity, suggesting that bringing Christianity to the Indians is a realistic and noble endeavor (even if, as depicted in the painting, some surly, bad Indians rejected it). Consider, on a more frivolous note, the costly jewelry made of diamonds and pearls that bears Pocahontas's name available at Amazon.com.

And what has the mythologizing of Pocahontas and the rescue story meant for understanding and capturing what really happened? Scholars like anthropologist Helen Rountree and historian Camilla Townsend argue that it has obscured and narrowed our vision of this past.[13] Focusing on an appealing picture of a romantic Indian princess and British captain has blotted out larger stories of British/Powhatan encounters and the groups' evolving relationship as the colonists began to make the Chesapeake their permanent home. Pocahontas's story, reduced to a fairytale, CliffsNotes form, leads students to miss out on learning significant things about this encounter and the peoples involved in it.

The fact that we do not have access to Pocahontas's words leaves us with a deafening silence about the complete story. In fact, all our written sources were composed by British men, and we have no access to the unmediated voices of Pocahontas's people. While Smith, William Strachey, and others left lengthy descriptions of the Indians of the Chesapeake, their accounts are necessarily filtered through the authors' cultural and personal prisms. Historians must read this written evidence closely. Townsend tells her readers that she culled the specifics of the event from reading Smith's accounts and "placing each statement in the context in which it was written and juxtaposing it against confirming or damning external evidence"–essentially doing what historians do best, contextualizing and corroborating text to understand what it tells us about the past.[14] Townsend's explicit treatment of "what the English knew" firmly establishes that we need to know how Smith's contemporaries and compatriots viewed and portrayed Indians and colonization to understand this event and Smith's rival accounts.

Similarly, knowing about the Chesapeake Indians' societies–their routines, rituals, and residences–sheds light on this event and the context in which it occurred. Archeologists and anthropologists have helped in building this knowledge. To document the scope and growth of Powhatan's chiefdom and relations between different Indian tribes and villages, E. Randolph Turner looked to archeological and geographical data to complement the English accounts.[15] He and others analyzed variations and consistencies between unearthed ceramics and their locations, as well as surviving trade goods like copper and sea shell artifacts. Evidence of defensive cliffs surrounding Indian settlements contributes to what we know about how the tribes of the Chesapeake got along. These scholars use the evidence available to them to reconstruct possible Indian perspectives on the encounter.

How much does this compensate for the silence of the peoples most embroiled in these early colonization efforts? It's not clear, but surely a more complete picture of the world of the John Smith/Pocahontas encounter contributes to understanding what is and isn't likely. Meanwhile, new information is being uncovered. In 2003, a site determined to be Werowocomoco, the village where the rescue would have happened, was discovered in Gloucester County, Virginia. Archeologists thrilled in discovering ditches predating the English by more than 150 years, a find that suggested a separation of secular and sacred spaces within the village. Thinner, more fragile pottery shards distinguish the sacred space; scholars have speculated that it may have been Powhatan's living quarters.[16] Archeologists continue to excavate that site for more clues to understanding this people who left no written record.

First, scholars have shown that the Powhatan were not an isolated or loner tribe, but part of an extensive intertribal network on the Chesapeake. Part of the Indian group called the Algonquian by virtue of a shared language and way of life, Chief Powhatan led something akin to a tribal federation. The federation extended more than 6,000 square miles in the Tidewater area of Virginia and grew to more than 30 tribes and 12,000 people under his leadership. Each of these tribes paid tribute to Powhatan and had a chief, or *werowance*, loyal to the federation and Powhatan. Tribes probably joined the federation through war, alliances, and intertribal marriage.

Further, Pocahontas's father was not new to the world of diplomacy or intergroup relations when the English arrived in Jamestown: He was already a powerful leader of diverse groups. Skilled and successful at diplomacy in his world, Townsend calls him "a brilliant strategist"[17] while Barbour uses the word "despotism" to describe his governance.[18] Nor were the British, with their foreign but useful tools, their big ships and strange ways, new to Powhatan. The Spanish had already been to the region and skirmished with the Indians: This was not the first time Europeans had arrived in their midst.

The British colonizers knew of the earlier Spanish efforts, and this influenced their plans and approach. When the *Susan Constant*, *Discovery*, and *Godspeed* arrived, the passengers had designs on colonizing the area, and in fact knew the region as a power vacuum that they hoped to fill. But the British didn't share this view with the natives, and their ineptness and trouble with creating a productive and self-sustaining settlement may have helped their cover story of being temporary visitors. However, it also led to what is now infamously known as "the starving times," and in the first winter of the settlement, Captain John Smith started making voyages upriver to trade tools and beads for corn to save his compatriots from starvation. In his furthest trip up the Chickahominy River, he was captured by Opechancanough, Powhatan's brother, and taken from village to village. In late December Smith was brought before Powhatan at Werowocomoco, 12 miles from Jamestown. This is the site of the rescue story and where the story of Pocahontas begins.

Given her status as icon serving multiple purposes, it is striking how little verifiable knowledge about Pocahontas we actually have. The daughter of Powhatan and an unknown mother was about 9 or 10 years old when she would have first seen the captive John Smith in her village–and when the supposed rescue happened. In the following year, Pocahontas was a frequent visitor to Jamestown. She brought the settlement provisions and was credited by Smith with being responsible for the safe return of some Indian hostages. She translated for the colonists and Indians, and Townsend conjectures that she may be responsible for the sole surviving Algonquian complete sentence recorded by Smith. While the exact nature of her visits is unknown, they seem to be friendly and helpful. However, before the year was up, she stopped visiting the colony and there is a single report that she married an Indian named Kocoom.

She did not appear again in British accounts until she was kidnapped in 1613 by an enterprising Englishman, Captain Samuel Argall. In the intervening years, Smith had returned to England with a gunpowder injury, and hostilities between the Indians and the colonists had accelerated. Hearing that Powhatan's daughter was near his ship, Argall seized the opportunity to use the Indian princess to British advantage. A member of a federation tribe, Patowomeck, helped lure Pocahontas aboard Argall's ship, where she was captured and held for ransom. For 3 months, Powhatan didn't respond to the ransom demands and then partially met them. Upon her release, Pocahontas stayed in Jamestown, under uncertain conditions, and within a year had converted to Christianity and met and married John Rolfe. In 1615, the two had a son, Thomas Rolfe, and the following year, they set sail for England. There, Pocahontas was regarded as an Indian princess and received at the court of King James I and Queen Anne. This is also when Simon Van de Passe produced the only existing portrait of her, an engraving that now hangs in the Smithsonian. Pocahontas's family set sail for their return to Virginia in the spring of 1617, but she fell ill and died before they cleared England. She would have been 19 or 20 years old.

Pocahontas is a romantic and popular historical figure for Americans today, and the rescue is what frames our perception of her. However, the common story that we know about this rescue may be more myth than history. Historians and scholars still debate the truth beyond the myth while pursuing an accurate telling of the story. In recent decades, new attention has been paid to understanding and incorporating Indian perspectives and cultural realities relevant to the event. Barbour, Lemay, Rountree, and Townsend–all of these scholars are attentive to this, but even so, they differ in their interpretations of the event. Questions persist. Is there evidence to convince us that Powhatan's tribe engaged in the kinds of ritual rebirths suggested by Barbour? And if we focus on the rescue, do we miss out on the true historical significance of Pocahontas–as a cultural broker whose interactions with the British, and eventual marriage to Rolfe, were more about diplomacy than affection? Is our focus on her misguided and overblown, given that she was a minor character in the events of the time? How did the rescue story eclipse all else in the American story of the British colonization of the Chesapeake region? At this point, the stories that we tell about Pocahontas and the rescue have taken on a life of their own, separate from any historical evidence. Helen Rountree adds still another twist on what Pocahontas teaches us.

> The story of a young woman firmly rooted in her own culture, held hostage by bellicose newcomers, forcibly and then willingly assimilated into their culture, killed by a mysterious disease, buried far from her homeland, and ultimately used by the dominant society as a symbol for the oppression of her own people is not only an authentic account of Pocahontas's experiences but is also emblematic of the histories of generations of Native people.[19]

The literature and scholarship concerning Pocahontas and John Smith are extensive and lively. From Barbour's compelling story and Lemay's careful and persuasive analysis to Rountree's ethnohistorical approach and Tilton's detailed telling of the making of a myth, the truth behind this story is worth investigating. More important, the story of John Smith's "rescue" lays bare history's weak points and shows us that what so many Americans have taken as fact relies, in fact, on a single (somewhat dubious) source. And when we compare this source to other documents from the same author, questions multiply. Genuine history is about asking questions, which makes the Pocahontas/John Smith story the ideal candidate for initiating our students into the art of historical detection.

Why Teach About John Smith and Pocahontas?

A Manageable Historical Problem to Start Your Course. The Pocahontas/John Smith rescue story is a compelling way to start teaching for historical thinking. While there is no shortage of interpretive work that has been done on the event, the actual documentary record is surprisingly thin. Essentially what this means is that over a few class periods, your students can encounter the main sources that fuel this debate. By reading John

Smith's two conflicting accounts, students are immediately thrust into the center of the controversy and confronted with a historical problem that is not easily solved. Having evaluated the primary documents behind this event, students can return to their textbook's narrative and look at it through new eyes: "How can they write something with such certainty when it's not even clear that it happened?!"

History presented as a series of problems to be explored, rather than a set of stories to be committed to memory, may be a new experience for your students. The early colonial setting of the John Smith/Pocahontas problem means that from the beginning of your course, students can encounter history as a different enterprise than what many of them expect. Identifying and working through a historical problem, complete with guiding questions, varied and contradictory sources, and no single right answer challenges students' ideas that history is static, where the only thinking involved is figuring out how so much material can be memorized. While the narrow question of whether Pocahontas actually rescued John Smith may seem expendable given the curricular terrain, the question's limited scope offers many instructional advantages. Students experience key facets of historical investigation with rich opportunities to think historically, but they are not overwhelmed by the historical record. Complex questions are easier for novices to grasp without dozens of documents.

Are Primary Sources Always "Primary"? Indeed, investigating the Pocahontas/John Smith story offers multiple avenues to developing students' historical understanding. The contrast in Smith's stories challenges students' ideas about first-hand or primary accounts–that is, that they are always the most reliable source for understanding the past. Often students privilege primary sources as reflections of historical truth and don't recognize the need to interrogate them. But here, the primary sources contradict one another, and these contradictions cannot be resolved by appealing to different writers with different perspectives. Why does the same source, John Smith, say different things? Working with the secondary historical interpretations introduces students to more complexity and challenges the simplistic notion that primary sources teach us more than the interpretations of modern-day historians. Scholarship done over the past few centuries provides alternative explanations to Smith's for what this event may have meant to the Powhatan, who, alas, left no written records of their own.

Starting with the Known. Finally, the topic's familiarity is another big advantage. It is the rare student who hasn't heard of Pocahontas or who cannot recite some version of the John Smith/Pocahontas story. This familiarity means that students are likely to be interested in the topic and problem, and be surprised by the fact that historians are still arguing about it. It is easier to work with contradictory sources when they take up a topic that students already know. Once students realize that the story they've been told may be more myth than history, questions about how we know the past take on new meaning. Instead of a numbing list of facts, history becomes an invitation to join a raucous debate about evidence and argument.

How Might You Use These Materials?

Scenario 1 (1–2 Hour Lesson). Did Pocahontas rescue John Smith? Use these sources and tools to engage students in reading and analyzing multiple accounts to create an evidence-based argument about the likelihood of the rescue.

Start off by asking students what they know about Pocahontas and John Smith. Elicit what students know about these individuals and their time, and where they learned it. Some will cite the 1995 Disney *Pocahontas* film. Show the Disney version of the rescue (Chapter 25 of the DVD, or approximately 1:09 into the movie). Use the timeline (Tool 1.1; all Tools are located at the end of chapters) along with any work you have done on the exploration and colonization of the Americas to briefly establish relevant background to the alleged event, then introduce the lesson's guiding question: Did Pocahontas rescue John Smith? In successive rounds, have pairs of students work with document sets and accompanying worksheets to help them answer this question. After each round of documents, lead a whole-class discussion. In this discussion, revisit the guiding question and prompt students to defend their answers with evidence from the documents. Listen for questions that students have generated to highlight how historical digging often leads to more questions.

In the first round, students work with Smith's accounts and accompanying tools (Sources 1.1 and 1.2, Tool 1.2). As they work, listen to whether students recognize that Smith tells contrasting stories in the two sources. Can they identify phrases and details that exemplify this difference? In the second round, students work with two historians' accounts and accompanying tools (Source 1.3, 1.4, Tool 1.3). Again, pay attention to whether students note differences between these accounts. In the optional third round, students tackle the final two historians' accounts and tools (Source 1.5, 1.6, Tool 1.4). Throughout the entire lesson, the question of whether Pocahontas rescued John Smith guides student work and class discussion. **Finally, students write an answer to the question with the requirement that they use evidence (e.g., direct quotes, details, and specifics) from the documents to**

support their argument. You may want to preface the writing assignment by revisiting the Disney movie and asking students to address how the historical sources challenge the well-known animated version of the event. Use Tool 1.5 to structure this assignment.

Targeted list of skills in this scenario

- Evidence-based thinking and argumentation
- Questioning sources
- Synthesizing multiple accounts

Scenario 2 (2–3 Hour Lesson). What is history anyway? Use these sources and tools to make explicit for your students some core features, materials, and vocabulary of historical investigation.

Replicating Scenario 1, begin to integrate direct instruction about the nature of history into your lessons. This additional instruction works best after students have completed the document analysis rounds but before they write their final essay, although it may be integrated after each step.

You might teach your students about the difference between Document Sets 1 and 2, i.e., secondary and primary sources. You could define "source," "evidence," and "interpretation." You can review the students' process of getting smarter about this lesson's guiding question, which included reading, analyzing, and synthesizing the multiple accounts; backing up assertions with evidence; and asking questions of the sources and of themselves to pinpoint what else they would like to know or what they indeed don't know. Point out that historians ask questions about what happened and what it meant. And help students recognize that historical investigation is a recursive process, where one has to continually check claims against the available evidence, and absolute answers are not always possible.

To check for understanding, students can answer the question in writing as they do in Scenario 1. Alternatively, they can address the following question: Why can't we know for certain whether Pocahontas rescued John Smith? Write down a minimum of three reasons.

- **For each reason write at least two specific details or quotes that support that reason.**
- **Compare sources to make your point in at least two instances.**

Students' responses could take the form of a paragraph, essay, talk show interview, or graphic organizer, among other possibilities. This question prompts students to think about what it means to "do" history and the role of historical texts in developing historical interpretations.

Targeted list of skills in this scenario

- Evidence-based thinking and argumentation
- Questioning sources
- Synthesizing multiple accounts
- Building vocabulary specific to the historical discipline
- Identifying how historical knowledge is produced

Scenario 3 (2–3 Hour Lesson). Myth or history, what's the difference? Use these sources and tools to make explicit the evidentiary nature of reconstructing the past and how this contrasts with myth-making.

Students participate in the reading and discussion rounds described in Scenario 1, experiencing how historians must analyze and synthesize multiple accounts to create coherent arguments. However, in this scenario, students subsequently analyze examples of myth-making, including the Disney movie and John Chapman's 1840 painting of Pocahontas that hangs in the Capitol Rotunda.

After looking carefully at each artistic piece, students consider the questions: What symbols are used? What larger messages (both to its contemporary audience and present-day audience) are embedded in this representation of Pocahontas? What purposes does this representation of Pocahontas serve (both at the time of its creation and present day)? **In a whole-class activity, guide students in making a chart comparing history to myth.** See David Lowenthal's essay "Fabricating Heritage" for help in considering what this comparison might look like.[20]

Targeted list of skills in this scenario

- Distinguishing between myth and history
- Close analysis of memorials and public history

Sources and Tools

Source 1.1: "True Relation" (Adapted)

Note: These are John Smith's own words about what happened.

Arriving at Werowocomoco, their **emperor** proudly lying upon a bedstead a foot high upon ten or twelve mats . . . with such grave and majestical **countenance**, as drove me into admiration. . . .

He kindly welcomed me with good words and great platters of sundry **victuals**, assuring me his friendship, and my liberty within four days. . . . He asked me the cause of our coming . . . demanded why we went further with our boat. . . . He promised to give me what I wanted to feed us, hatchets and copper we should make him, and none should disturb us. This request I promised to perform. And thus having all the kindness he could devise, sought to content me, he sent me home.

Source: Excerpt adapted from John Smith (1608), A true relation of such occurrences and accidents of note as hath happened in Virginia since the first planting of that colony. In *Narratives of Early Virginia, 1606–1625,* ed. L. G. Gardiner (New York: Charles Scribner's Sons, 1907), 48, 50.
Online facsimile edition available at www.americanjourneys.org/aj-074/

WORD BANK

emperor–ruler, king
countenance–face
victuals–foods

(Original)

Arriving at Weramocomoco, their emperour proudly lying uppon a Bedstead a foote high upon tenne or twelve Mattes . . . with such a grave and majesticall countenance, as drave me into admiration. . . . hee kindly welcomed me with good wordes, and great Platters of sundrie victuals, assuring mee his friendship, and my libertie within foure days. . . . Hee asked mee the cause of our comming . . . demaunded why we went further with our Boate. . . .

. . . Hee promised to give me Corne, Venison, or what I wanted to feede us: Hatchets and Copper wee should make him, and none should disturbe us. This request I promised to performe: and thus, having with all the kindnes hee could devise, sought to content me, hee sent me home. . . .

Source 1.2: "General History" (Adapted)

Note: These are John Smith's words about what happened from a later version of his experiences.

At last they brought [Smith] to Meronocomoco, where was Powhatan their Emperor. At his entrance, all the people gave a great shout . . . and . . . having feasted him after their best barbarous manner they could, a long **consultation** was held. But the conclusion was, two great stones were brought before Powhatan. Then, as many as could laid hands upon him, dragged him to them, and thereon laid his head, and being ready with their clubs, to beat out his brains. Pocahontas, the King's dearest daughter, when no **entreaty** could **prevail**, got his head in her arms, and laid down her own upon his to save him from death; whereat the Emperor was contented Smith should live.

Two days after, Powhatan having disguised himself in the most fearful manner he could, caused Captain Smith to be brought forth to a great house in the woods, and there upon a mat by the fire to be left alone . . . then, Powhatan, more like a devil than a man, came unto him and told him how they were friends, and presently he should go to Jamestown, to send him two great guns, and a grindstone, for which he would forever **esteem** him as a son. . . .

Source: Excerpt adapted from John Smith (1624), *General History of Virginia, New England and the Summer Isles*. In *The Complete Works of Captain John Smith (1580–1631)*, Vol. 2, ed., P. L. Barbour (Chapel Hill: University of North Carolina Press, 1986), 151.

WORD BANK

consultation–discussion
entreaty–request, plea
prevail–succeed
esteem–value, respect

(Original)

At last they brought him to Meronocomoco, where was Powhatan their Emperor. . . . At his entrance before the King, all the people gave a great shout . . . and . . . having feasted him after their best barbarous manner they could, a long consultation was held, but the conclusion was, two great stones were brought before Powhatan: then, as many as could layd hands on him, dragged him to them, and thereon laid his head, and being ready with their clubs, to beate out his braines, Pocahontas, the Kings dearest daughter, when no intreaty could prevaile, got his head in her armes, and laid her owne upon his to save him from death; whereat the Emperour was contented he should live. . . .

Two dayes after, Powhatan having disguised himselfe in the most fearefullest manner he could, caused Captaine Smith to be brought forth to a great house in the woods, and there upon a mat by the fire to be left alone . . . then Powhatan more like a devill then a man . . . came unto him and told him now they were friends, and presently he should goe to James towne, to send him two great gunnes, and a gryndstone, for which he would . . . for ever esteeme him as his sonne. . . .

Source 1.3: "Adams's Interpretation" (Adapted)

Note: Here is how one historian interprets John Smith's two accounts.

John Smith's two completely different versions don't match up. The later one, *A General History of Virginia,* exaggerates a lot of details in *A True Relation*, and brings up new information Smith never mentioned in the 16 years between the publication of the two.

When Smith describes his captivity (winter of 1607–1608) in *A True Relation*, he says Powhatan was kind and generous. He says he found no cause to fear for his life. (This proves Smith thought it was wrong to doubt Powhatan's goodwill.) Plus, Smith never mentioned Pocahontas in *A True Relation.* Therefore, a thinking person can't believe it.

A True Relation mentions Pocahontas coming to Jamestown later in 1608. Smith says he gave her gifts in return for her father's kindness. Wouldn't he have been thanking her for saving his life (*if it happened*)?

Finally, Smith wrote in 1612 (in *A Map of Virginia*) that while he was in captivity he witnessed a method of execution practiced by the tribe. He describes a prisoner's head being placed on a sacrificing stone, while "one with clubs beats out their brains." Isn't it rather odd that he didn't mention his own experience here, since it sounds just like what happened to him?

Source: Summary adapted from Henry Adams (1867, January), "Captain John Smith," *The North American Review 104*(214).

Source 1.4: "Lemay's Interpretation" (Adapted)

Note: Here is how another historian interprets John Smith's accounts.

John Smith had no reason to lie. In all of his other writing about native customs and geography, he is very accurate and observant. For 250 years after his captivity, no one questioned his story.

The reason the two versions differ is that their purpose is different. In *A True Relation*, Smith didn't want to brag about his adventures; he wanted to inform readers about the land and people of Virginia. In the *General History*, his goal was to promote **colonization** in Virginia (and added stories might get people interested in the activities of the Virginia Company).

And to those critics who say Smith never mentioned Pocahontas's bravery until 1624–after some of her fame would enhance his status–he did write about her before she came to England. In 1616, Smith wrote to Queen Anne to tell her of Pocahontas's bravery and other rare qualities, and he described how Pocahontas rescued him from Powhatan, and how she saved all Jamestown from starvation.

There is no doubt that the event happened. Smith may have **misinterpreted** what the whole thing *meant.* I think it was probably a ritualistic death and rebirth, with Pocahontas acting as his sponsor into Indian identity.

Source: Summary adapted from J. A. Leo Lemay, *The American Dream of Captain John Smith* (Charlottesville: University Press of Virginia, 1991).

WORD BANK

colonization–settlement, domination
misinterpreted–misunderstood, got the wrong idea about

Source 1.5: "Lewis's Interpretation" (Adapted)

Note: Here is how another historian interprets these events.

Why is it that none of the other members of the Virginia Company who kept diaries ever wrote about Pocahontas saving Smith's life? (Ten fellow Virginia company members kept journals in 1608.) Surely someone would have written about it if Smith came back to Jamestown and shared his story.

Thus, no one in England had ever heard of her until 1617 when she was a big media event in London. She was a "princess" (daughter of "King" Powhatan), and the first Indian woman to visit England. Because she had converted to Christianity, people high up in the church, as well as the King (James I) and Queen (Anne), paid attention to her.

While all this was going on, John Smith published a new edition of *A True Relation* that now had footnotes in the part about his capture. These notes mention Pocahontas throwing herself on Smith to beg his release, and her father giving in to her request. Smith even goes on to take credit for introducing Pocahontas to the English language and the Bible.

In 1624, Smith polished this story in his *General History*. This version expands the details of his rescue, saying Pocahontas risked her life to save his. He also describes Chief Powhatan providing the Jamestown colonists with Indian guides. Would the same chief who wanted to kill Smith now try to help him?

Source: Summary adapted from Paul Lewis, *The Great Rogue: A Biography of John Smith* (New York: David McKay Company, 1966).

Source 1.6: "Barbour's Interpretation" (Adapted)

Note: Here is how another scholar interprets the disputed event.

The bringing in of two big stones, and forcing John Smith to stretch out on them, seemed to Smith like he was about to be executed. When a young girl (Pocahontas) knelt and placed her head on Smith, he was released. The way he saw it, she saved his life.

What almost certainly happened was that Smith was the center of a **ritual** similar to what young boys in the tribe went through before entering manhood. They have a pretend execution or death and then are reborn as men. Pocahontas was preselected to be his protector. She did not actually save his life because the Powhatan were not really going to kill him.

Source: Summary adapted from Philip Barbour, *Pocahontas and Her World* (Boston: Houghton Mifflin, 1969).

WORD BANK

ritual–custom, ceremony

Tool 1.1: Timeline of Events Related to Pocahontas and John Smith

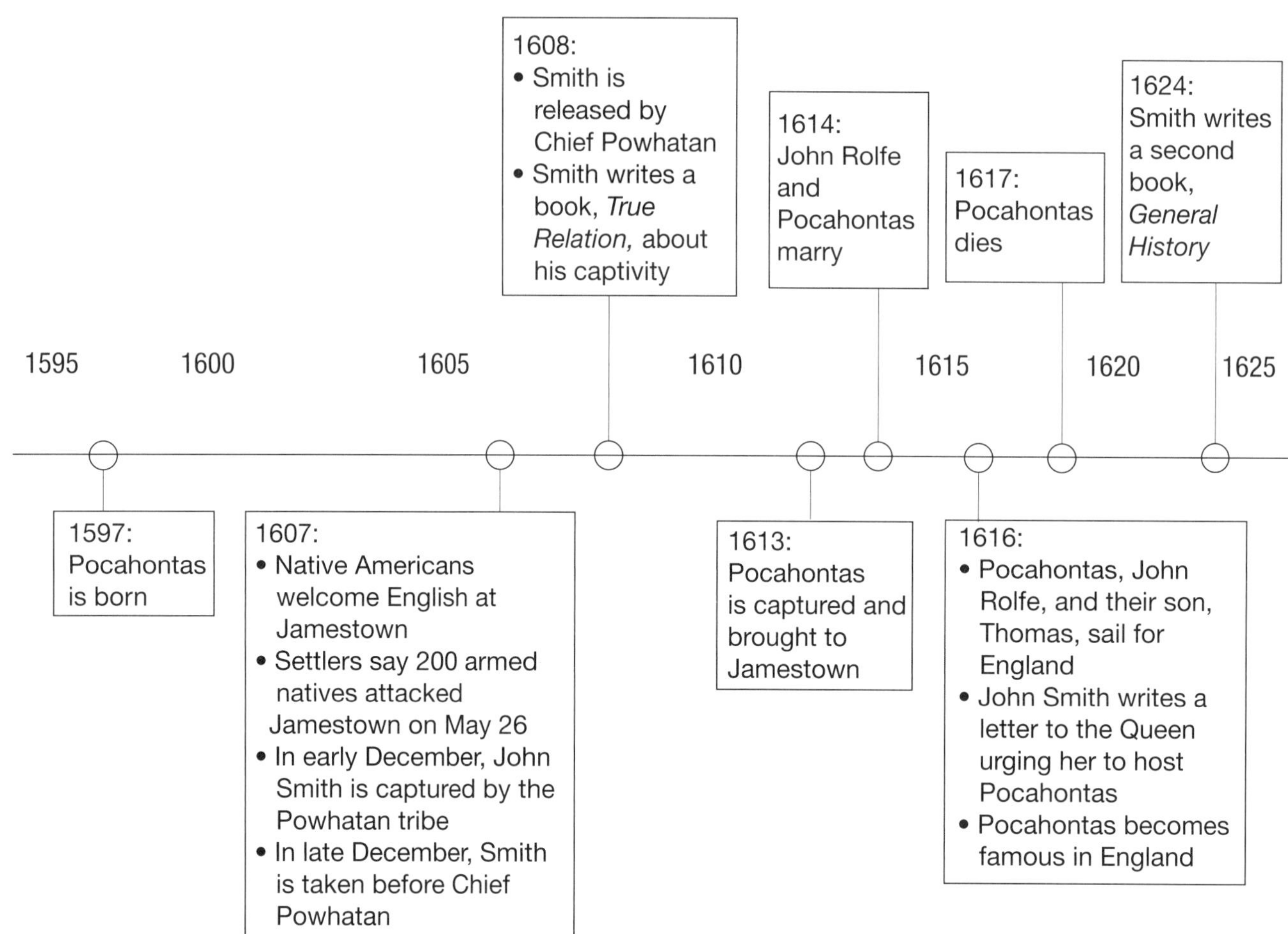

Tool 1.2: Comparing Smith's Accounts

1. What are the different facts in Smith's two accounts of his captivity in December 1607? (Use the space below to answer or create a Venn diagram on the back of this sheet.)

   A True Relation (Source 1.1) says:

   General History (Source 1.2) says:

2. Why would Smith add on to his earlier story?

3. Why might he lie or exaggerate and invent new information?

4. Why wouldn't he lie about the story?

Tool 1.3: Comparing Historians and Smith

Assuming that the basic facts (though not necessarily the interpretation of the facts) in Smith's latest account (the *General History of Virginia*) are true, record below a "play-by-play" description of the facts in the passage:

1.

2.

3.

4.

5.

Which historians believe that the basic sequence above did occur?

Describe what they think the facts (above) mean:

1. Historian ____________________ believes . . .

2. Historian ____________________ believes . . .

Tool 1.4: Comparing Historians and Smith

Refer to the "play-by-play" description of the facts in Smith's latest account. Compare this to Lewis's and Barbour's interpretations of these facts.

Which historians believe that the basic sequence above did occur?

Describe what they think the facts (above) mean:

1. Historian ____________________ believes . . .

2. Historian ____________________ believes . . .

Tool 1.5: Analytical Essay
Did Pocahontas Save John Smith?

1. Watch the Disney clip of Pocahontas saving John Smith again. Disney claims that its film is "responsible, accurate, and respectful." Do you agree? Why or why not? Explain your position in an essay. Use evidence from the documents to support your analysis of this film clip.

2. Write an outline of your essay and share it with your teacher.

   a. Include a clear *position.*

   b. List the *points* you want to make to support your position.

   c. Cite key pieces of *evidence* that support your position.

3. Write your essay.

   a. Convey your position in the introductory paragraph.

   b. Explain your points and your evidence.

   c. Conclude with a wrap-up of your argument.

Suggested Resources

http://www.virtualjamestown.org/
This site, created through collaboration between Virginia Tech and the University of Virginia and its Center for Digital History, includes a rich set of teaching and learning resources, including first-hand accounts and video interviews with local Indians.

http://historicjamestowne.org/
Maintained by the Association for the Preservation of Virginia's Antiquities and the National Park Service, this site includes biographies of the early colonists and teaching resources for involving students with the ongoing archeological digs and the area's geography.

http://www.apva.org/jr.html
Maintained by the Association for the Preservation of Virginia's Antiquities, this is the home page for the archeological efforts at the Jamestown site. It includes exhibits and updates about the ongoing digs and brief histories relevant to Jamestown.

http://chnm.gmu.edu/loudountah/exploresources.php
A unique site that shows a video of an elementary teacher planning and using John Smith's 1612 map of Virginia with her students as well as a scholar's analysis of the map.

http://xroads.virginia.edu/~CAP/POCA/POC-home.html
This site focuses on Pocahontas and representations of her over time. Here you can find the Baptism painting.

http://www.pbs.org/wgbh/nova/pocahontas
This companion site to the PBS video *Pocahontas Revealed* includes a feature on the "science of Jamestown," interviews with a historian and a Tidewater Indian chief, and an interactive exhibit of the changing images of Pocahontas.

http://digital.lib.lehigh.edu/trial/pocahontas/
An archive maintained by an English professor, this site has an extensive variety of resources concerning Pocahontas.

http://www.nps.gov/jame/historyculture/index.htm
Maintained by the National Park Service, this site includes fact sheets about many aspects of Jamestown and its residents.

http://www.learner.org/channel/courses/amerhistory/interactives/
Users can match representations of Pocahontas with descriptions and then access lively contextual clues to place them on a timeline. This interactive web-based activity uses changing representations of Pocahontas to introduce chronological thinking.

CHAPTER 2

"Standing Tall" or Fleeing the Scene?

Jacob Douglas and Sam Wineburg

Cornelius Tiebout, Battle of Lexington, 1790. Engraving. Accessed at http://www.loc.gov/pictures/item/2004669978/

For the 150th anniversary of the Battle of Lexington–the "shot heard 'round the world"–the U.S. Postal Service produced a two-cent commemorative stamp (Source 2.3). Issued in 1925, the stamp depicts a solid line of Minutemen resolutely facing superior British forces. Portraying the Minutemen in various stages of returning fire, reloading, and defiantly shaking their fists, the image projects a heroic version of the story that Americans had proudly come to regard as fact.

There was only one little problem: The stamp was based not on eyewitness accounts of the battle, but on an 1886 painting by Henry Sandham. Completed well over a century after the actual event (Source 2.2), Sandham's painting showed rebellious Americans defying orders to leave Lexington Green. However, if we look at another rendering of the event, one created weeks after the event, not years, a different impression emerges. In the fall of 1775, a 21-year-old silversmith named Amos Doolittle created a metal engraving depicting the encounter that had taken place that April (Source 2.1). Doolittle's etching has British regulars firing on a ragtag group of fleeing Minutemen, with not a single member of the Lexington militia showing the slightest sign of resistance. The colonists in Doolittle's engraving are not standing tall in the face of overwhelming odds. They are fleeing for their lives.

The striking contrast between these two images–the first carrying the weight and legitimacy of the United States Postal Service, the second drawn by an obscure Connecticut craftsman–brings us to a critical question: What happened at Lexington Green on the morning of April 19, 1775? Is it even appropriate to call this encounter a "battle"? Would it be better labeled a "massacre" or even an unfortunate but bloody misunderstanding? Would it be preferable, for simplicity's sake, to refer to this event neutrally as the "Incident at Lexington"?

Historiographical Debate

The question of what really happened at Lexington came to light some 50 years after the event as the towns of Lexington and Concord fought over the distinction of who spilled the first British blood of the American Revolution. In 1825, Lexington's Elias Phinney published his *History of the Battle at Lexington*, an effort to refute claims that the first American resistance actually occurred at neighboring Concord. Using depositions of eyewitnesses taken 50 years after the fact, Phinney describes the Battle of Lexington in ways consistent with Sandham's 1886 painting (and, for that matter, the 1925 postage stamp). According to Phinney's account, John Parker, the Minutemen's captain, ordered "every man to stand his ground" and threatened to shoot the first man who left his post. Phinney then lists each Minuteman who stood his ground and returned fire on the British, including several who continued fighting after sustaining wounds. No wonder, then, that Henry Sandham's 1886 painting corresponds to Phinney's work: It was commissioned by the Lexington Historical Society, which paid Sandham $4,000 for an illustration that portrayed Lexington's sons in a courageous light.[1]

Seven years after Phinney's account, Concord's Ezra Ripley issued a rebuttal. Arguing that the first armed resistance to the British had taken place at Concord, Ripley contended that Lexington's Minutemen never returned fire on the British. Instead, he claimed that the Lexington militia scattered in disarray as soon as the British started firing (a depiction that corresponds with the 1775 Doolittle engraving). Little evidence existed to support the notion that Americans fought back at Lexington. Those descriptions that did substantiate that claim, Ripley argued, were by British officers who had a vested interest not only in showing that the Americans had fired their weapons, but fired first. Ripley suggested that the incident at Lexington could be called a massacre or a melee, but not a battle. Instead, he asserted that the first real battle of the American Revolution took place at Concord.[2] Despite its strengths, Ripley's account was a thinly veiled attempt to win Concord the honor of being the first to fight back against the British in the American Revolution, just as Phinney's was an attempt to claim that distinction for Lexington.

Nearly a century later, at a meeting of the Massachusetts Historical Society, Harold Murdock, a banker and amateur historian from Boston, delivered a paper that called into question the traditional account of the Battle of Lexington. The story of Americans defiantly resisting a British advance, he argued, was due to "the accumulation of a mass of questionable evidence" that had gradually become accepted as truth. "Tradition, legend, tune, and song all played their part in the reconstruction of the Lexington story."[3] In making the argument for what happened at Lexington, Murdock began with the Doolittle engraving, noting that "even the magnifying glass fail[ed] to reveal any member of that company in an attitude of resistance; no suggestion of a return fire, or even of loading."[4] Over time, Murdock explained, artistic renderings depicted greater levels of resistance on the part of the Americans, culminating in Sandham's 1886 painting in which the colonists emerged as musket-toting rebels. While Murdock introduced no new information to the body of historical evidence, he painstakingly detailed the discrepancies in Phinney's account, Sandham's painting, and other evidence, such as the remarkably few casualties sustained by the British (one superficially wounded soldier and a wounded horse).

In 1959 Arthur Tourtellot supported Murdock's arguments with evidence that had become available in the intervening years. While conceding that the Americans might have actually fired on the British, he noted that "the American fire did not come close to matching the British in volume, and it was extremely erratic and irregular"—clearly not a solid line of Minutemen reloading their firearms at close range.[5] Based on the claims of these scholars, the "Battle" of Lexington, a tale worthy of commemorative postage stamps, would seem to be more myth than history.

What Do the Primary Sources Say? To be sure, disagreement remains over what exactly happened on Lexington Green on the morning of April 19, 1775, but the consensus points away from an epic battle and more toward the chaotic retreat depicted in Doolittle's 1775 engraving. This version is strengthened by the primary accounts of the Lexington Minutemen themselves. On April 23–25, 1775, several days after the events at Lexington and Concord, the Massachusetts Provincial Congress, an extralegal governing body set up by the colonials, arranged for justices of the peace (favorable to the Minutemen's cause) to take depositions from those present on Lexington Green. These depositions were sent to Parliament and published throughout England in an effort to portray the colonials as innocent victims of the British army's barbarism. Colonial justices of the period took 21 depositions from 97 individuals; while some of the depositions bore the name of only 1 or 2, some contained the names of over 30 deponents.

One such deposition, taken from Nathaniel Mulliken, Philip Russell, and 32 other members of the Lexington militia, described the scene at Lexington Green as follows (see Source 2.5):

> About five o'clock in the morning, hearing our drum beat, we proceeded towards the parade [Lexington Green] and soon found that a large body of troops were marching towards us, some of our company were coming up to the parade and others had reached it, at which time the company began to disperse, whilst our backs were turned on the [British] troops, we were fired on by them, and a number of our men were instantly killed and wounded, not a gun was fired by any person in our company on the regulars to our knowledge before they fired on us, and [they] continued firing until we had all made our escape.[6]

Like the other depositions taken at this time, the account adamantly held that the British fired first, and not on a firmly planted line of Minutemen, but on a dispersing crowd fleeing with their backs turned. While not flattering to the Lexington militia, such an image would have been useful in convincing the other colonies, as well as members of Parliament, of the cruelty of the British troops. While the deposition presents compelling evidence, it may also have been tainted by the political interests of colonials seeking to portray themselves as victims of a one-sided massacre. We should consider additional perspectives on the same events.

Lieutenant John Barker, a member of the British Light Infantry Company of the Fourth Regiment and one of the officers present on Lexington Green that morning, recorded in his diary a surprisingly similar account of these events (see Source 2.4):

> 19th. At 2 o'clock we began our march by wading through a very long ford up to our middles: after going a few miles we took 3 or 4 people who were going off to give intelligence; about 5 miles on this side of a town called Lexington which lay in our road, we heard there were some hundreds of people collected together intending to oppose us and stop our going on; at 5 o'clock we arrived there and saw a number of people, I believe between 200 and 300, formed on a common in the middle of the town; we still continued advancing, keeping prepared against an attack tho' without intending to attack them, but on our coming near them they fired one or two shots, upon which our

> men without any orders rushed in upon them, fired and put 'em to flight; several of them were killed, we cou'd not tell how many because they were got behind walls and into the woods. . . . We then formed on the Common but with some difficulty, the men were so wild they cou'd hear no orders; we waited a considerable time there and at length proceeded on our way to Concord.[7]

In looking at both American and British versions of the events at Lexington Green, we might expect some differences. It is not surprising, for instance, that each report claimed that the other fired first. But more striking is where these accounts match up: *Neither side describes significant resistance by the Minutemen.*

When historians try to discover what happened in the past, they rely on *corroboration,* the careful consideration of points of contact across different sources. When multiple sources agree, particularly when they come from opposing sides, we can take greater stock in their accuracy. The fact that a British officer's diary corroborates the deposition given by the Minutemen lends greater credibility to this version of the event.

Primary sources are the raw materials that get distilled into the textbook narratives served up to students in history classes. But myth creeps into textbooks as well. Consider the following passage taken from a 1963 American history textbook for middle school students:

> In April 1775 General Gage, the military governor of Massachusetts, sent out a body of troops to take possession of military supplies at Concord, a short distance from Boston. At Lexington, a handful of "embattled farmers" who had been tipped off by Paul Revere, barred the way. The "rebels" were ordered to disperse. They stood their ground. The English fired a volley of shots that killed eight patriots. Paul Revere spread the news of this new atrocity to the neighboring colonies. The patriots of New England, although still a handful, were now ready to fight the English.[8]

The textbook repeats the claim that the Minutemen "stood their ground" when ordered to disperse. Yet neither the Minutemen's own depositions nor Barker's diary say anything about the Minutemen "standing their ground."

If we look at yet another source, the diary of Ezra Stiles, the president of Yale College at the time of the events at Lexington Green, we gain a deeper understanding of what may have happened (Source 2.6). According to an account Stiles received from Major Pitcairn, who commanded the British troops, the American colonists *did* "stand their ground" when they were ordered to disperse. However, once firing commenced, they ran for their lives. As Stiles recorded it:

> [Pitcairn's] account is this–that riding up to them he ordered them to disperse; which they not doing instantly, he turned about to order his troops so to draw out as to surround and disarm them. As he turned, he *saw* a gun in a peasant's hand from behind a wall, *flash in the pan* without going off; and instantly or very soon two or three guns went off.[9]

Pitcairn did not say that he saw the Americans fire first. Nor does he say that once the firing began they stood their ground. What he does say is that the colonists defied an order to quit Lexington Green. Stiles's version does not necessarily contradict those of Barker or Mulliken. Perhaps the Minutemen did stand their ground, but when shots were fired, they may have fled without returning fire.

Unanswered questions continue to swirl about the events on Lexington Green, especially concerning who fired the first shot. Barker claimed that as troops approached the Green, the Minutemen "fired one or two shots" at the British; the Minutemen argued that they were fired upon when their backs were turned. While not surprising, the discrepancy actually tells us more about the purpose of each document than the actual events described–a point to keep in mind when judging a document's trustworthiness. No document is written in a vacuum. What exactly *were* the historical circumstances, or context, for each document?

We know that the Minutemen's statement was sent by the Provincial Congress to Parliament and the British people, hoping to portray themselves as innocent victims of British aggression, not rabblerousing revolutionaries. For his part, Barker likely didn't keep a diary simply to record his innermost feelings, but because it might serve to exonerate him if he had to justify his actions to higher authorities. Indeed, in a study we did using these documents with a group of historians and a group of high school students, one of the historians suggested to us that Barker may have been trying to "cover his backside." Caught between two unflattering alternatives–admitting that he issued an order to fire or admitting that he lost control over his troops–the latter option was preferable.[10] Thus, Barker's diary would provide an alibi if the lieutenant had to defend himself against a charge of issuing an order to shoot. If he was at fault, it wasn't because he issued an order to fire, but because his men, tired and soggy after a 3-hour march, were guilty of firing back when fired upon.

Challenges for Students. When historians review evidence about Lexington or any historical event, they begin by using a common set of problem solving strategies. First, they ask about the *source,* a process we refer to as "sourcing." Who was Lt. John Barker and how do we know he can be believed? What do we know about the deponents Nathaniel Mulliken, Philip Russell, and the group they assembled to testify before three Justices of the Peace? Next, historians consider a document's *context*: Why, for example, did the Minutemen seek justices of the peace to take depositions for what happened at Lexington? How did knowing that their testimony would be sent to Benjamin Franklin, the colonial representative to Parliament, influence what they did and did not say to the justices? Finally, how does examining multiple documents, the act of *corroboration*, permit a broader understanding of these events, even when these documents disagree on key details?

In the study we referred to above, we compared a group of professional historians to a group of talented high school students using these Lexington documents. We purposely selected historians with specialties outside of American history, and we purposely selected students enrolled in Advanced Placement classrooms who had scored well on a test of facts about the American Revolution. Given the same sources and textbook passage used here, each group ranked each document in terms of its reliability. For historians, the textbook passage ranked dead last, because its claims could not be verified.[11] Students, on the other hand, tended to view the textbook as *most* reliable, observing in one case that the book was "just reporting the facts."[12] Neither the lack of corroborating evidence nor the source information for each document seemed of great importance to the students, but those factors were of utmost importance to the historians. Even though the high school students were skilled readers, they had not yet acquired the habits necessary for engaging in historical inquiry.

The question of what happened on Lexington Green on the morning of April 19, 1775, provides a ripe opportunity for students to begin to develop historical reading skills and habits of mind. Part of Americans' collective memory is the image of the Minutemen standing strong at Lexington as they fired, in Ralph Waldo Emerson's words, the "shot heard 'round the world." But an examination of the evidence from Lexington raises troubling questions about this heroic depiction. The discrepancies between image and evidence provide students with an entry point into doing history: investigating and evaluating evidence, placing individual accounts into a larger context, and corroborating documents, all with the purpose of constructing a picture of what happened in the past. Here the task for students is deceptively straightforward: to determine whether the Battle of Lexington was, in fact, even a battle!

Concluding Questions. So let's step back and consider what we know about the events on Lexington Green, what we will never be able to know, and what is still up for grabs. We know that when the British troops arrived in Lexington en route to Concord shots were fired on the Green that left eight Minutemen dead and ten wounded, and that the British for their part sustained minimal casualties (possibly caused by friendly fire). We do not know who fired the first shot and probably never will. Different sources contradict one another on this point, and each has a strong motive for making the claim that it does.

In between these claims are questions that students can debate as they work to construct an accurate historical narrative: Was the battle at Lexington really a battle? Did the Minutemen intend to resist the British that morning? If not, what was their goal? What was the intention of the British? What did these events mean for both the Americans and the British in the context of the ensuing struggle for American independence?

Why Teach About the Battle at Lexington Green?

An Opportunity to Teach About What Is Knowable. Some events in history are well-established and there is little debate about what happened. For this topic, there is no question that a conflict took place on Lexington Green on April 19, 1775. Yet other aspects lie beyond our immediate understanding. No matter how much we do, we will never know with absolute certainty what happened.

It is in this space–between the well-established and the unknowable–that historians toil. Struggling to understand what can and can't be known forces students to wrestle with the messiness of evidence, and gives them a chance to engage in legitimate historical work.

A Chance to Explore How Myth Becomes Interwoven with History. Every nation's history is full of legends, distortions, and myths. Teaching students how factual inaccuracies creep into the historical record, even becoming enshrined on a postage stamp, is essential to helping them develop a sense of skepticism and a keen eye for evidence. Equally important, this approach turns students into historical detectives in search of truth, a task far more motivating than filling in a worksheet.

Corroborated neither by British nor American primary sources, the image of Minutemen "standing tall" at Lexington has been shaped by personal interest, dubious scholarship, and local concerns. Consequently, it presents an opportunity to teach students to think about the motives of authors, the importance of evidence, and the ever-present tendency to rewrite the past to suit the needs of the present.

An Opportunity to Use Visual Sources. Primary sources are the raw materials of history. More often than not, historians rely on written documents to piece together the events of the past. But visual sources can be primary sources, too. Amos Doolittle's 1775 engraving is every bit as much a primary source as the diary of Ezra Stiles. Both were created in the same year as the event itself, and both attempted to record the events at Lexington Green for the sake of posterity.

Using visual sources is invaluable to the process of history inquiry. Even students struggling with written sources can productively locate the visual discrepancies between Amos Doolittle's engraving and Henry Sandham's oil painting, and generate hypotheses for why the two images might disagree. But beware: When you use visual sources, students will invariably mistake visual accuracy–how realistic a picture looks–with historical accuracy. Because Sandham's painting "looks more real," with more lifelike depictions than Doolittle's stick figures, some students will judge it to be the more accurate of the two, even in the face of overwhelming evidence to the contrary.

How Might You Use These Materials?

Scenario 1 (1–2 Hour Lesson). Was the battle at Lexington Green truly a battle? Analyze and compare images of the conflict at Lexington Green to figure out what might have happened (see Tool 2.1).

Begin this lesson with three images: the Doolittle engraving, the Sandham painting, and the image of the U.S. postage stamp (Sources 2.1, 2.2, 2.3). Without recourse to the dates of each image, ask students to describe what they see. They will notice that the postage stamp is based on the Sandham painting, which in students' minds may confer the image with special legitimacy. (Why else would the postal service choose to feature it?) Help students establish that these two images provide different versions of the same event. Because Sandham's painting benefits from artistic advances in portraying perspective and depth, some students will judge it to be the more accurate of the two. Part of developing historical judgment is resisting what appeals to the eye, and learning that vividness and artistic realism are no substitute for truthfulness.

Ask students to interpret what they see. Do they detect differences in appearance, posture, or organization between the combatants on Lexington Green? Students will notice some consistencies–a tree, buildings, troops arrayed in a line–as well as some contradictions, such as whether the Minutemen fled or held their ground. While some students will try to create stories that reconcile the images, others will assume that one image is accurate and the other not.

At this point, introduce into the discussion the dates of the Doolittle engraving and the Sandham painting, reminding students that the events took place in 1775. Help them to mine the importance of this new information. What happens to human memory the more distant we become from actual events? Organize students into groups to examine the two written primary source documents (Sources 2.4, 2.5) with the aim of confirming or reevaluating their positions on the guiding question.

To assess students' reading of visual documents, ask them to consider images from another event in pre-Revolutionary America, the Boston Massacre. Using Stephen Mintz's "Exploration 2" on the excellent "Digital History" website (see http://www.digitalhistory.uh.edu/learning_history/revolution/revolution_art.cfm), consider Paul Revere's famous 1770 engraving alongside a lithograph from 1770 and another from 1868. Which depicts the Boston Massacre most accurately? How do visual accuracy and historical accuracy differ?

Targeted list of skills in this scenario

- Analyzing images
- Distinguishing between visual and historical accuracy
- Contextualizing sources
- Corroborating sources
- Evidence-based thinking and argumentation

Scenario 2 (1 Hour Lesson). Focus on sourcing. This scenario teaches students to privilege the information that typically appears at the end of a document–information about who wrote a document and the circumstances of its composition. Novices typically skip this information or give it little heed. Historians, on the other hand, zoom in on it immediately, often using it as a framework for their ensuing analysis.

Begin with the textbook account (Source 2.7). This excerpt provides you with an excellent opportunity to teach your students how to read closely and to focus on how words convey feeling and emotion. Ask them to track how the Minutemen undergo a metamorphosis in this short paragraph, moving from "embattled farmers" (an allusion to Emerson's "Concord Hymn") to "rebels" (Why would the textbook author put this word in quotes and what do they signify?), only to emerge as "patriots of all New England." Ask them to think about the title of this textbook. What is the relationship between the kind of narrative presented here and the book's title? Questions like these sensitize students to reading their textbooks for more than the information they present. It helps them understand their textbook as another kind of historical source, one that also carries a perspective and reflects a particular point of view.

Introduce students to Sources 2.4 and 2.5 (depending on their reading level, you can choose to use the adapted or the original documents). Provide explicit instruction about sourcing by explaining that historians, even before they study the substance of a document, ask questions about a document's author, the circumstances of its creation, and the relationship between a document's creation and the event it describes. Typical questions include: Who wrote (or created) this document? What is the author's perspective? Why did the author write this? Is this author trustworthy (e.g., what does the author stand to gain or lose by writing this)? See Tool 2.2 with questions tailored to the particular documents in this lesson.

After students have completed this Tool, **return to the textbook excerpt and evaluate its claim that the Minutemen "stood their ground." How does this claim hold up compared to what two documents, written from opposing sides, say? To see how students' reasoning about sources develops, ask them to explain which sources are the most and least trustworthy in evaluating the claim that the Minutemen "stood their ground." This will help you assess whether students can source, contextualize, and corroborate primary documents.**

Alternately, give students two sources they have not seen: the Ezra Stiles document (Source 2.6) and the excerpt from Jeremy Lister (Source 2.8). Have them compare the two documents, focusing on how sourcing information informs notions of trustworthiness. How, exactly, did Stiles get his information? How many hands did this information pass through before it reached him? Can we know for sure? How much time has passed between the event Lister records and when the actual events happened? What might be Lister's motivation for recording these events so long after they occurred?

Targeted list of skills in this scenario

- Sourcing documents
- Understanding sourcing and why it is necessary
- Determining reliability of sources
- Questioning narrative accounts
- Evidence-based thinking and argumentation

Scenario 3 (2–3 Hour Lesson). How does myth become history? For this lesson, lead students through the analysis and discussion rounds described in Scenario 1, and the focus on sourcing described in Scenario 2. However, rather than asking students to produce a final project in which they detail elements that make a source credible, this scenario culminates in a project in which students explore the various forces that allow myth to creep into the historical record.

After students discuss which sources they found *most* and *least* reliable, ask them to pinpoint the qualities of reliable and unreliable sources. What were the motives of the unreliable sources? What did these sources stand to gain from their inaccuracies? To which audience did such inaccuracies appeal? How did certain stories about the events at Lexington get passed down? Which versions were likely to be recorded, and which were unlikely? Remind them of the original guiding question ("Was the battle at Lexington Green really a battle?") and of the notion portrayed in the postage stamp that the Minutemen stood tall against British troops. Now, ask them to complete a final project such as a short essay or oral presentation that details the elements and forces that help turn myth into history.

Targeted list of skills in this scenario

- Determining reliability of sources
- Distinguishing between myth and history

Sources and Tools

Source 2.1: Doolittle Painting

Source: The Battle of Lexington, April 19th, 1775, by Amos Doolittle, 1775, public domain image, http://images.nypl.org/?id=54426&t=w

Source 2.2: Sandham Painting

Source: Birth of Liberty by Henry Sandham, 1886, http://www.mce.k12tn.net/revolutionary_war/lexington.gif

Source 2.3: U.S. Postage Stamp

Source: U.S. Postage Stamp, 1925, http://hubpages.com/hub/US-Postage-Stamps-1925

Source 2.4: Barker Diary (Adapted)

19th. At 2 o'clock in the morning we began our march by wading through a river that came up to our middles; after going a few miles we came to a town called Lexington. We heard there were hundreds of people gathered there who planned to oppose us. At 5 o'clock we arrived and saw a number of people, between 200 and 300, formed in a field (Lexington Green) in the middle of the town.

We continued marching, keeping prepared against an attack though without intending to attack them. On our coming near, they fired one or two shots. As soon as that happened, our men without any orders, rushed in upon them, fired and put them to flight.

We regrouped, but with some difficulty because our men were so wild they could hear no orders.

Source: Entry for April 19, 1775, from the diary of Lieutenant John Barker, an officer in the British army; R. H. Dana, Jr., A British Officer in Boston. *The Atlantic Monthly, 39*, 1877, 389–401.

(Original)

19th. At 2 o'clock we began our march by wading through a very long ford up to our middles; after going a few miles we took three or four people who were going off to give intelligence; about five miles on this side of a town called Lexington, which lay in our road, we heard there were some hundreds of people collected together intending to oppose us and stop our going on; at 5 o'clock we arrived there and saw a number of people, I believe between 2 and 300, formed on a common in the middle of the town; we still continued advancing, keeping prepared against an attack th'o without intending to attack them; but on our coming near them they fired one or two shots, upon which our men without any orders, rushed in upon them, fired and put them to flight; several of them were killed, we cou'd not tell how many, because they were got behind walls and into the woods; We had a man of the 10th light Infantry wounded, nobody else hurt. We then formed on the Common but with some difficulty, the men were so wild they cou'd hear no orders; we waited a considerable time there, and at length proceeded on our way to Concord.

Source 2.5: Minutemen's Depositions (Adapted)

We Nathaniel Mulliken, Philip Russell (followed by the names of 32 other men present on Lexington Green on April 19, 1775) All of lawful age, and inhabitants of Lexington, do testify and declare, that on April 19th, at about 1 or 2 am, we were told that British soldiers were marching from Boston towards Concord.

We were ordered to meet at the field at the center of town [Lexington Green], where we were told by our captain to go back home, but to be ready to come back when we heard the beat of the drum. We further testify and declare that about 5 o'clock in the morning, hearing our drumbeat, we returned, and soon found a large body of troops marching towards us.

At that point, some of our group was making its way toward Lexington Green, and others had reached it. Our men began to disperse [leave]. While our backs were turned on the [British] troops, we were fired on by them, and a number of our men were killed and wounded. To our knowledge, not a gun was fired by any person in our group on the British soldiers before they fired on us. The British continued firing until we had all made our escape.

Source: Lexington, April 25, 1775, Nathaniel Mulliken, Philip Russell, [and the 32 men] [Duly sworn to by 34 minutemen on April 25 before three justices of the peace]; C. C. Sawtell. *The Nineteeth of April, 1775: A Collection of First Hand Accounts* (Lincoln, MA: Sawtells of Somerset, 1968).

(Original)

We Nathaniel Mulliken, Philip Russell, (Followed by the names of 32 other men present on Lexington Green on April 19, 1775) . . . all of lawful age, and inhabitants of Lexington, in the County of Middlesex . . . do testify and declare, that on the nineteenth of April instant, about one or two o'clock in the morning, being informed that . . . a body of regulars were marching from Boston towards Concord . . . we were alarmed and having met at the place of our company's parade, were dismissed by our Captain, John Parker, for the present with orders to be ready to attend at the beat of the drum, we further testify and declare, that about five o'clock in the morning, hearing our drum beat, we proceeded towards the parade and soon found that a large body of troops were marching towards us, some of our company were coming up to the parade, and others had reached it, at which time, the company began to disperse, whilst our backs were turned on the troops, we were fired on by them, and a number of our men were instantly killed and wounded, not a gun was fired by any person in our company on the regulars to our knowledge before they fired on us, and they continued firing until we had all made our escape.

Source 2.6: Stiles Letter (Adapted)

Descriptions of the beginning of the firing are relatively unclear. Major Pitcairn, who was a good man fighting for a bad cause, insisted to the day he died that the colonists fired first. . . . He does not say that he saw the colonists fire first. Had he said it, I would have believed him, because he is a man of integrity and honor. He expressly says he did not see who fired first; but he believed the American peasants began the shooting.

His account is that he rode up to the peasants and ordered them to disperse. Because they did not do so instantly, he ordered his troops to spread out and surround the colonists and disarm them. As he turned, he saw a gun in a peasant's hand from behind a wall. The gun misfired without firing a bullet; and instantly two or three guns went off, wounding Major Pitcairn's horse and also a man near him. He did not see those guns, but he believed they could not have been from British troops and that it must have been the American colonists who began the attack.

The British troops were so eager and impulsive that they began shooting without orders and Major Pitcairn could not keep them from shooting. Pitcairn struck his staff or sword downwards with all seriousness as a signal to his men to stop firing.

Major Pitcairn told this story to Mr. Brown of Providence who went to Boston a few days after the battle and told Governor Sessions, who then told it to me.

Source: From the diary of Ezra Stiles, president of Yale College, entry for August 21, 1775; In F. B. Dexter, ed., *The Literary Diary of Ezra Stiles* (New York: Charles Scribner, 1901).

(Original)

There is a certain sliding over and indeterminateness in describing the beginning of the firing. Major Pitcairn, who was a good man in a bad cause, insisted upon it to the day of his death, that the colonists fired first. . . . *He does not say that he saw the colonists fire first.* Had he said it, I would have believed him, being a man of integrity and honor. *He expressly says he did not see who fired first;* and yet believed the peasants began. His account is this–that riding up to them he ordered them to disperse; which they not doing instantly, he turned about to order his troops so to draw out as to surround and disarm them. As he turned, he *saw* a gun in a peasant's hand from behind a wall, *flash in the pan without going off*; and instantly or very soon two or three guns went off by which he found his horse wounded and also a man near him wounded. These guns he did not see, but believing they could not come from his own people, doubted not and so asserted that they came from our people; and that thus they began the attack. The impetuosity of the King's Troops were such that a promiscuous, uncommanded but general fire took place, which Pitcairn could not prevent; though he struck his staff or sword downwards with all earnestness as a signal to forbear or cease firing. This account Major Pitcairn himself gave Mr. Brown of Providence who was seized with flour and carried to Boston a few days after the battle; and Gov. Sessions told it to me.

Source 2.7: Textbook Version of Lexington

In April 1775, General Gage, the military governor of Massachusetts, sent out a body of troops to take possession of military stores at Concord, a short distance from Boston. At Lexington, a handful of "embattled farmers," who had been tipped off by Paul Revere, barred the way. The "rebels" were ordered to disperse. They stood their ground. The English fired a volley of shots that killed eight patriots. It was not long before the swift-riding Paul Revere spread the news of this new atrocity to the neighboring colonies. The patriots of all of New England, although still a handful, were now ready to fight the English.

Source: From a high school textbook: Samuel Steinberg, *The United States: Story of a Free People* (Boston: Allyn and Bacon, 1963).

Source 2.8: Lister's Account

To the best of my recollection about 4 o'clock in the morning being the 19th of April the 5 front companies was ordered to load which we did. . . . It was at Lexington when we saw one of their companies drawn up in regular order. Major Pitcairn of the Marines second in command called to them to disperse, but their not seeming willing he desired us to mind our space which we did when they gave us a fire then run off to get behind a wall. We had one man wounded of our Company in the leg, his name was Johnson, also Major Pitcairn's horse was shot in the flank; we returned their salute, and before we proceeded on our march from Lexington I believe we killed and wounded either 7 or 8 men.

Source: Ensign Jeremy Lister, youngest of the British officers at Lexington, in a personal narrative written in 1782. Reprinted in J. Lister, *Concord Fight* (Cambridge, MA: Harvard University Press, 1931).

Tool 2.1: Image Analysis Worksheet

Directions: Look at the three images of the Battle at Lexington Green (Sources 2.1, 2.2, 2.3) and consider these questions.

A) What details do you notice in each image?

Image	Artist/ Date	What people do you see?	What objects do you see?	What actions do you see?
2.1				
2.2				
2.3				

B) What details are the same in each image?

C) What details are different?

Tool 2.1: Image Analysis Worksheet (continued)

D) How are the British troops portrayed in each image?

E) How are the patriots portrayed?

F) Based on these images, do you think the "Battle at Lexington" was really a battle? What details lead you to your conclusion?

G) What new questions do you have after looking at these images?

H) Read Sources 2.4 and 2.5. What details in the images do these sources support?

Tool 2.2: Sourcing Worksheet

Refer to the diary entry of John Barker and the deposition of Nathaniel Mulliken and the other Minutemen (Sources 2.4 and 2.5).

1. What do we know about the author(s) of each of these documents?

2. How does this information influence whether or not we believe the authors?

3. Explain the difference between the genres of these two documents: How is a diary different from a sworn deposition?

4. Regarding Barker's diary, provide one reason that you might trust it. What is one reason you might *distrust* it?

5. On what day was Barker's diary entry written? How much time elapsed between Barker writing in his diary and the event he describes? Is there any way to be absolutely sure? Could this entry have been written days later?

6. Regarding Mulliken's deposition, provide one reason that you might trust it. What is one reason you might distrust it?

7. How does knowing that this deposition was sent to the colonial representative in Parliament, Benjamin Franklin, inform your judgment of its trustworthiness?

Suggested Resources

http://www.nps.gov/mima
This National Park Service page offers a variety of resources from "Minute Man" National Historical Park, including a historical overview, photographs and multimedia, and curricular materials and professional development opportunities for teachers.

http://memory.loc.gov/ammem/today/apr19.html
This page, run by the Library of Congress, offers rich primary source material, including access to maps, personal papers, and the original depositions taken after the conflict on Lexington Green took place.

http://www.lexingtonhistory.org/
This site is run by the Lexington Historical Society and offers photographs and descriptions of historic buildings in Lexington such as Buckman Tavern, best known as the headquarters of the Minutemen.

http://www.masshist.org/revolution/lexington.php
This site, maintained by the Massachusetts Historical Society, features a historical overview of the events at Lexington and Concord, supporting primary documents, and lesson plans focusing on the onset of the American Revolution.

http://teachingamericanhistory.org/library/index.asp?subcategory=74
This page, created in partnership with the Ashbrook Center, features a number of primary source documents related to the onset of the American Revolution, including the documents of General Thomas Gage and Major John Pitcairn.

http://edsitement.neh.gov/view_lesson_plan.asp?id=679#01
This site, created by a partnership among the National Endowment for the Humanities, the Verizon Foundation, and the National Trust for the Humanities, features a lesson on the American Revolution in the North. The first of the suggested activities focuses on "The Shot Heard 'Round the World" and utilizes a number of primary sources.

http://historicalthinkingmatters.org/why/
This page, featured on the Historical Thinking Matters website, uses the case of the battle at Lexington Green to show and explain historical reading and thinking, and includes historians thinking out loud as they analyze primary source documents.

CHAPTER 3

Lincoln in Context

I have no purpose to introduce political and social equality between the white and black races. There is a physical difference between the two, which in my judgment will probably forever forbid their living together upon the footing of perfect equality, and inasmuch as it becomes a necessity that there must be a difference, I . . . am in favor of the race to which I belong, having the superior position. (Abraham Lincoln's reply to Stephen A. Douglas at Ottawa, Illinois, August 21, 1858)[1]

Samuel Alschuler. Photograph of Lincoln. 1857. Urbana, IL.
Available at http://memory.loc.gov/service/rbc/lprbscsm/scsm0971/001r.jpg

Today these words sound offensive, a relic of bygone times that few mourn or romanticize. They broadcast an attitude that is anathema to American ideals, and many readers will be shocked to learn that they were uttered by Abraham Lincoln. How could the man who wrote the Emancipation Proclamation and the stirring words at Gettysburg be responsible for words that convey a racial superiority so distasteful to our modern ears?

These words fly in the face of Americans' understanding of Abraham Lincoln as the "Great Emancipator." They prompt readers to embrace another vision of Lincoln: "White Supremacist." In fact, *Ebony* magazine editor Lerone Bennett, Jr. made that very call in 1968 with a famous article asking, "Was Abe Lincoln a White Supremacist?"[2] Bennett claimed that Americans' Lincoln was a feel-good creation, and that Lincoln was actually a White supremacist, albeit a well-intentioned one. He was a conservative politician who responded only to political necessity, and showed his true colors through racist jokes.

Bennett's article prompted scholars to confront the question of Lincoln's racism. A deeper and more extended conversation ensued, with eminent historians revisiting and seriously considering the question of Lincoln's views on slavery and race. Historians wondered if this paradox (Lincoln as author of the Emancipation Proclamation and as believer in White supremacy) was a matter of judging the man more than a century after the fact, or whether Lincoln also appeared paradoxical to his contemporaries. What did these words mean to those who heard them in 1858?

Historians worked to understand Lincoln's views in the *context* of his own time, and this required making connections. Lincoln did not live in a vacuum; his speeches and actions were deeply intertwined with the particulars of his world. The word *context* has Latin roots that mean "to weave together." *Contextualizing* in history is about working to understand historical phenomena–speeches, people, events–as they existed in their original worlds in order to understand them on their own terms rather than through a modern lens.

We cannot separate the words that began this chapter from the occasion on which they were uttered (a debate with Stephen A. Douglas for a fiercely contested senatorial seat); the location of this debate (Ottawa, Illinois, a hotbed of anti-Black sentiment); the kinds of people who heard the debate (largely supportive of Douglas and suspicious of Lincoln); and the fact that both Lincoln and Douglas addressed their audience not as prophets or moralists but as candidates courting votes. Nor can we ignore what Douglas said to spark this response, or the words Lincoln uttered that immediately follow the excerpt at the start of this chapter. The act of contextualizing requires considering a wide-ranging variety of factors, from the ideologies of the day to a particular sequence of phrases and sentences. But in all cases, it demands that historical artifacts and sources be recognized as human constructions that existed within a particular social world, and as such, cannot be considered as free-floating evidence that speaks for itself.

Was Lincoln a Racist? Analyzing the Question

The question of whether Lincoln was a racist is no ordinary one. It links one of America's favorite icons with one of its most reprehensible legacies and ideas. The question alone can elicit passionate responses, and answering it convincingly is neither easy nor quick.

First there is the difficulty of uncovering a person's sincere beliefs. Even in the best cases, this is not an easy task for the historian–how do you get inside a man's mind? Moreover, who does not change his or her mind over a lifetime? Does expressing something one year mean that the speaker believes it the next? And then there is the matter of consistency. Is a man all or nothing–racist or egalitarian? Can we discern when a man is absolute in his views and when those views may be mixed, tentative, or uncertain?

Questions also arise about the term "racist," a word that didn't exist in Lincoln's time.[3] Is its use anachronistic? Are we imposing modern ideas on past situations in an ahistorical way? Racism has enormous relevance to today's America and to understanding our past. But phrasing the question in present-day terms raises a central tension in history: While today's concerns may prompt historical investigations, they should not swamp or distort the realities of the past.

Still, even given these limitations, historians have pursued the question.[4] And to discern meaning and uncover Lincoln's views, they strive to analyze his words within their original context.

The Sources

What sources illuminate Lincoln's views on race? He produced a huge cache of documentary evidence. He wrote constantly and left behind letters, notes and memos, speeches, legal arguments, policy statements, and revisions and drafts of many of these.[5] Historian Douglas Wilson explained that "[Lincoln] responded to almost every important development during his presidency, and to many that were not so important, with some act of writing."[6]

Then there is the reminiscent testimony. After Lincoln's death, William Herndon, his law partner for more than 15 years, collected stories from many who knew him. He then wrote a biography of his former partner. Historians are skeptical of this work, given the cool personal relationship he maintained with Lincoln, as well as the financial opportunities bound up with writing about the slain president. Nevertheless, the stories Herndon collected add to the evidence about Lincoln. Historians can also look at all the source material available from the time to understand Lincoln (e.g., newspapers, other people's papers, legal briefs and decisions).

Even with this large pool of primary sources, it is hard to pin down Lincoln when it comes to race. Historians have had to disentangle the mythic Lincoln from the man. Lincoln biographer David Herbert Donald described him as a versatile icon, that for different groups "he was a Communist . . . also a vegetarian, a socialist, a prohibitionist, a greenbacker, and a proponent of Union Now."[7] Because Lincoln has become the "central symbol" of American ideals, historians have to work to distinguish the real Lincoln from the symbolic.[8] They have been doing this work for decades and have produced a vast body of scholarship.

Still, the "real" Lincoln remains elusive. Described as a "puzzling mixture" by historians, "reticent" and "secretive" by his contemporaries, it is with good reason that an acclaimed book in the Lincoln pantheon is called *The Lincoln Nobody Knows*.[9] Author Richard Current described certain topics in the Lincoln literature as controversial, explaining that the "evidence is tangled in contradictions, and equally fair-minded and well-informed students disagree in their interpretation of it."[10] Lincoln's views on race and slavery exemplify a tangled topic.

We discuss below four sources that are central to the study of Lincoln's views, and a fifth that can help put Lincoln's words in perspective. These sources span the period 1841–1863, a time of significant change in American history. The three decades preceding the Civil War saw Nat Turner's Rebellion, the birth of William Lloyd Garrison's newspaper *The Liberator*, legislative acts meant to settle the question of slavery in the territories, the Dred Scott decision denying Blacks citizenship, and acts of violence from Harpers Ferry to the riots of "Bloody Kansas." Different groups adopted extreme positions: On the one hand, the abolitionists called for an immediate end to slavery; on the other, pro-slavery factions praised slavery as a blessed institution sanctioned by the Bible. It is against this backdrop that these sources must be considered.

Lincoln-Douglas Debates. The 1858 Lincoln-Douglas debates are one of the most famous events in political history. Lincoln, an Illinois state legislator, challenged incumbent U.S. Senator Stephen Douglas to a series of debates. Douglas agreed to debate Lincoln in seven Illinois towns.[11] The debates were elaborate events, complete with marching bands, picnics, fireworks, and banners–a major source of entertainment for the 19th-century crowds. Each debate followed the same format: three hours of rousing oratory punctuated by the crowd's cheers, laughter, jeers, and applause.[12] The reporters in attendance filed stories that were printed in newspapers around the country, and the debates drew a national audience.

While the Lincoln-Douglas debates are routinely included in history textbooks, their accounts focus on "appearances and voices," with little if any attention paid to the words spoken or the ideas espoused.[13] What were the great issues being debated?

The expansion of slavery into the Western territories was at the heart of the debates. In the 1850s, the Missouri Compromise, which declared territories north of the 36°30" latitude forever off limits to slavery, was repealed. Douglas, the architect of this change, supported popular sovereignty in the territories, making it possible for Western settlers to approve slavery in their region. New territories could hold elections to establish their status as slaveholding or free soil. The Kansas-Nebraska Act of 1854 escalated tensions over westward expansion and slavery, the most violent manifestation being "Bleeding Kansas." Given this backdrop, historians agree that the 1850s was a time of virulent racism, when the very humanity of dark-skinned people was denied in many quarters.

"The Equal of the White Man." The first document (Source 3.1), an excerpt from the first debate in Ottawa, Illinois, on August 21, 1858, begins with Douglas's claim that Lincoln (and the "Black Republican party") supported Black citizenship and rights, including the right to vote and serve on juries and in elected office. Douglas established his own position as being "in favor of confining citizenship to white men," and opposed to Negro citizenship "in any and every form." He went on to claim that Lincoln (alongside the abolitionists) believed that the "Negro was born his equal" and was "endowed with equality by the Almighty."

Douglas set up a contrast between himself and his challenger in what is a familiar context to the modern reader: the political campaign. Although a 3-hour 19th-century debate may seem a bit much to us, we can relate to the campaign stump speech and candidates who calibrate their words to win audience approval.

Historian Eric Foner called charges that the Republicans were pro-Negro the 1850s' most utilized "weapon in the Democrats' political arsenal."[14] Especially in the West, the Democratic Party bet that linking the Republicans to "Negro equality" would win the Democrats the election. People on all sides of the political spectrum saw advocacy of Negro equality as political suicide: Not enough voters supported this platform. More common were feelings of hate and fear toward Blacks, and this held true in all regions of the country, not just in the slaveholding South.

This was an era when "racial prejudice was all but universal" and four "free" states wouldn't even let Negroes into their territory.[15] Evincing support for the prohibition of slavery, or even abolishing it altogether, did not equate to advocating Negro rights, let alone equality. White workers did not want to compete with slave labor nor compete with free Blacks for available jobs. Keeping the West free of slaves had more to do with the Free Soil Party's political platform in the 1840s than it did with anti-slavery passion. Free Soilers emphasized hard work and fair competition as the key to economic self-improvement for White men. Keeping the Western territories free of slave labor would ensure this "fair" competition, and fulfill the promise of a land where perseverance and ability paid off. In short, the people who voted down slavery in the territories often did so based on self-interest, rather than moral qualms about slavery.

In the first document, we hear Stephen Douglas's attention to this mindset. His words jar and upset us. It is hard to imagine a world in which the words "I am in favor of confining citizenship to White men, men of European birth and descent, instead of conferring it upon Negroes, Indians and other inferior races" get votes. But we can't forget the outcome of the Senate election. Douglas won.

We hear Lincoln considering this ideological climate, this context, in his reply (Source 3.2). He carefully distanced himself from the "little abolition orators" whom Douglas ungraciously dumped in his corner, and stated that he would not interfere with slavery where it already existed. Lincoln focused on the question of slavery's westward expansion. This allowed any voter against expansion of slavery, regardless of the reason, to give his support to Lincoln. It is moves like this one that prompted historian and classicist Garry Wills to credit Lincoln with "defining the issue of slavery in politically manageable terms."[16] Lincoln made distinctions and qualified his statements in ways critical to that accomplishment.

Natural Rights and Political Rights. Initially, Lincoln denied any desire to introduce political and social equality between the races, a message that must have drawn relief and applause from his audience. He acknowledged physical differences between the races and credited these with stacking the odds against a society where Blacks and Whites could share "perfect equality." Here he marked himself in agreement with Douglas that, given such odds, the White population would have the superior position. But the contingency of Lincoln's remarks stands in contrast to Douglas's.

Lincoln took a different tack on the question of equality, away from social and political equality, toward natural rights and the right to enjoy the fruits of one's labor. In these, he asserted, the Negro is "as much entitled . . . as the White man." Social, political, natural, economic–all these different kinds of rights. Why did Lincoln make these distinctions?

The anti-Black ideology of the day partly answers this question. Lincoln crafted an ideology that focused on the humanity of the Black slave, in contrast to those who saw slaves as subhuman. In Lincoln's law practice he called getting at the core issue in a case "getting at the nub." The "nub" of Lincoln's stated position on Blacks in 1858 was that as human beings, they were due natural rights as stated in the Declaration of Independence.

Lincoln's distinctions between kinds of equality are accompanied by hedging and careful language. While he does admit a physical difference between the two groups, he equivocates in his other comparisons. There is only "perhaps" a difference in moral or intellectual endowment. Even raising the possibility that the two races were morally and intellectually equivalent would go squarely against the prevailing winds of his day.

Lincoln's distinctions and qualifications might seem trivial and even deceptive to the modern ear, the workings of a politico willing to say whatever was needed to best his opponent. But given his world, his publicly expressed ideas were more progressive than those of most other Whites (abolitionists being the significant exception). The views that Lincoln articulated in these debates would unify the Republican party.[17] As historian Eric Foner notes, the Republicans

> did develop a policy which recognized the essential humanity of the Negro, and demanded protection for certain basic rights which the Democrats denied him. Although deeply flawed by an acceptance of many racial stereotypes, and limited . . . the Republican stand on race relations went against the prevailing opinion of the 1850's, and proved a distinct political liability in a racist society.[18]

Lincoln's stance was obviously not as radical as the abolitionism of his day, but its focus on the shared humanity of the slave was non-negotiable and a logical necessity if any eventual emancipation were to be accepted. Always attentive to public opinion and existing law, Lincoln neither pushed too hard nor conceded too much with his stance on equality. Instead, he took a path that allowed anti-slavery voters of all stripes to join him. He might have lost a Senate election in 1858, but his careful path allowed him to be elected president in 1860.

Letter to Mary Speed. The third document in the set (Source 3.3) takes us back to 1841, more than 15 years before the Lincoln-Douglas debates. It is a private letter Lincoln wrote to the half-sister of Joshua Speed, one of his closest friends. Different in style and form from Lincoln's public words at the senatorial debates, it reveals little about Lincoln the politician and more of the private man known by his friends. But if we look closely, we see a consistency with his 1858 statements regarding the humanity of the slave. That said, this letter also includes passages that shock the modern reader.

The letter describes a journey on a Mississippi riverboat on which a group of slaves were literally being sold down the river, "separated forever," Lincoln writes, "from the scenes of their childhood, their friends, their fathers and mothers, and brothers and sisters, and many of them, from their wives and children." But as the letter continues, it presents a perplexing contrast that has prompted debate about its exact meaning. As he recalled the spectacle of slaves chained together in close quarters, Lincoln was moved to remark not on human misery, but on human happiness. The same scene that would have provoked fury and outrage in any abolitionist inspired Lincoln to write words that can be read as "ameliorat[ing] slavery's horror with an inference that blacks have a special capacity to deal with captivity."[19]

However, on closer inspection, we see that Lincoln's description of the slaves' happy activities communicates a belief that slaves shared a common humanity with Whites. The slaves' response to their situation is presented as "a fine example . . . for contemplating the effect of condition upon human happiness . . . [and that God] renders the worst of human conditions tolerable." Such phrases won't still a modern-day reader's discomfort over enslaved people described as happy and cheerful. But considered in the context of mid-19th-century ideas about slavery and the Negro, they are significant.

After 1830, tensions over slavery and westward expansion grew. Publication of *The Liberator*, William Lloyd Garrison's abolitionist magazine, and Nat Turner's slave rebellion in 1831 sharpened the divide between North and South. Abolitionist rhetoric and assaults on the institution of slavery propelled pro-slavery thinkers and factions to develop theories to justify the institution and its permanence.[20] These included arguments that slavery actually benefited its captives and that Blacks were genetically different and inferior to Whites. In his 1841 letter, Lincoln embraces neither stance. Rather, he declares slaves to be human beings and slavery responsible for "the worst of human conditions."

The Speed letter raises other questions. It serves as an example of how historians continue to interrogate sources to uncover Lincoln's views on race, while finding few *prima facie* answers. Because Lincoln's words show little concern for slaves' suffering, they can be read as callous and unconcerned with the human costs of slavery. However, to Lincoln scholar Philip Paludan, what this shows is the need to ask more questions.[21] In writing to Mary Speed, a woman who lived in the slaveholding state of Kentucky, was Lincoln loath to rail against slavery for fear of offending her? Was Lincoln doing what his wife identified as his true nature–talking the least about what he felt the most? Or did he really believe that Blacks suffered less than others in "the worst of human conditions"? Paludan wonders if Lincoln's musings on the slaves' suffering were tempered by his audience or his own sense of privacy. Still, the question of Lincoln's insensitivity doesn't change the ideas undergirding his words. He considered Blacks as human and slavery as a cruel system.

Colonization. On August 14, 1862, President Lincoln addressed a delegation of free Black men, the first ever invited to the White House. Lincoln shook their hands and delivered his "Address on Colonization" (Source 3.4). The pairing of these factors is puzzling. Is welcoming Blacks into the White House consistent with a message of mass Black emigration?

Colonization. The emigration of Black Americans to other lands–in this case, Central America–to create a separate society from the one they had built with their forced labor, blood, sweat, and tears. How can we judge this plan as anything but segregation at its most extreme?

The idea of colonization had been around since the birth of the Republic. Following the British example in Sierra Leone in the late 18th century, the American Colonization Society founded Liberia on the west coast of Africa in 1821. Before the 1830s colonization was the "main embodiment of white anti-slavery sentiment," but Black opposition to the policy and the rise of radical abolitionism changed that.[22] However, colonization continued to have its supporters, and the years immediately before the outbreak of war saw increased attention to it as a practical policy. When President Lincoln addressed Congress for the first time in December 1861, he asked them to authorize funds to carry out a colonization plan and Congress responded by appropriating $600,000.

Historians agree that the colonization movement was riddled with conflicting purposes from its start. Some supported the idea because they saw it as the only way that Blacks could live in an equitable society–they judged White America so hostile to Blacks that equal rights and privileges would always be out of reach. For others, colonization was what Lerone Bennett called a "white dream," a movement to make the United States and its territories free of Blacks.[23] Still others saw colonization as the opportunity to spread Christian ideals while forging economic ties with far-off populations.

Lincoln supported colonization, but his views on it continue to divide and perplex historians.[24] Why did he support this policy? Was Lincoln's support for colonization a "psychological safety valve" meant to reassure fearful Whites that emancipation would be accompanied by colonization?[25] Or was he against the races mixing and so advocated removing the freedmen? Did he change his mind about colonization during his political career?

Columbia's Eric Foner argued that Lincoln's views on colonization did indeed change during his administration, and that the Emancipation Proclamation was a turning point. Lincoln went from supporting a colonization program that accompanied a plan of gradual emancipation to abandoning the policy altogether.[26] At the beginning of his administration, Lincoln advocated the gradual freeing of slaves, compensating their owners, and coupling this with colonization. Following the Emancipation Proclamation and a failed experiment of Black colonization on Île à Vache, a small island near Haiti, he abandoned his support for the policy. Lincoln eventually endorsed the Thirteenth Amendment and extended the franchise to Black veterans–demonstrating that he could envision freedmen as American citizens. The fact that he spent only $38,000 of Congress's $600,000 also shows that the colonization policy dropped from his favor.

Lincoln's words of August 1862 (Source 3.4) preceded the Emancipation Proclamation, and historians will, no doubt, continue to argue their intent and meaning. However, they do reiterate important ideas present in the previous documents, including a belief that conditions matter to human development (in his use of the term "systematically oppressed"). Lincoln also goes further than his equivocation at Springfield (that Blacks may "perhaps" be his intellectual equal) and uses the phrase "intelligent colored men." Even so, the address made many Blacks angry, not only for what they saw as a denial that they were as American as the White man, but also for statements (not included here) they understood to mean that Blacks were the cause of the Civil War.[27]

Perspectives and stances regarding colonization, an idea intimately linked to slavery and abolition, changed in the 25 years leading up to the Civil War, just as political movements regarding the institution of slavery had. While Lincoln's stance may have been progressive in earlier decades, it was conservative when compared with the post-1830s radical abolitionist stance.

"Us to Rule, and the Negroes to Serve." On first reading, the 1863 words of John Bell Robinson (Source 3.5), a White author from the northern state of Pennsylvania, may seem irrelevant to this investigation; after all, they mention neither Lincoln nor his policies. However, Robinson provides a lens into what many Whites were thinking, reading, and publishing at the time, in effect providing the reader with a context for Lincoln's own views.

In this document we see a racialized ideology that was so common it was considered neither shocking nor lunatic. John Bell Robinson claimed that the "advantages of Negro slavery" went beyond free labor and amounted to a sacred obligation. He wrote of God's plan for White people "to rule, and the Negroes to serve," warning that tampering with these "holy arrangements" would result in eternal degradation, if not worldly subjugation. Robinson also mentioned colonization, asserting that any attempt would fail, as Negroes "would fall back into heathenism and barbarism in less than fifty years."

This Northerner's words provide a sharp contrast to Lincoln's, by asserting that Blacks were inherently inferior and not equipped to rule themselves. They offer a necessary context for understanding the world in which Lincoln lived and spoke.

Corroborating Sources. While Sources 3.1 to 3.4 are fixtures in historians' ongoing conversations about Lincoln's views, other documents and events appear repeatedly. For example, Lincoln's August 1862 letter to *New York Tribune* editor Horace Greeley is frequently used to show that Lincoln was concerned only with the nation's unity, not with abolishing slavery. Lincoln wrote:

> My paramount object in this struggle is to save the Union, and is not either to save or destroy slavery. If I could save the Union without freeing *any* slave I would do it, and if I could save the Union by freeing *all* the slaves I would do that and if I could do it by freeing some and leaving others alone I would also do that.

Often the quote ends there. But to understand Lincoln's sentiments, it is wise to read what he goes on to say: "I have here stated my purpose according to my view of *official* duty; and I intend no modification of my oft expressed *personal* wish that all men everywhere could be free"[28] [emphases in original].

Two events also appear repeatedly in a discussion of Lincoln's views: General Fremont's August 30, 1861, proclamation freeing the slaves in Missouri, and General David Hunter's 1862 order to emancipate slaves in South Carolina, Georgia, and Florida. Some argue that when Lincoln overrode Fremont's orders, he signaled a lack of intent to free the slaves. Others argue that this was more about Lincoln the politician and lawyer: Fremont didn't have the constitutional power to issue such an order and Lincoln did not see even his own power as extending that far. What mattered here was his respect for his position as executor of the laws, not as writer of the same. Additionally, given Chief Justice Taney's Supreme Court–a court that had shown itself friendly to both pro-slavery and anti-Black ideology–Lincoln was wary of any moves that might involve them.

Contextualizing Lincoln doesn't provide pat answers. Historical inquiry teaches us to tolerate complexity, not shy away from it. One thing we can say for sure is that Lincoln's ideas are more complex than any simple label. Historian James Leiker talks about the discrepancies and contradictions in Lincoln's thought–other historians would emphasize the nuances and distinctions in Lincoln's prose.[29] An absolute label, racist or egalitarian, doesn't begin to capture the historical evidence.

It's more instructive to think about Lincoln as existing along a continuum between these two absolutes of racist and egalitarian. We could assert that compared to his White peers, Lincoln was not racist for his time, or certainly less so than others. We could also assert that like most if not all Whites in antebellum America, Lincoln was in fact a racist.

Which leads us to the second answer to our question. Lincoln's America was an incredibly racist place. Discussing the abolitionist movement and regional splits over slavery can lull us into a false sense that racism was confined to a particular region and population. But reading these documents historically reveals a world in which Blacks were denied their humanity, and people justified the barbarism of slavery with theories that repel us today. Was Lincoln a racist? It depends. Was his time? Yes, more than we would like to think possible.

Why Teach About Lincoln and Race?

Learning That Context Matters. We can't help judging the past. Every history teacher has had the student who rushes in to share the revelation, "Jefferson owned slaves! Columbus cut off the ears of natives!" Such students are eager to share this information that proves that their past teachers not only left out part of the story, they whitewashed these figures and turned knaves into heroes. But how should we judge the past and its actors? By our contemporary standards or by the standards of their day? While there is not one way to answer this question, *history demands that we know the difference between the two.*

What was Lincoln's world like? Very different from our own, so different that we might feel like aliens if we were to take an "excellent adventure" Bill-&-Ted style. It was in this foreign world that Abraham Lincoln lived, spoke, and led. If we are to think historically about Lincoln's words, we must resist easy judgments and ask questions about historical context. What were the setting and purpose of these words? And how do his words and ideas compare to those of his contemporaries?[30]

For historians, context lies at the epicenter of historical reasoning. Engaging students in Lincoln's views and words on race presents them with powerful opportunities to learn what "contextualizing" is all about.

Analyzing Ideas About Race. Race is a topic too often glossed over or omitted in our classrooms. There is no denying that race matters to understanding the American past–the crimes that have been done in its name, the ideologies that justified those crimes, the institutions that reified those ideologies–the list goes on. Racism has influenced how our country has developed and who we have become. These documents engage students in thinking specifically about racialized ideas and prompt analysis of them.

Learning that statements that sound offensive to our ears could have been judged progressive in another time opens up an important lesson for our students: Don't be too quick to assume that the meaning you ascribe to a statement is the same one the speaker intended. Some students are reluctant to acknowledge that race is important to the study of America. Others quickly dismiss an untoward word as just more home-grown racism. A focused consideration of Lincoln's distinctions and purposes gives both groups practice in analyzing this volatile and necessary topic.

Slowing Down Student Reading. These documents demand analysis. They require that students read slowly and pay attention to word choice and nuance. In a single "perhaps," an easily missed equivocation in the debate with Douglas, historians open up a world of possibilities. Lincoln was a careful wordsmith; examining his words is an opportunity for students to see how qualification and distinctions matter to meaning. If students read these documents on a surface level, without wondering who is presenting what to whom, they will miss key aspects of historical context and won't be able to answer the question satisfactorily. Understanding Lincoln means slowing down and asking why he used one word and not another. This careful attention to text is central to understanding history and how we know what we know about the past.

Challenging Student Misconceptions. As students consider the world in which these words were uttered, flawed ideas about the past are challenged. Although Illinois was a Northern free state, racial superiority still played very well in Peoria. Students learn that racial prejudice was not limited to the South, but existed throughout antebellum America.

Misleading ideas about documentary evidence will also be challenged. John Bell Robinson's document (Source 3.5) makes no mention of Lincoln. Students often infer that this makes it irrelevant to questions about Lincoln's views.[31] But Robinson provides a vital lens for what people of this time were thinking, reading, and publishing. By examining Robinson's words, students will be better able to locate Lincoln on a spectrum of opinion in the 1850s and 1860s.

How Might You Use These Materials?

Scenario 1 (2–3 Hour Lesson). Was Lincoln a racist? Engage students in a "Structured Academic Controversy" where they analyze documents in order to answer the focus question and craft a warranted conclusion.[32]

Open the lesson with Lincoln's words from Springfield in 1858 (Source 3.2), but omit any identifying information (speaker, year, place). Ask students how they would describe the passage and what else they want to know about it. Would they describe it the same way given any speaker, time, and place? Then share with them the identifying information. Are they surprised to find out that these are Lincoln's words?

Tell students that they will be investigating the question, Was Lincoln a racist? Review the structure of the activity (Tool 3.1). Organize students into groups of four and assign one pair in each group Side A (Yes, Lincoln was a racist) and the other pair Side B (No, Lincoln was not a racist). Pass out document packets (Sources 3.1–3.5) with the document analysis chart (Tool 3.2). In pairs, students work through the documents, finding and recording evidence for their assigned position. They should also record any questions that arise during this process. After pairs have gathered evidence for their position, they will convene in groups of four. The first pair shares their position and the supporting evidence while the other pair listens in order to restate that position. Then reverse the roles. Remind students that in this listening and restating activity, students are *not* debating. After this, students give up their assigned positions and discuss the best answer to the question, that is, the one that is best supported by the evidence and other background knowledge students bring to the activity.

Finally, **ask students to write independent answers to the question, using documentary evidence to support their answers.**

Targeted list of skills in this scenario

- Evidence-based thinking and argumentation
- Questioning sources
- Contextualizing sources
- Synthesizing multiple accounts
- Listening carefully

Scenario 2 (2–4 Hour Lesson). Extend Scenario 1 by including the question, How should we judge the past?

Include this second focal question in the lesson and have students consider it after they have addressed the question about Lincoln and race. They can **write a separate paragraph explicitly addressing this question or include it in their written analysis of the first.**

Targeted list of skills in this scenario

- Evidence-based thinking and argumentation
- Questioning sources
- Contextualizing sources
- Synthesizing multiple accounts
- Listening carefully

Scenario 3 (1 Hour Lesson). Reading for context: see it, do it, know it. Use modeling and guided practice to teach students how to contextualize historical sources.

Introduce the question of whether Lincoln was a racist with the explanation, "You will be trying to answer this question, but to do so you must carefully read the historical evidence." Make sure every student has a copy of Source 3.2, then model how a historian would read and approach this document. First read aloud the source information and head note, pausing to generate questions and comments. Then read the contents of the document aloud, again pausing to parse a phrase, question a term, or wonder aloud. The point of this modeling is to "think aloud," and make visible for students the active questioning and thinking that historians do as they read.[33]

After you work through the document, identify what questions you asked to establish the historical context. These will include: Who was he talking to? What were his purposes in making this speech? What else was happening at the time? What were existing racial attitudes and laws in Illinois in 1858? How might these factors have shaped Lincoln's word choice and message? Reading this chapter's historiographical essay will help you answer these questions. However, also include questions you don't have answers for; these may be used to show students that closely reading a historical document means specifying your ignorance and identifying what you need to know to understand it.

Define historical context as "imagining the setting," and show students some beginning questions to contextualize documents (Tool 3.3). Make the points that in order to contextualize:

1. Historians use what they know about the time and place to help them understand the document;
2. Historians ask questions about what they don't know and what else they need to know, to try to more fully understand the document.

With your guidance, students can use the reading practices you modeled to help them to understand and analyze Source 3.3. You can walk them through this process by asking questions such as "What should we do first when reading a historical document?" and prompting them to use contextualizing questions at key places in the document. After this guided practice, **students can read and analyze Source 3.5 independently as homework.**

Targeted list of skills in this scenario

- Contextualizing sources
- Understanding contextualization and why it's necessary

Sources and Tools

Source 3.1: Douglas's Speech (Modified)

Note: In 1858 Abraham Lincoln ran against Stephen A. Douglas for a seat in the U.S. Senate. The two engaged in a series of seven public debates that attracted national attention. The following is an excerpt from Douglas's address to Lincoln in their first debate at Ottawa, Illinois, on August 21, 1858.

If you desire Negro citizenship, if you desire to allow them to come into the State and settle with the White man, if you desire them to vote on an equality with yourselves, and to make them **eligible** to office, to serve on juries, and to judge your rights, then support Mr. Lincoln and the Black Republican party, who are in favor of the citizenship of the Negro. For one, I am opposed to Negro citizenship in any and every form. I believe this government was made . . . by White men, for the benefit of White men and their **posterity** forever, and I am in favor of confining citizenship to White men, men of European birth and descent, instead of conferring it upon Negroes, Indians and other inferior races.

Mr. Lincoln, following the example and lead of all the little abolition **orators**, who go around and lecture in the basements of schools and churches, reads from the Declaration of Independence, that all men were created equal, and then asks how can you **deprive** a Negro of that equality which God and the Declaration of Independence awards to him. He and they maintain that Negro equality is guaranteed by the laws of God, and that it is **asserted** in the Declaration of Independence. . . . I do not question Mr. Lincoln's **conscientious** belief that the Negro was made his equal, and hence is his brother, but for my own part, I do not regard the Negro as my equal, and positively deny that he is my brother. . . .

[Lincoln] holds that the Negro was born his equal and yours, and that he was **endowed** with equality by the Almighty, and that no human law can deprive him of these rights. . . . Now, I do not believe that the Almighty ever intended the Negro to be the equal of the White man. . . . For thousands of years the Negro has been a race upon the earth, and during all that time, in all latitudes and climates, wherever he has wandered or been taken, he has been inferior to the race which he has there met. He belongs to an inferior race, and must always occupy an inferior position.

Source: Excerpt from Douglas's address to Lincoln in their first debate at Ottawa, Illinois, August 21, 1858. Cited in D. E. Fehrenbacher, ed., *Abraham Lincoln, Speeches and Writings, 1832–1858* (New York: Library of America, 1989), 504–505.

WORD BANK

eligible–qualified, fit to be chosen
posterity–descendents, future generations
orators–speechmakers
deprive–deny, rob
asserted–stated
conscientious–careful, moral
endowed–provided, gifted

Source 3.2: Lincoln's Response to Douglas (Modified)

Note: Read how Lincoln carefully compares Blacks and Whites in his reply to Douglas at the Ottawa, Illinois, debate.

I will say here . . . that I have no purpose directly or indirectly to interfere with the institution of slavery in the States where it exists. I believe I have no lawful right to do so, and I have no **inclination** to do so. I have no purpose to introduce political and social equality between the white and black races. There is a physical difference between the two, which in my judgment will probably forever forbid their living together upon the footing of perfect equality, and inasmuch as it becomes a necessity that there must be a difference, I, as well as Judge Douglas, am in favor of the race to which I belong, having the superior position. I have never said anything **to the contrary**, but I hold that notwithstanding all this, there is no reason in the world why the Negro is not **entitled** to all the natural rights **enumerated** in the Declaration of Independence, the right to life, liberty and the pursuit of happiness. I hold that he is as much **entitled** to these as the White man. I agree with Judge Douglas [that the Negro] is not my equal in many respects–certainly not in color, perhaps not in moral or intellectual **endowment**. But in the right to eat the bread . . . which his own hand earns, he is my equal and the equal of Judge Douglas, and the equal of every living man.

Source: Excerpt from Abraham Lincoln's reply to Stephen A. Douglas at Ottawa, Illinois, August 21, 1858. Cited in D. E. Fehrenbacher, ed., *Abraham Lincoln, Speeches and Writings, 1832–1858* (New York: Library of America, 1989), 512.

WORD BANK

inclination–preference, tendency
to the contrary–different
entitled–due, permitted
enumerated–listed
endowment–gifts

Source 3.3: Letter to Mary Speed (Modified)

Note: Read Lincoln's words to his personal friend about seeing slaves on a riverboat.

By the way, a fine example was presented on board the boat for **contemplating** the effect of *condition* upon human happiness. A gentleman had purchased twelve Negroes in different parts of Kentucky and was taking them to a farm in the South. They were chained six and six together. A small iron clevis was around the left wrist of each . . . so that the Negroes were strung together precisely like so many fish upon a trot-line. In this condition they were being separated forever from the scenes of their childhood, their friends, their fathers and mothers, and brothers and sisters, and many of them, from their wives and children, and going into **perpetual** slavery . . . yet amid all these distressing circumstances . . . they were the most cheerful and apparently happy creatures on board. One, whose offense for which he had been sold was over-fondness for his wife, played the fiddle almost continually; and the others danced, sung, cracked jokes, and played various games with cards from day to day. How true it is that . . . [God] renders the worst of human conditions tolerable.

Source: Excerpt from Abraham Lincoln's letter to Mary Speed, a personal friend, September 27, 1841, cited in *Collected Works of Abraham Lincoln* (Vol. 1). (Ann Arbor: University of Michigan Digital Library Production Services, 2001), 260. Available at http://quod.lib.umich.edu/l/lincoln/

WORD BANK

contemplating–considering, reflecting on
perpetual–lasting, permanent

Source 3.4: Address on Colonization

Note: Colonization of freed Blacks was an idea that had been around since the 1700s. Many Whites who opposed slavery actively supported colonization, maintaining that true freedom and equality could be realized only by relocating the Black population. Abraham Lincoln long favored the idea, and in 1862 Congress allocated a sum of money for a colonization program. The following is from Lincoln's "Address on Colonization," delivered to a group of free Black men at the White House on August 14, 1862.

Why . . . should the people of your race be colonized, and where? . . . If we deal with those who are not free at the beginning, and whose **intellects** are clouded by Slavery, we have very poor materials to start with. If intelligent colored men . . . would move in this matter, much might be accomplished. It is exceedingly important that we have men at the beginning capable of thinking as White men, and not those who have been systematically **oppressed**. . . . The place I am thinking about having for a colony is in Central America. . . . The country is a very excellent one for any people, and with great natural resources and advantages, and especially because of the similarity of climate with your native land–thus being suited to your physical condition.

Source: Lincoln's "Address on Colonization" delivered to a group of free Black men at the White House on August 14, 1862, cited in *Collected Works of Abraham Lincoln* (Vol. 5). (Ann Arbor: University of Michigan Digital Library Production Services, 2001), 371–372. Available at http://quod.lib.umich.edu/l/lincoln/

WORD BANK

intellects–minds
oppressed–dominated in a cruel, unfair way

Source 3.5: John Bell Robinson

Note: Read John Bell Robinson's theories about race and race relations. Robinson was a White man who lived in Pennsylvania.

God himself has made them for usefulness as slaves, and requires us to employ them as such, and if we betray our trust, and throw them off on their own resources, we **reconvert** them into barbarians. Our Heavenly Father has made us to *rule*, and the Negroes to serve, and if we . . . set aside his holy arrangements for the good of mankind and his own glory, and **tamper** with his laws, we shall be overthrown and **eternally degraded**, and perhaps made subjects of some other civilized nation. . . . Colonization in their native land of all the Negroes would be so nearly impracticable, that it will never be done, and no other spot on this green earth will do for them. It would be the height of cruelty and barbarism to send them anywhere else. If they could all be colonized on the coast of Africa, they would fall back into **heathenism** and barbarism in less than fifty years.

Source: Excerpt from J. B. Robinson, *Pictures of Slavery and Anti-Slavery: Advantages of Negro Slavery and the Benefits of Negro Freedom Morally, Socially, and Politically Considered* (Philadelphia, 1863), 42.

WORD BANK

reconvert–to change back
tamper–interfere, mess
eternally degraded–forever damaged, lowered in rank
heathenism–un-Christian state of things, paganism

Tool 3.1: Structured Academic Controversy Directions

Question: Was Abraham Lincoln a Racist?

Side A	**Side B**
Yes, Lincoln was a racist	**No, Lincoln was not a racist**

I. Partners Prepare

   a. Find evidence to support your side of the argument. Craft position.

II. Position Presentation

   a. Side A presents their position using supporting evidence from the texts.

   b. Side B *restates* to Side A's satisfaction.

   c. Side B presents their position using supporting evidence from the texts.

   d. Side A *restates* to Side B's satisfaction.

III. Consensus-Building

   a. Abandon roles.

   b. Build consensus regarding the question (or at least clarify where your differences lie), using supporting evidence.

   c. Consider the question:

   How should we judge people from the past?

Tool 3.2: SAC Document Analysis Chart

Was Lincoln a Racist?

Position: YES, Lincoln was a racist.

Document:

Evidence 1:

Document:

Evidence 2:

Document:

Evidence 3:

Document:

Evidence 4:

What questions do you have about these sources and ideas?

Tool 3.2: SAC Document Analysis Chart (continued)

Was Lincoln a Racist?

Position: NO, Lincoln was not a racist.

Document:

Evidence 1:

Document:

Evidence 2:

Document:

Evidence 3:

Document:

Evidence 4:

What questions do you have about these sources and ideas?

CONSENSUS:

WRITING PROMPT

Was Lincoln a racist?

Use evidence (quotes, information) to support your answer. Include an evaluation of the question if you wish.

Tool 3.3: Context Questions

1. When and where was this source written or produced?
2. What else was happening at the time this was written?
3. Why was it produced?
4. What was different back then? What was the same?
5. What would it look like through the eyes of someone who lived back then?

Suggested Resources

http://lincoln.lib.niu.edu/aboutbiovideo.html
Maintained by the Abraham Lincoln Historical Digitization Project, this site has a wealth of materials focused on Lincoln's life prior to his presidency. Resources include interpretive essays, lesson plans, videos of scholarly lectures, primary source archives, maps, and images. These can be browsed by format or theme.

http://www.gilderlehrman.org/institute/lincoln.html
This gateway to resources on teaching and learning about Lincoln, housed at the Gilder Lehrman Institute, includes invaluable (and brief!) scholarly essays on Lincoln and video lectures. Of special interest is the online exhibition "Lincoln and the Emancipation Proclamation," which includes explanatory notes, and images and transcripts of key documents.

http://memory.loc.gov/ammem/alhtml/alhome.html
Mr. Lincoln's Virtual Library
The Library of Congress's large collection of manuscripts, sheet music, and memorabilia regarding Lincoln and his times.

http://www.history.umd.edu/Freedmen/index.html
Supported by the University of Maryland, the Freedmen and Southern Society Project uses documents from the National Archives to vivify the drama of emancipation through the words of its participants. Of special interest may be the detailed "Chronology of Emancipation during the Civil War" (http://www.history.umd.edu/Freedmen/chronol.htm).

http://www.abrahamlincoln.org/
This home page for the Lincoln Institute links directly to its six websites focused on different aspects of Lincoln's life. Interpretive essays and selected primary sources make it easy to pursue a Lincoln topic in depth.

http://www.learner.org/workshops/primarysources/emancipation/introduction.html
Produced by Annenberg Media, this professional development workshop explores Lincoln's role in the ending of slavery. Participants are prompted to consider Lincoln's beliefs on African Americans and slavery using a video lecture, primary sources, and guiding questions.

http://quod.lib.umich.edu/l/lincoln/
Here, the multivolume classic *The Collected Works of Abraham Lincoln*, edited by a team led by Roy P. Basler, is available online in searchable form.

CHAPTER 4

Columbus Day: 1892, *Not* 1492

Jack Schneider

Columbus Day Memorial Celebration, Union Station, Washington, DC, 1912. Published by Bain News Service. Available at http://www.loc.gov/pictures/resource/ggbain.11303/

In the summer of 1892, President Benjamin Harrison was locked in a fierce campaign for reelection to a second term. On July 21, he issued a proclamation calling for a new national holiday: "Discovery Day" (see Source 4.1). To be observed in schools, churches, and other places of assembly, Discovery Day honored Christopher Columbus as a symbol of "progress and enlightenment." Over a century later, Columbus Day is one of only two American holidays (along with the birthday of Dr. Martin Luther King, Jr.) that honor an individual.

While previous generations viewed Columbus as an intrepid explorer and courageous risk-taker, today's historians tend to be less generous. Kirkpatrick Sale's *Christopher Columbus and the Conquest of Paradise* describes Columbus's legacy as one of violence, colonialism, greed, and racism. Howard Zinn, whose *A People's History of the United States* has sold well over a million copies, casts the mariner as a monomaniacal fiend driven by the pursuit of gold in the Indies. Not finding the riches he sought, Zinn's Columbus resorted to brutality and eventual human trafficking, writing: "Let us in the name of the Holy Trinity go on sending all the slaves that can be sold."[1]

Alas, Columbus has not fared well of late. Like the rhyme about his sailing "the ocean blue" for previous generations, historians' bleak portrait of Columbus has penetrated popular consciousness. South Dakota and the city of Berkeley, California, even abrogated Columbus Day in the 1990s, renaming it "Native American Day" and "Indigenous People's Day," respectively.

Given Columbus's falling stock, it is hardly surprising that in a recent study we completed, high school history students bristled when reading the original Columbus Day decree.[2] These students were asked to read a series of documents and to place each in historical context. As they read through the texts, students talked about what they thought the documents were about and any other associations that came to mind.

When they reached Harrison's "Discovery Day" proclamation, some students wasted no time getting down to Columbus-bashing. Jacob, a high school student in an Advanced Placement U.S. history class, began his comments thus:

> The first thing that jumps out is that Columbus is a pioneer of "progress and enlightenment," which was certainly one way of looking at it, but from what I've learned, his goals were not entirely noble. Just get rich, whatever. Find a way to the Indies. Show that the earth wasn't flat.

Further, Jacob complained, the document "praises Columbus for his devout faith." Columbus "claimed to be a true Christian, but he also captured and tortured Indians, so he wasn't maybe as noble as this is having him be." Asked if anything else occurred to him, Jacob responded: "And the fact that it's becoming a holiday that we're supposed to revere, that's even worse!"

Jacob's response was common among this group of bright, articulate high school students. Drawing on background knowledge, Jacob went right at the explorer, engaging in what some might view as "critical thinking." Critical, without a doubt.

President Harrison's proclamation, it turns out, has little to do with 1492, or even Columbus himself. Capable and articulate as he was, Jacob had missed the document's real story.

How Did Historians Read It?

Asked what the same document was about, a group of doctoral candidates in history saw it quite differently, citing such things as:

- The "expansion of the heroic pantheon to include former undesirables."
- A "shameless appeal to superheroes in order to gain votes in urban centers."
- "The beginning of Pan-Whiteness in post-bellum America."[3]

Unlike the high school students, who alighted on Columbus's name and never budged, the graduate students viewed the document as a reflection of identity politics and good old electioneering. In fact, the historians hardly mentioned Columbus at all. How was it that the two groups saw such different things in the same text?

The easy answer would be to say that the historians simply know more American history. Obviously that's true, but only to a point. Having studied such topics as gender relations among French colonialists and Arab nationalists in Tunisia, the relationship between the Siege of Paris and German unification, and doctrinal schisms in Islam after Ali's death, the young historians possessed no factual knowledge of this time period in American history that would change their readings of the text. What they did possess, however, was a "historical approach" to the document, an orientation to documentary evidence that almost seems like common sense to those practiced in it. This orientation unlocks a world closed to untutored readers.

While the high school students responded to the document's most pronounced feature–the polarizing figure of Christopher Columbus and his changing fortunes in the court of public opinion–the historians employed a different approach. For them, reading a historical document meant putting sources on the stand and demanding that they yield their truths or falsehoods. To be sure, the historians were experts at employing disciplinary canons of evidence and rules of argument. Still, nothing about their approach was particularly complicated. In fact, some of the deepest things they did were also the most basic.

Consider their opening gambit. When historians sat down with the document, their first words were something along the lines of: "Okay, it's 1892."

A simple move, really–a recognition that the Harrison proclamation was not a free-floating utterance echoing from the ether. To the historians, the document was an artifact located in a unique time and place, a moment in history unlike any other. For them, this moment was not about 1492, or even 2002. It was about 1892.

Which immediately raises the question: What does 1892 mean?

President Harrison in Context

To the historians, President Harrison's proclamation was more about 1892 than it was about Columbus. Consequently, their questions focused on the late 19th century rather than the 15th. Why would Harrison have honored Columbus? Did he harbor some personal affinity for the explorer? Did Harrison consider Columbus a role model? Or was there something more to this move that doesn't immediately strike the eye? Surely, there must have been some reason.

The historians brainstormed what little they could remember about the era's historical context (recall that none was an expert in American history). Most, in fact, could remember only what they had covered in high school and undergraduate survey courses. In thinking about the United States in the 1890s, they tried to recall major events, themes, and people: the Progressive Era, the closing of the frontier, Frederick Jackson Turner, Populism, William Jennings Bryan, the "Cross of Gold" speech–the kinds of references found in any high school textbook. But as the historians continued to talk about the period, they inevitably arrived at the topic of immigration. When they did, light bulbs clicked on.

At the end of the 19th century, the United States was getting a makeover. Unprecedented waves of immigration transformed the country overnight (see Source 4.4). In the 30 years between 1880 and 1910, 18 million newcomers came to America's shores. And they were immigrants of a different breed–in the terminology of the time they were "Slavs," "Alpines," "Hebrews," "Iberics," or "Mediterraneans." They were from Europe, mostly, but not the Europe most American immigrants had come from previously. They were from farther east and farther south. They were swarthy and spoke strange languages. They worshipped differently from the indigenous Protestant majority.[4]

The most numerous of these new arrivals were Catholics. At the beginning of the 1880s, there were about 300,000 Italians in the United States, almost all of them Catholic. By 1910 that number had reached 2 million out of a population of 92 million Americans. As the Italians joined the Irish American community that had formed during the previous three decades, urban Catholics became a political bloc with the potential to swing elections. But though their numbers were strong and growing, they remained a much-maligned minority.

Throughout the 19th century, Catholics were attacked as un-American "papists," accused of being more loyal to Rome than to the United States. The Know-Nothing movement that sprang up before the Civil War and sent dozens of its members to Congress was founded in large part in order "to resist the insidious policy of the Church of Rome and all other foreign influence"[5] (see Source 4.6).

Catholics faced prejudice and suspicion everywhere they went, most egregiously in schools and at the workplace. Opponents of Catholic immigration included well-known figures like Samuel F. B. Morse, inventor of the telegraph, and Lyman Beecher, a religious leader and father of Harriet Beecher Stowe. Morse, in fact, penned a tract titled "Foreign Conspiracy against the Liberties of the United States," which warned Protestant Americans of a plot to control them hatched by the Vatican bishops and their American agents–Irish and Italian immigrants.

When their children were harassed in the public schools and subjected to a Protestant-leaning curriculum, Catholics responded by creating separate systems of parochial schools. But even though the Catholic schools received no public money, they remained visibly different from public schools: They used a Catholic bible rather than the King James version, classes were often led by members of the clergy, and instruction was frequently in foreign languages for the benefit of the immigrant pupils. As a result, Catholic schools were portrayed as breeding grounds of anti-Americanism.

In the workplace the story was much the same. Like many 19th-century immigrants, the Catholic newcomers were often desperately poor and willing to work for reduced wages. Consequently, they were scorned for driving down the earning power of American-born workers. When strikes shut down urban factories, owners frequently turned to Catholics as strikebreakers, providing them with temporary employment but further stigmatizing them in the eyes of the native-born. Whether they were Irish, Italian, or some other ethnic origin, Catholics often got the message that they did not belong.

Not surprisingly, Catholics were eager to improve their social and economic standing, and worked overtime to express their patriotism. Many Catholics, particularly Italians and Portuguese, promoted their connection to Columbus, discoverer of the New World and a devout Catholic. An 1878 editorial in the *Connecticut Catholic* put it succinctly: No one was more deserving "of grateful remembrance than the great and noble man–the pious, zealous, faithful Catholic . . . Christopher Columbus."[6]

To further their image, American Catholics created a feast day in Columbus's honor, named schools and hospitals after him, and sought his official canonization by the Pope. The University of Notre Dame commissioned twelve murals in its Main Building honoring "Columbus the Catholic," and in 1882, 10 years before Harrison's proclamation, Catholics from New Haven, Connecticut, founded the Knights of Columbus, which eventually became the nation's largest pan-Catholic fraternal organization. Its members believed that as Catholic descendants of Columbus, they were "entitled to all the rights and privileges due such a discovery by one of our faith."[7] Thus, despite disparate national origins and different customs, the Catholic minority drew on their connection to the famous and still-beloved explorer both as a means of creating pan-Catholic unity and to show how American they really were (see Sources 4.2 and 4.3).

In the mid-1860s New Yorkers hosted Columbus-themed festivities. San Francisco's Italians celebrated their first Discovery Day in 1869, and Philadelphians erected a statue of Columbus in Fairmount Park in 1876. Well before the 1892 proclamation, celebrations of Columbus were already on the calendar in St. Louis, Boston, Cincinnati, and New Orleans. And so, when Benjamin Harrison proclaimed October 21, 1892, "Discovery Day," he wasn't creating anything new. Rather, he was sanctioning the many celebrations already in place, according recognition to grassroots efforts by Catholics around the country. According to Thomas J. Schlereth, for Catholics, Columbus had become "an American ethnic saint in an era of unprecedented immigration."[8]

The proclamation had a political angle, too. Harrison was engaged in a battle for his political life. By formally recognizing Columbus, he sought to bring legions of new voters into the fold. Thus, "Discovery Day" may have been less about hero worship than tried and true party politics. Harrison's public recognition of Columbus was an astute political appeal to a special-interest group–urban Catholics–whom he believed had the power to swing the election in his favor.

It was an election with many strange twists, pitting the incumbent Harrison against Grover Cleveland, himself a former president. After becoming the first Democrat elected to the office since the Civil War, Cleveland lost his 1888 reelection bid to Harrison, despite narrowly winning the popular vote. Four years later, the same two opponents were locked in a battle for reelection. Neither the sitting president nor the former leader was a runaway favorite.

Thanks to Cleveland's resurgent popularity, and third-party candidate James B. Weaver, Harrison faced an uphill battle in the traditionally Republican Midwest. Looking to secure those states, along with the Eastern cities, Harrison and his Republican allies decided to go all out in their pursuit of the immigrant vote.

In the Midwest they courted Scandinavian- and German-Americans, as well as the Irish and Italian groups in the East. To appeal to ethnic Americans who were often taught in their mother tongue, Harrison openly advocated local control of public and parochial schools. To appeal to Irish Catholics, Republicans organized the Irish-American Protective Tariff League and the Irish-American Republican League, inserting an endorsement for Irish home rule in the 1892 Republican Platform–a symbolic gesture if there ever was one. While recognition of Columbus was an appeal to all Catholics, it particularly targeted Italian-Americans, who had been celebrating Cristoforo Colombo as their own for as long as they had been in the New World.

In the end, Harrison's "Discovery Day" was celebrated less than 3 weeks before the voters went to the polls. Despite its timing, the move was not enough to secure Harrison's victory. Cleveland was returned to the White House in a landslide.

Even though "Discovery Day" failed to produce Harrison's second term, it proved to be a success in its own right. A slate of patriotic activities accompanied celebrations of Columbus Day across the nation, including one that would become an enduring school ritual: the Pledge of Allegiance, written by Francis Bellamy. On Discovery Day, 1892, 10 million schoolchildren proudly swore their loyalty to the United States, regardless of religion or national origin. While the practice was more symbolic than substantive, it resonated powerfully at a time when immigrants sought to display their patriotism. This was especially true for those facing the charge of being foreign agents of the Vatican. The pledge soon became a daily classroom fixture.

Although other Discovery Day activities didn't share the pledge's staying power, including the "Song of Columbus Day," celebrating Columbus certainly did. In 1905, Colorado Governor Jesse F. McDonald declared the first official noncentennial Columbus Day, a practice taken up by other states. Thirty years later, at the urging of the Knights of Columbus, President Franklin D. Roosevelt and Congress made Columbus Day a federal holiday, moving the official celebration to October 12.

Puzzles, Questions, and the Process of History

When they first encounter the Harrison proclamation, many students become so fixated on 1492, they never notice that this document appeared 400 years *later.* Putting Harrison's declaration in the context of 1892 changes a reader's next steps in exploring the story of Columbus Day.

The historians who read the Discovery Day proclamation wanted to understand this historical puzzle. They wanted to know if there was a precedent to Harrison's declaration, whether Discovery Day had ignited opposition or anti-Catholic backlash. They were curious to know if other states had made October 21 a holiday before the federal declaration, and if so, whether those states had large Catholic populations. Finally, they wanted to know how and when the event had gone from a proclamation to a national celebration.

In thinking historically about the document, historians ended up going down a different path from the high school students. While the students revisited what they already knew about Columbus and repeated politically correct slogans, historians found themselves dealing with puzzles and questions, the unexplored and the unknown. As a result, they were challenged to think more critically, more creatively, and more *historically.*

In the end, the historians uncovered new information–not only about immigration and identity politics but also about Columbus's evolving legacy. Whatever positions they may have today, in the late 19th century Americans held a uniformly positive view of Columbus. Understanding that, students are less likely to interpret celebrations of Columbus solely through the lens of the present. By putting documents like Harrison's proclamation into context, a new world opens up–one filled with unanswered questions and new ways of looking at the past.

Why Teach About "Discovery Day"?

An Opportunity to Teach About Understanding Sources in Context. Many students are so blinded by Columbus's name in the Discovery Day document that they never get past it. Historians, on the other hand, begin their reading by situating a document in place and time. They begin by "sourcing" and "contextualizing" a document, asking who wrote it, where it appeared, when it was published, and what the burning issues of the day were. By asking such questions, historians develop a better understanding of a document's significance and the real motives of its author.

In the case of the Discovery Day proclamation, many students drew on 20th-century interpretations of Columbus's voyage to critique Harrison's proclamation. Inevitably, they overlooked that the document was signed in 1892, a fact that invites a host of questions about why public figures issue proclamations when they do. Teaching about Discovery Day provides an opportunity to help students situate documents in time and place. It can show them how developing historical habits of mind will instinctively point them to the context of a document's creation.

A Chance to Explore the Uses to Which History Is Put. History is constantly being put to various uses; the same historical figure or event may be used for different purposes at different times. Such changes can occur when new information comes to light, producing the need for reevaluation. At other times, shifts in political and cultural developments make us look anew at our previous interpretations. In the case of Discovery Day, both forces are at work. On one hand, present-day scholarship is more critical of Columbus than it was in the 19th or even 20th centuries. On the other, while modern celebrations of Columbus are seen as insensitive to native peoples, in 1892 they were a way of reaching out to the maligned urban Catholic.

A Chance to Teach About Change over Time. Students often assume that the layout of the world into which they are born is the way things have always been. An America in which Catholics faced constant discrimination and charges of disloyalty is hard to imagine. The distinctions between Protestant and Catholic rarely matter today, except as they touch on issues like abortion or same-sex marriage. But even here, the Catholic vote is hardly monolithic: There is considerable overlap between their stances and those held by Americans from other religions. The 19th-century fear that American Catholics were receiving marching orders from Rome seems like the stuff of wacko fringe groups with little influence on public life. Still, as late as 1960, presidential hopeful John F. Kennedy was obliged to defend himself against charges that his Catholicism rendered him unfit to be president (Source 4.7). An excursion into the 1890s helps students understand how far America has come in its journey from being a Protestant country that faintly tolerated outsiders to a multicultural nation with a wide range of religious faiths.

Connection to Today. Discovery Day shows how a presidential platform addressed the demographic upheavals of America, prefiguring a tactic that has become a fixture in the political landscape: reaching out and courting votes among varied constituencies. Harrison's campaign opens a window on why politicians court voters from different backgrounds–racial, ethnic, and religious–and how this practice has increased as America has become more diverse. Considering Harrison's motives in the 1890s raises questions about today's immigration and presidential politics, including how contemporary candidates tailor their message to curry favor with different groups.

How Might You Use These Materials?

Scenario 1 (1–2 Hour Lesson). What date matters most, 1492 or 1892? Learn to put a document in context and understand what influenced Harrison to make his "Discovery Day" proclamation.

Ask students to read the Discovery Day proclamation (Source 4.1), but first eliminate the document's date and author. Have students write down their responses to the document and jot down questions they would ask about its historical context. Unless you've already done some work on placing documents in context, many students will zoom in on Columbus's troubled legacy and never think to ask when the document was written or for what purpose. After briefly discussing students' responses, give them the document's date and author, and ask them to write down ideas that these new pieces of information may prompt.

After pointing out that 1892 was an election year, divide students into groups to consider Harrison's motives in proclaiming "Discovery Day" a national holiday (see Tool 4.1). Give each group Sources 4.1, 4.2, 4.3, and 4.4. Depending on how much time you have, provide additional documents, such as Source 4.5. **Assign an essay in which students explain why Harrison issued his "Discovery Day" proclamation when he did, and how the events of 1892 shape how the document should be read.**

Targeted list of skills in this scenario

- Contextualizing sources
- Questioning sources
- Corroborating sources
- Evidence-based thinking and argumentation

Scenario 2 (2–4 Hour Lesson). Focus on context. This scenario expands on the previous one, and is designed to give students more practice reading documents in context.

First, lead them through the analysis and discussion described above, using Sources 4.1, 4.2, 4.3, 4.4, and 4.5. In this scenario, students will confront the issue of anti-Catholic prejudice, as seen in the Civil War-era excerpt about the Know-Nothing Party (Source 4.6) and John F. Kennedy's 1960 speech that confronted the issue of anti-Catholicism head-on (Source 4.7). **Consider having students compare issues of immigration policy across time. In what ways are issues the same and different? Give students an opportunity to consider how the issue of religion has influenced debates about immigration during the last hundred years.**

Alternately, go deeper with the particular era of immigration and Harrison's proclamation. Once students are acquainted with the broader issues of the 1890s, read them Jacob's response to the Harrison proclamation at the beginning of this chapter. Ask them to consider what Jacob is missing. **Have students write an essay about what Jacob, the high school student, missed when he commented on the Harrison proclamation.**

Targeted list of skills in this scenario

- Contextualizing sources
- Questioning sources
- Corroborating sources
- Evidence-based thinking and argumentation
- Making connections to more recent history

Scenario 3 (1–2 Hour Lesson). This scenario will help students analyze an editorial cartoon from a different era. We use an illustration by Thomas Nast (Source 4.8), who was not only one of the most famous editorial cartoonists in America, but also the man largely responsible for making the elephant and donkey the symbols of two major political parties.

We sometimes assume that cartoons are easy for students to understand because they make their point in pictures, not in words. While this might hold true for contemporary images, trying to decode a cartoon from the distant past is a different story. The very features that make an image easy to understand today–George W. Bush's huge floppy ears–are what will trip up students when trying to decipher an editorial cartoon from a different era. Codes and symbols that readers would recognize in 1870 will often be indecipherable to today's students (and often to us as well).

Editorial cartoons employ a series of conventions that are unfamiliar to many students. For this purpose, we have developed a mnemonic tool, "B.A.S.I.C." (Tool 4.2), to help students crack a cartoon's code.

The goal of an editorial cartoon is different from regular cartoons (think Gary Larson or *Dilbert*) that seek to amuse or entertain. If an *editorial* cartoon makes us smile, it's a side effect, not the primary goal. First and foremost, editorial cartoons convey messages that carry a trenchant political or social critique. Editorial cartoons have a point, sometimes a very sharp one.

Source 4.8 displays one of Nast's most famous cartoons, "The American River Ganges," published in *Harper's Weekly* on September 30, 1871, and again, in a slightly different form, in 1875. Despite its ubiquity (the cartoon appears on dozens of websites), few students will be able to unlock its meaning without a carefully scaffolded entree to this unfamiliar world.

"The American River Ganges" appeared during a debate over public funding of Catholic schools in New York State. In 1869, William "Boss" Tweed, whose powerful Democratic headquarters, Tammany Hall, symbolized graft and corruption, authored a bill to allow New York City to fund parochial schools of 200 students or more (in general, this applied only to Catholic schools, as Protestant and Jewish schools were typically much smaller). When the press learned of Tweed's scheme, they tarred and feathered it with anti-Catholic taunts of "Popery." Although the Republican majority in the New York legislature killed the bill, the die was cast: People feared that Catholics were determined to take money away from the public schools to promote a sinister "Roman" agenda.[9]

Before asking students to tackle the riddle that is "The American River Ganges," begin by going over the B.A.S.I.C. acronym (Tool 4.2). First, try practicing it on contemporary editorial cartoons, whose meanings are more transparent to modern audiences. In our teaching, we have found that a three-part sequence is useful when decoding visual evidence such as cartoons, artwork, and photographs. We begin by asking students to *describe* what they see, staying close to the details of the image. By doing this as a whole-class activity, students can collectively glimpse more than whatever first meets their individual eyes. Once students have exhausted the details of the image, we move on to *interpreting* what we see. For this stage Tool 4.3 will be crucial, familiarizing students with symbols and indicators used by Nast (mitres, St. Peter's Basilica, and so on).

During the final stage–*speculating*–students are ready to tackle the cartoonist's argument. **Tool 4.4 includes questions that guide students through this analysis. Using this set of questions will allow students to make observations about "The American River Ganges" without unnecessarily forming conclusions or interpretations.**

Draw students' attention to the crocodiles shown in the cartoon: Are they real? What are they wearing? Make sure students note the difference between the boy onshore with smaller children huddled behind him, and the other children in the background. Do they notice the book protruding from the older boy's pocket? What does the book say? Finally, when students speculate about the meaning of the cartoon, help make the connection between the Ganges River and Catholicism (i.e., the Ganges is sacred to the Hindus, a religion considered by many 19th-century Americans to be foreign and "barbaric").

Targeted list of skills in this scenario

- Analyzing political cartoons
- Contextualizing sources
- Questioning sources

Sources and Tools

Source 4.1: Harrison's Proclamation (Modified)

By the President of the United States of America
A Proclamation

Now, therefore, I, Benjamin Harrison, President of the United States of America, in pursuance of the aforesaid joint resolution, do hereby appoint Friday, October 21, 1892, the four hundredth anniversary of the discovery of America by Columbus, as a general holiday for the people of the United States. On that day let the people, so far as possible, cease from toil and devote themselves to such exercises as may best express honor to the discoverer and their appreciation of the great achievements of the four completed centuries of American life.

Columbus stood in his age as the pioneer of progress and enlightenment. The system of universal education is in our age the most prominent and salutary feature of the spirit of enlightenment, and it is peculiarly appropriate that the schools be made by the people the center of the day's demonstration. Let the national flag float over every schoolhouse in the country and the exercises be such as shall impress upon our youth the patriotic duties of American citizenship.

In the churches and in the other places of assembly of the people let there be expressions of gratitude to Divine Providence for the devout faith of the discoverer and for the divine care and guidance which has directed our history and so abundantly blessed our people.

Source: President Benjamin Harrison's Proclamation, July 21, 1892.

Source 4.2: Catholicism in America

As American Catholics we do not know of anyone who more deserves our grateful remembrance than the great and noble man–the pious, zealous, faithful Catholic, the enterprising navigator, and the large-hearted and generous sailor: Christopher Columbus.

Source: Excerpt, unknown author, "Christopher Columbus–Discoverer of the New World," *Connecticut Catholic,* May 25, 1878, 4.

Source 4.3: Knights of Columbus

4 *The* COLUMBIAD

The Knights of Columbus

First meeting of the Order—Determination to have ritualistic ceremonies—The adoption of a name

By Daniel Colwell, Historian of the Order

(Continued from last issue)

The first subject taken up was the selection of a name for the new society. Father McGivney suggested as a name "Sons of Columbus," stating that by the adoption of this name, we would be indicating in a way the Catholic and American character and tendency of the Order. James T. Mullen took the floor, and in his remarks said that if he understood the situation correctly, the new society was to be a ritualistic one. If such were the case, he would offer an amendment to Father McGivney's suggestion, and that the society should be known as the *Knights* of Columbus.

Transcript:

"The first subject taken up was the selection of a name for the new society. Father McGivney suggested as a name 'Sons of Columbus,' stating that by the adoption of this name, we would be indicating in a way the Catholic and American character and tendency of the Order. James T. Mullen took the floor, and in his remarks said that if he understood the situation correctly, the new society was to be a ritualistic one. If such were the case, he would offer an amendment to Father McGivney's suggestion, and that the society should be known as the *Knights* of Columbus."

Source: Excerpt from Daniel Colwell, "The Knights of Columbus: First Meeting of the Order," *The Columbiad*, March 1910.

Source 4.4: Immigration to the United States by Nationality: 1850–1930

Year	Total Immigration	Ireland	Italy
1850	2,244,602	961,719	3,679
1860	4,138,697	1,611,304	11,677
1870	5,567,229	1,855,827	17,157
1880	6,679,943	1,854,571	44,230
1890	9,249,547	1,871,509	182,580
1900	10,341,276	1,615,459	484,027
1910	13,515,886	1,352,251	1,343,125
1920	13,920,692	1,037,234	1,610,113
1930	14,204,149	744,810	1,790,429

Source: U.S. Census Bureau. Available at http://www.census.gov/population/www/documentation/twps0029/tab04.html

Source 4.5: Harrison Speech (Adapted)

Some may suggest that the question of the pending legislation relating to Ireland, which is being debated in the British Parliament, is not a proper subject of discussion in an American town meeting. We have no official say in what the British government does. It can take notice or not of what we do and say here, but all the same we will exercise the liberty of saying it. We are not here to suggest to Great Britain that shc shall grant the Irish their independence. We are here simply to say that, in our opinion as American citizens, what Ireland needs is not **coercion**, is not the **constable**, is not the soldier with musket and bayonet. What Ireland needs is liberal laws, that **emancipate** her people from the results of long centuries of ill government. When this British Ministry starts in the direction of coercion, and postpones suggestions for reform, it is traveling in the wrong direction.

Source: Campaign speech made by Benjamin Harrison in Indianapolis, April 8, 1887.

WORD BANK

coercion–the act of being forced
constable–a policeman
to emancipate–to free

(Original)

It may be suggested that we are engaged to-night in an act that savors somewhat of impertinence–that the question of the pending legislation relating to Ireland, which is the subject of discussion in the British Parliament, is not a proper subject of discussion in an American town meeting. . . . We have no official representations to make to the British government. It can take notice or not of what we do and say here, but all the same we will exercise the liberty of saying it. . . . We are not here to suggest to Great Britain that she shall concede Irish independence. . . . We are here simply to say that, in our opinion as American citizens, what Ireland needs is not coercion, is not the constable, is not the soldier with musket and bayonet; but liberal laws, tending to emancipate her people from the results of long centuries of ill government, and that when this British Ministry starts in the direction of coercion, and postpones suggestions for reform until a coercion bill has been enacted, it is traveling in the wrong direction.

Source 4.6: Know-Nothing Party

The object of this organization shall be to protect every American citizen in the legal and proper exercise of all his civil and religious rights and privileges; to resist the **insidious** policy of the Church of Rome and all other foreign influence against our republican institutions in all lawful ways; to place in all offices of honor, trust, or profit, in the gift of the people or by appointment, none but native-born Protestant citizens and to protect, preserve, and uphold the Union of these States and the Constitution of the same.

Source: Article II of the National Council of the United States of North America, otherwise known as the Know-Nothing Party. Circa 1855.

WORD BANK

insidious–evil

Source 4.7: Kennedy Speech

Note: On September 12, 1960, presidential candidate John F. Kennedy gave a speech to the Greater Houston Ministerial Association. Many at the time questioned whether Kennedy's Catholic faith would interfere with his ability to lead the country.

Because I am a Catholic, and no Catholic has ever been elected president, the real issues in this campaign have been obscured, perhaps deliberately, in some quarters less responsible than this. So it is apparently necessary for me to state once again not what kind of church I believe in–for that should be important only to me–but what kind of America I believe in. . . .

I believe in an America that is officially neither Catholic, Protestant nor Jewish . . . where no religious body seeks to impose its will directly or indirectly upon the general populace or the public acts of its officials. . . .

Finally, I believe in an America where religious intolerance will someday end; where all men and all churches are treated as equal; where every man has the same right to attend or not attend the church of his choice; where there is no Catholic vote, no anti-Catholic vote, no bloc voting of any kind; and where Catholics, Protestants and Jews . . . will refrain from those attitudes of disdain and division which have so often marred their works in the past, and promote instead the American ideal of brotherhood. . . .

If I should lose on the real issues, I shall return to my seat in the Senate, satisfied that I had tried my best and was fairly judged. But if this election is decided on the basis that forty million Americans lost their chance of being president on the day they were baptized, then it is the whole nation that will be the loser–in the eyes of Catholics and non-Catholics around the world, in the eyes of history, and in the eyes of our own people.

Source: Excerpt from a speech given by presidential candidate John F. Kennedy, September 12, 1960.

SOURCE 4.8: NAST CARTOON

Source: Thomas Nast, "The American River Ganges," *Harper's Weekly*, September 30, 1871 (see also http://www.aoh61.com/images/ir_cartoons/river_ganges.htm).

Tool 4.1: Putting a Source in Context

Directions: Use Sources 4.2–4.5 to help you understand why Harrison established Discovery Day in 1892.

1. What does this source tell us was going on in 1892?

Source 4.2:

Source 4.3:

Source 4.4:

Source 4.5:

2. How might the events or issues presented in this source have influenced Harrison?

3. After reading these sources, why do you think Harrison established "Discovery Day" in 1892?

Tool 4.2: B.A.S.I.C.

B.A.S.I.C.: Steps to Interpreting Editorial Cartoons

Editorial cartoons use features that pack dense information into a small space. The acronym B.A.S.I.C. reminds you what to look for when exploring a cartoon from a different time.

B: Background Knowledge

Cartoonists make certain assumptions, and one of them is that they and their readers share a common world. In a cartoon about strip searches by Homeland Security agents, an artist can depict two burning buildings, and we'll immediately recognize them as the Twin Towers of the World Trade Center. These features are so basic that we take them for granted, yet in another generation or so they won't be. When we interpret a cartoon from a hundred years ago, we often lack necessary background knowledge to crack the cartoon's code. Studying the period in which a cartoon appeared can help you figure out what the artist is trying to say.

A: Argument

The A in B.A.S.I.C. stands for "argument." Although editorial cartoons can make us laugh or smile, they have a more serious goal: to convey a point and convince us to adopt a position. When you look at a cartoon, ask yourself, "What does the artist want me to think?" Try to state the artist's point, or thesis, in a short statement, e.g., "From this cartoon, it is clear that the author thinks dependence on foreign oil will ruin America."

S: Symbolism

Cartoons use symbols to pack a lot of information into a single frame. Symbols are designations that point to something broader than themselves. A crescent, a six-pointed star, and a cross are more than moons, stars, or geometric figures. They stand for entire religious civilizations: Islam, Judaism, and Christianity, respectively. Symbols are part of the toolbox of every editorial cartoonist.

I: Indicators

But symbols can't do it alone. Cartoonists use *indicators*, or written labels, that point us in a certain direction. Often, indicators tell us directly what something stands for (and may be the only words used in the cartoon). In addition to the cartoon's title and caption, be on the lookout for other indicators, sometimes found in small print in the body of the cartoon itself.

C: Caricature

Cartoons follow the adage, "What's worth stating is worth overstating," and caricature exemplifies such exaggeration. When we're stuck in a traffic jam, we might say, "There are a million cars in front of us! It'll take years to get out of here." In the same spirit, cartoonists compare a bad government policy to one of the Ten Plagues, or an aging candidate to the Thousand-Year-Old Man. Caricature can also employ stereotypes, distorted images that exaggerate the features of entire groups. Such images, particularly those from a different era, often seem racist or bigoted to our modern eyes.

Tool 4.3: Decoding Thomas Nast's "The American River Ganges"

This background information will help you answer questions in the following handout.

1) **Mitre**: a religious head covering worn by the Pope, as well as bishops and cardinals.

A mitre (head covering) worn by the Pope, http://www.godsonlygospel.com/POPE~4.JPG

2) **Basilica of St. Peter**: Located in Vatican City, St. Peter's Basilica is the Pope's principal church, and home to official ceremonies of the Roman Catholic Church. Catholic tradition holds that this church is the burial site of its namesake, Saint Peter, one of the Twelve Apostles and the first Bishop of Rome.

Saint Peter's Basilica in Rome (i.e., the large building with a dome), symbolic "Mother Church" of the Catholic Church. Photograph available at http://countries-of-europe.com/wp-content/uploads/2011/02/St.-Peters-Basilica1.jpg

3) **Columbia**: A late-17th-century synonym for the New World, "Columbia," for which the District of Columbia is named, is symbolically represented as a female figure. Depicted in a simple white gown, she is frequently shown holding the liberty pole, the American flag, or the Constitution, and is often accompanied by an eagle. As an icon, Columbia evokes Christopher Columbus, the ostensible "discoverer" of America, from whom she derives her name, while also functioning as an allegorical figure who represents liberty and progress.

Tool 4.3: Decoding Thomas Nast's "The American River Ganges" (continued)

Image of Miss Columbia in a World War I recruiting poster. "Columbia calls–Enlist Now for U.S. Army," designed by Frances Adams Halsted; painted by V. Aderente. 1916. Library of Congress Prints and Photographs Division, Washington, D.C., http://lcweb2.loc.gov/service/pnp/cph/3g00000/3g03000/3g03600/3g03685v.jpg

4) **Tammany Hall**: Founded in 1789, the Tammany Society (alternately known as "the Sons of St. Tammany" and "the Columbian Order") was at the heart of New York City politics throughout the 19th century. Operating out of Tammany Hall, the organization was the city affiliate for the Democratic Party and grew in influence as it gained the loyalty of immigrants, many of whom were Irish Catholics. Governing through a system of public outreach, political patronage, and corruption, Tammany "bosses" were among the most powerful politicians in New York State. The most famous of them, William "Boss" Tweed, even won a seat in the New York State Senate before ending his days in prison.

5) **The Inverted Flag**: An upside-down national flag is a common symbol of distress. According to *Admiral Smyth's Sailor's Word Book of 1867*, when a ship is "in imminent danger," its crew "hoists her national flag upside down, and if she is armed, fires minute guns."

6) **The Ganges River**: The Ganges runs roughly 1,500 miles through India. It is considered a holy river by the Hindus, who make pilgrimages to bathe in its waters by descending the stone steps called "ghats" along its banks. Hindus attribute special powers to the Ganges waters. In the 19th century, many Americans considered Hindus and their religious practices not only strange and exotic, but inferior to the more "developed" religious traditions of the West.

Source: "Benares: View Taken from the Ghats," Elisee Reclus, *The Earth and Its Inhabitants*, 1884.

Tool 4.4: Thomas Nast's "The American River Ganges"

1. Look carefully at the crocodile-infested waters. What do the crocodiles have on their heads? What does this symbolize?
2. What do the crocodiles in this cartoon represent?
3. Who are the people casting the children off the cliff?
4. Who is the woman being dragged to the gallows?
5. There are two buildings in this cartoon; both contain "indicators" to help the reader correctly interpret the cartoon. What are these indicators and what do they tell you about the cartoon's message?
6. What is the argument of this cartoonist? What does he want the reader to think after viewing this cartoon?
7. Why do you think Nast titled the cartoon "The American River Ganges"? By connecting Catholic symbols with a river sacred to the Hindus in India, what do you think the cartoonist wanted people to think about American Catholics?

Suggested Resources

http://www.loc.gov/teachers/classroommaterials/primarysourcesets/immigration/
This is the home page of a primary document set, "Immigration Challenges for New Americans," created and maintained by the Library of Congress. In addition to primary source materials like audio and video footage, photographs, and cartoons, teacher materials are available as well.

http://www.digitalhistory.uh.edu/modules/immigration/index.cfm
This page from Stephen Mintz's Digital History website offers a range of resources about the history of immigration to the United States.

http://www.fordham.edu/halsall/mod/modsbook28.html
This page from Paul Halsall's Internet Modern History Sourcebook lists document and website links that focus on the American immigration of various ethnic groups.

http://avalon.law.yale.edu/19th_century/harris.asp
Read Benjamin Harrison's inaugural address at The Avalon Project, an online archive of legal and political documents housed at Yale University.

http://historymatters.gmu.edu/mse/sia/cartoon.htm
See how a historian interprets another Thomas Nast cartoon at History Matters, a website developed and maintained by the Center for History and New Media at George Mason University.

http://cartoons.osu.edu/nast/portfolio.htm
Find other Thomas Nast cartoons on this site hosted by Ohio State University.

CHAPTER 5

Electricity and Women's Work: Who Really Benefited? And When?

Theodor Horydczak, advertisement of Electric Institute of Washington, August 8, 1946. Available at http://memory.loc.gov/ammem/today/sep30.html

In a 1921 letter to Thomas Edison, Mrs. W. C. Lathrop, a housewife from Kansas, thanked the inventor for the electricity and time-saving appliances in her home (see Source 5.1).[1] From Norton, Kansas, she wrote:

> Dear Sir,
>
> It is not always the privilege of a woman to thank personally the inventor of articles which make life liveable for her sex. . . . I am a college graduate and probably my husband is one of the best known surgeons between Topeka and Denver. . . . [Our] house is lighted by electricity. I cook on a Westinghouse electric range, wash dishes in an electric dish washer. An electric fan even helps to distribute the heat over part of the house. . . . I wash clothes in an electric machine and iron on an electric mangle and with an electric iron. I clean house with electric cleaners. I rest, take an electric massage and curl my hair on an electric iron. Dress in a gown sewed on a machine run by a motor. Then start the Victrola and either study Spanish for a while or listen to Kreisler and Gluck and Galli. . . . Please accept the thanks Mr. Edison of one most truly appreciative woman. I know I am only one of many under the same debt of gratitude to you.

We recently observed a class of 11th-graders who examined this letter. With this letter in hand, they pondered the question, "How did Edison's inventions change American life?" Carried away by Mrs. Lathrop's exuberance, students gushed, "In every way," "A lot," "They made life easier–especially for women." The vividness of Mrs. Lathrop's words led students to believe electricity and appliances had improved life for all women, just as they had for her.

Not until the teacher asked, "How typical was Mrs. Lathrop? How much can we say from this one letter?" did the students move from glib first impressions to begin the work of real historical analysis. Census data and historians' work on electrification, technology, housework, and women's roles all indicate that Mrs. Lathrop was not a typical 1920s woman. Nor did her household represent the majority of households of the time. Investigating the typicality of Mrs. Lathrop thus becomes a lesson in social class, regional differences, life in the 1920s, and the transition from pre-industrialized to industrialized housework.

The first thing we need to do is source this document by focusing on two core aspects of historical understanding: time and place. The year is 1921. The many inventions Mrs. Lathrop mentions–sewing machine, dishwasher, and so on–had *just* come out the previous year or so. Who, in fact, owned these devices? How widespread were they? Second, where exactly is Norton, Kansas? Kansas is in the American heartland, obviously, but where is Norton? Is it a suburb of an urban area like Wichita or Topeka? Or is it distant from a big city, part of the rural landscape that still constituted a majority of the American population in the 1920s?

Years ago, trying to answer these questions would have meant long hours spent in the stacks of a library, hunting through piles of reference books hoping to find answers. But thanks to the wonders of the Internet and the proliferation of easy-to-use databases, these questions can be answered by any student with a high-speed connection. Drawing on these resources, we can quickly get an idea of just how unusual Mrs. Lathrop was, and just how perilous it is to generalize from her to all American women in the 1920s.

Using Google Maps (http://maps.google.com), we can quickly see that Norton, Kansas, is in the northwest corner of Kansas, just south of the Nebraska border and far from major population centers–290 miles from Topeka, 350 from Kansas City, 270 from Wichita, and 310 from Denver. A look at the 1920 Federal census at the University of Virginia library's website (http://mapserver.lib.virginia.edu) gives us more information about Lathrop's hometown. By specifying Kansas, we learn that in 1920, Norton County accounted for 11,423 Kansans out of a state population of 1,769,257 (or less than 1%). Indeed, the census shows that Norton County had 130 people per square mile, putting it in the bottom half of the state's counties in terms of population density. Mrs. Lathrop, it appears, lived in a fairly rural region when she wrote to Thomas Edison in 1921.

Compared to her rural peers, the fact that Mrs. Lathrop even had electricity in 1921 was highly unusual. David Nye, a historian of American technology, notes that in 1935 (14 years *after* Mrs. Lathrop wrote her letter) only 5 to 15% of rural Kansas had electricity; most rural areas with electricity lay in the Northeast or Far West.[2] Clayton Brown, a historian of 20th-century Southern economic development, cites a 1920 Federal census showing that of 6 million farms, only 452,620 (less than 8%) had electric lights and only 643,899, roughly 10%, possessed running water.[3] Brown concludes that most of these advancements took place in New England and the Far West: "The Midwest and South ranked lowest, ranging from 10 percent to less than 1 percent."[4] Electrification didn't come to most rural areas until the New Deal of the 1930s.

In contrast to Lathrop, most rural women endured backbreaking work to keep their households running. Doing laundry was particularly odious.[5] Historian Susan Strasser gives a description based on the treatises of home economists Catharine Beecher (1841) and Helen Campbell (1881).

> Without running water, gas, or electricity, even the most simplified hand-laundry process consumed staggering amounts of time and labor. One wash, one boiling, and one rinse used about fifty gallons of water–or four hundred pounds–which had to be moved from pump or well or faucet to stove and tub, in buckets and wash boilers that might weigh as much as forty or fifty pounds. Rubbing, wringing, and lifting water-laden clothes and linens, including large articles like sheets, tablecloths, and men's heavy work clothes, wearied women's arms and wrists and exposed them to caustic substances. They lugged weighty tubs and baskets full of wet laundry outside, picked up each article, hung it on the line, and returned to take it all down; they ironed by heating several irons on the stove and alternating them as they cooled, never straying far from the hot stove.[6]

Brown's work supports these analyses. In 1919, the U.S. Department of Agriculture (USDA) reported that "rural families spent over 10 hours per week pumping water and carrying it from source to kitchen."[7] Brown contends, "Farmwives spent twenty days more per year washing clothes than women in the city using electric washers."[8] In his biography of Lyndon B. Johnson, American biographer Robert Caro describes the intensive labor involved in doing laundry in the rural hill country of Texas–just 816 miles south of Norton–before LBJ orchestrated the advent of electricity in the region in 1938 (see Source 5.5).[9]

The process of doing laundry was largely unchanged across generations until electrical lines and indoor plumbing were extended to people's homes and people purchased washing machines. Mrs. Lathrop's use of an electric washing machine, vacuum cleaner, iron, and electric lights in rural America in 1921 did not represent the experiences of her rural peers. Although by 1930 most urban dwellers had such conveniences, it would be years before farm families could take similar advantage of household technology.[10]

If Mrs. Lathrop could enjoy such amenities in rural America, why couldn't others? Using a washing machine required indoor plumbing, and hot and cold running water. And you needed the money to buy the appliance in the first place, pay utility bills, wire the house, and bring electrical lines to it. Power companies had no incentive to extend lines to rural areas where only small numbers could tap into them. Most rural residents were too poor to pay for appliances or daily electricity (see Source 5.3). Nye stipulates that the 10% of American farmers who had distribution lines to their homes by the end of the 1920s had paid double the urban rate to get connected to the grid.[11] If Lathrop had electricity in rural Kansas in 1921 while others didn't, it is because she was in a rare position. She was rich!

Mrs. Lathrop's rural peers had to wait until the New Deal before they could hope for electricity. Begun in 1938, the Rural Electrification Administration (REA) lent money, equipment, and expertise to farmers' cooperatives. A year later, a quarter of all farms had electrical service.[12] World War II slowed the pace; only 45% of U.S. farms had received electricity by 1944.[13] In contrast, spurred by business and civic interests, electricity came quickly to cities. Urban dwellers benefited from lines that connected businesses and factories, while suburban residents took advantage of electrical trolley lines connecting them to city centers.

The sharp contrast between Mrs. Lathrop's home and the majority of rural households shines a light on her upper-class background. Given that 35% of *all* American households had electricity in 1920, Mrs. Lathrop enjoyed a higher standard of living than most Americans.[14] The chief beneficiaries of these new electrified gadgets were the wealthy. Historian Ruth Schwartz Cowen found that of the affluent households in 36 American cities, 80%

had vacuum cleaners and washing machines in 1926.[15] Electric ranges and washing machines were more often found in upper-class homes in 1921.[16] In 1935, 60% of families in Muncie, Indiana, owned a gas or electric range and 50% had a vacuum cleaner.[17] Mrs. Lathrop had *both* appliances in a rural area 14 years earlier (compare with Source 5.2).[18]

What was life like for a woman of means in 1921? Mrs. Lathrop's letter indicates that she didn't work to make ends meet. She mentions her roles as officer in the District of Women's Club, President of the Town Organization, and hostess. According to Cowen, these are the kinds of activities that an upper-class housewife of this era might have engaged in.[19]

But changes were afoot. In some cases, new time-saving devices meant that rich women were doing *more* housework rather than less. How is that possible? From 1900 to 1920, a woman with a high standard of living most likely had domestic help to complete housework such as washing and ironing laundry or cleaning rooms–tasks involving such heavy labor were considered demeaning for women of this class.[20] Mrs. Lathrop's statement about "doing *practically* all my own work"[21] suggests that she may have had domestic help. However, from 1920 to 1940, upper-class housewives had less and less help in the home as ownership of electric appliances grew. Even genteel ladies could use a washing machine and vacuum cleaner without much toil.[22] Compared to the turn of the century, "the average comfortable housewife of this generation learned to organize the work in her household without the assistance of servants or with far fewer hours of assistance than her mother had had."[23]

Mrs. Lathrop was different from her peers in another crucial way: she was a college graduate. As historian of education Patricia Albjerg Graham notes, few people attended college at the turn of the century–in 1920, only 8% of men *and* women from the "traditional college age group" attended college.[24] In 1900–10, when Mrs. Lathrop likely attended, that figure was only 4–5%.[25] These students came from families with "greater wealth and higher social status than the population at large."[26] In 1837, Oberlin was the first college in the United States to open its doors to women. By 1910, women made up almost 40% of the undergraduate population.[27] By 1920, when Mrs. Lathrop wrote Edison, a total of 34% of American women had received a bachelor's degree or professional degree.[28] Historian Barbara Solomon notes that while most college women married, they did so in fewer numbers than those who didn't attend college, and at a later age.[29] Many married graduates focused on domestic duties and volunteer work rather than a career. In 1920, only 9% of American women worked outside the home, up 3.4% from 1900.[30] Mrs. Lathrop was unusual for having gone to college, but fairly typical in using her degree for volunteer and domestic work rather than a profession.

What else does Mrs. Lathrop represent? She certainly represents the positive reaction of women once electricity and household appliances changed the nature of women's work. Residents' reactions to an early Alabama experiment in rural electrification were overwhelmingly positive. D. Clayton Brown reports, "Electricity had [the] greatest impact in easing the burden of keeping house. Wives mentioned freedom from carrying water and caring for kerosene lamps as their most prized releases from drudgery. Participants devoted more time to evening activities such as reading and listening to the radio."[31] When electricity reached more rural residents in 1939 and beyond, reactions were similar.[32] Lighting, time for leisure, and a break from the grueling toil of fetching water for drinking, cooking, bathing, and laundry were all welcome changes in rural homes.

Was life more "livable" for Mrs. Lathrop once the new technology entered her home? Was she truly "rested and ready to serve" her husband at the end of the day? Though scholars agree that electricity reduced backbreaking labor, several point to unexpected consequences it had on women's role in the home. The impact of electricity and appliances was greater and more varied than either Lathrop's letter or people's immediate reactions might suggest (see Source 5.4). Historians Cowen and Strasser argue that women's work was in the midst of fundamental changes, and the ramifications had not yet been fully realized.

Mrs. Lathrop's letter suggests that households in the 1900s were no longer units of production, but had become units of consumption. For Ruth Schwartz Cowen this notion is misleading, as it suggests that women had gained new leisure time as a result of technological changes. Cowen argues that electricity only changed the nature of housework; it didn't eliminate it. Rising standards of cleanliness now added to the amount of housework women were expected to complete. Because technology made tasks easier, they were expected to be done more often. Although vacuum cleaners made cleaning rugs much easier, women were now expected to vacuum weekly and have no dust in the home rather than clean the rugs a few times per year and not worry about the dust. New standards of cleanliness applied to laundry as well. And because new technology made such tasks seem easy, they were expected to be done more often. Strasser explains,

> Over the long run, the automatic washer probably restructured rather than reduced laundry time. . . . Encouraged by advertisements for these machines and for the detergents, fabric softeners, bleaches, and static reducers they used, Americans began to make quicker decisions about what to throw in the hamper. No individual laundry load caused as much fatigue or took as much time as hand-done laundry. . . . But it changed the laundry

> pile from a weekly nightmare to an unending task, increasing the size of the pile, the amount of water and fuel and laundry products most households used, and possibly even the housewife's working time, which was now spread out over the week.[33]

Decreasing immigration, the onset of war, economic depression, and emerging ideology about women's roles led to a sharp decline in the number of servants employed by households.[34] At the same time, returning certain tasks to the home (washing and ironing laundry, carpet cleaning) filled any time gained by the new equipment. As Cowen explains,

> The woman endowed with a Bendix would have found it *easier* to do her laundry but, simultaneously, would have done *more* laundry, and more of it herself, than either her mother or her grandmother had.[35]

In earlier times, tasks like laundry were deemed too labor-intensive or demeaning for upper-class women. Once the new technology eased the drudgery, it became acceptable for all women to do this kind of work.[36] The net effect was that American women were more engaged in housework than ever. The labor saved was hired workers', not their own.[37]

When Cowen examined time studies of affluent housewives in the 1920s and 1930s, she found that the average time spent on housework did not change markedly.[38] Again, women's class background reflected the impact of electricity and technology on housework. Rural women without means saw no change until about 1939; most would not experience major changes until after the war. Only then did working-class women feel a boost from technology that made housework less laborious.

Urban women of the poorer and middle classes probably experienced an improved standard of living around the time Mrs. Lathrop wrote. These women often earned wages beyond their housework, and would have been less likely to pay others to complete basic household tasks. But even as new technology, running water, and electricity were notable improvements, increasing standards of cleanliness and an ideology that linked domesticity and womanhood put additional pressure on all women.

Cowen argues that as their roles became more fixed in the home, regardless of class, women became more isolated. Since the onset of the industrial age, women had worked less alongside their husbands and children than in pre-industrial times. With the advent of electricity, this trend continued. The tasks men and children used to perform (cutting and hauling wood for stoves) were now obsolete. This freed men's time and enabled them to find work outside the home. Children, freed by industrialization, spent time at school or wage-earning labor. Meanwhile, tasks like cleaning and cooking remained—and they fell to women.[39] Thus, some historians argue that even though the immediate impact of electricity and household technology was stunning, in the long run, they simply rearranged, rather than reduced, housework. And for many women, the consequences were not nearly as positive as Mrs. Lathrop's letter would have us believe.

In comparing this one letter to a range of sources, we can appreciate Mrs. Lathrop in her historical context, and better understand both the period and the individual source. Understanding Mrs. Lathrop makes us consider regional and class differences. This broader context is necessary to see Mrs. Lathrop as both similar to and different from other women in the 1920s. We tend to think of the technological changes as improvements without fully considering how they affected different groups. Though Mrs. Lathrop was thrilled with her new technology, over time it meant she probably had to do more housework than before. In contrast, the poor and rural women who were yet to receive power in 1921 likely benefited the most, given that they had always done their own housework. Regardless, the new technology altered women's work in more profound ways than Mrs. Lathrop's letter indicates. Her letter is a window on an era, but only that. We can see just as much as that one window allows. But beyond that window is a broader, more complex world that resists facile generalizations. Mrs. Lathrop's story and the accompanying sources help our students navigate these complexities.

Why Teach About Mrs. Lathrop?

Representativeness: How Much Can We Learn from One Letter? When students first read Mrs. Lathrop's letter to Thomas Edison, many conclude that electricity positively influenced everyone in 1921. They take Mrs. Lathrop's impressions and assume that all people at this time had the same reaction to electrification and new appliances. The tendency to generalize is natural, but in doing so, students miss the complexities of the time period and miss the long-range impact of electricity and new technology.

Social psychologists talk about a "vividness effect" in which the color and immediacy of data skew our judgments of typicality and representativeness. To be sure, Mrs. Lathrop's letter provides a vivid peek inside her life—as a source, it is expressive and memorable, and given Edison's handwritten note at the top, it possesses an authenticity shared by few secondary sources.

But the very qualities that attract us to this letter can lead us astray. Mrs. Lathrop's letter tells how Edison's inventions transformed the life of an educated woman of privilege who in 1921 owned appliances that most Americans did not own until much later.

No doubt Edison's inventions transformed Lathrop's life. But it would be many years before these inventions would reach the average American, particularly in rural areas. Corroborating Mrs. Lathrop's letter with other documents and data sources pushes students to read more critically and place Mrs. Lathrop's experience into historical context. Once they begin to see Mrs. Lathrop's experience as one of many, they gain a more complex view of the time period, women's history, and technology. One letter tells us about Mrs. Lathrop; it does not tell us about the country as a whole.

Point of View: Comparing Historical Perspectives. We tend to view historical change as progress from a less enlightened state to an advanced state. U.S. history textbooks support the notion that the American story is one of unending progress: With each event we move closer to the ideals set out in the founding of this nation. In reality, historical changes affect people differently. Portraying historical change as completely good or bad oversimplifies the matter. Life is more complicated.

To understand the impact of any technology, we must ask: Who benefits? As students corroborate historical sources, they see beyond Mrs. Lathrop and gain a glimpse of other women's experiences in the 1920s. Multiple historical perspectives can give a more complete view of history and help students see complex cause-effect relationships.

Historical Evidence: Using Numerical Data and the Internet to Understand the Past. This lesson not only gives students the chance to read written documents, but also presents an opportunity to use numerical data and the Internet. Through simple web searches and reading accompanying historical sources, students encounter statistical data that allow them to compare Lathrop to her contemporaries. Because the historical record is incomplete–we don't know exactly who had and didn't have electricity and appliances in Norton, Kansas, in 1921–this lesson uses data from places like Philadelphia and rural farms to study the difference between urban and rural areas. Drawing conclusions from incomplete data always involves making inferences. But there is a big difference between a wild guess and an educated one. This lesson gives students the opportunity to engage with new forms of evidence and teaches them to be tentative in the conclusions they draw.

How Might You Use These Materials?

Scenario 1 (1–2 Hour Lesson). How representative was Mrs. Lathrop of women in the 1920s? Use these sources and tools to engage students in reading and analyzing multiple sources and creating an evidence-based argument about her representativeness.

Read Mrs. Lathrop's letter (Source 5.1) with students and ask what it tells them about women in the 1920s. Use Tool 5.1 to help students set Mrs. Lathrop into a broader picture of American women at this time. Using Tool 5.1, students will use the World Wide Web to examine the region Mrs. Lathrop came from and access 1920 Census data at the University of Virginia's online library database. We suggest having students work in pairs or groups to encourage discussion of discoveries and to give students opportunities to help each other. After consulting various resources and reading Mrs. Lathrop's letter, students are then asked to make an argument about Lathrop's representativeness. This is a good starting point for a whole-class discussion. Following the discussion, ask students to write a brief essay giving their conclusions with supporting evidence.

Students can continue this inquiry by reading Sources 5.2 and 5.3, which give statistics for one urban area and an overview of rural America at the time. Tool 5.2 helps students use these new sources to explore Mrs. Lathrop's typicality against a much broader portrait of the United States in the 1920s. The sources direct students to consider not only regional differences but class differences, too. At the end of the lesson, discuss students' ideas about Mrs. Lathrop. Ask students to cite evidence to support their conclusions. Compare these responses to earlier ones (at the end of Tool 5.1) and see how and if the evidence has altered their conclusions. **After the discussion, ask students to write a revised conclusion to Question 8 at the bottom of Tool 5.2. Students should use evidence from the sources to explain whether their conclusions have changed and why.**

Targeted list of skills in this scenario

- Corroborating sources
- Contextualizing sources
- Questioning sources to identify representativeness
- Evidence-based thinking and argumentation
- Perspective recognition

Scenario 2 (1–2 Hour Lesson). How did electricity and new technology influence people in the 1920s? Use these materials to engage students in reading and analysis to create an evidence-based argument about the impact of technology in the 1920s.

Ask students to reread Mrs. Lathrop's letter (Source 5.1) before starting this lesson, or complete Scenario 1 and then move on to this lesson, which combines Sources 5.4 and 5.5 with Tool 5.3 to consider the effects of electricity in the 1920s as students ponder the impact of electricity on women from different backgrounds.

Begin with Mrs. Lathrop's letter. As a class or in groups, create a schedule of Mrs. Lathrop's daily life as reported in her letter. Have students list words and phrases from the letter that indicate how Lathrop feels about her life. Have students read Sources 5.4 and 5.5 to compare laundry tasks for affluent women vs. the rural poor. Ask students to imagine how different housewives would describe their lives. What evidence will students use to construct these images? Using a Venn diagram, ask students to work with a partner to contrast the lives of upper-class women before and after electricity. This will give students a sense of change and continuity for one social class, and the ways electricity altered their housework.

A major focus of this chapter is to understand the impact of technology in the 1920s through corroborating sources. Tool 5.3 will assess this objective. In addition, students could create a T chart, with positive influences of technology on women in the 1920s on one side and negative influences on the other. Ask students to give their initial impression and then add ideas, quotations, and information to this chart as they work with the sources. Ask students to revisit their initial responses and revise them periodically throughout the lesson as they learn more. Follow this up with a paragraph or full essay in response to the question: Was the impact of technology on women in 1921 mostly positive or negative? As with every essay, ask students to draw on evidence from sources to support their arguments.

> **Targeted list of skills in this scenario**
>
> - Corroborating sources
> - Identifying consequences of new technology (cause-effect relationships)
> - Evidence-based argumentation

Scenario 3 (1 Hour Lesson). What were housewives concerned about in the 1920s? Use online resources to examine the challenges housewives faced in the 1920s.

Read Mrs. Lathrop's letter and ask students what it says about Mrs. Lathrop's lifestyle. To consider multiple housewives' perspectives from this era, go to the History Matters website at George Mason University's Center for History and New Media. There, search for a source housed at History Matters entitled, "'I am only a piece of machinery': Housewives analyze their problems."

Here students may read letters sent to the *Woman's Home Companion* in 1923 in which housewives shared household problems and solutions (our favorite is entitled "The Unbroken Circle"). **Give students a focus question like "What conclusions can you make about housewives in the 1920s? Cite evidence from the sources to support your conclusions."** You can return to Mrs. Lathrop's letter to see how Lathrop compares to the women of the Woman's Home Companion. What might Mrs. Lathrop have written to the Woman's Home Companion? Would her tone have remained as upbeat and happy, regardless of audience? This lesson models the process of historical investigation, questioning, and comparison of sources.

An alternative assignment (see Tool 5.4) asks students to select four groups of women in 1921 (poor urban, poor rural, wealthy rural, wealthy urban) and schedule a day from each woman's life. Students should construct a daily schedule for each woman. Sources from this chapter, as well as those from the Center for History and New Media website, should be consulted and cited to ground students' work in the realities of 1920s America. Students could then write a response to the question: How representative was Mrs. Lathrop of women in 1921?

> **Targeted list of skills in this scenario**
>
> - Corroborating sources
> - Perspective recognition
> - Evidence-based argumentation

Sources and Tools

Source 5.1: Dear Mr. Edison (Modified)

Norton, Kans.
March 5, 1921

Mr. Edison *Thank her very much Etc—*

Dear Sir:

It is not always the privilege of a woman to thank personally the inventor of articles which make life liveable for her sex. . . . I am a college graduate and probably my husband is one of the best known surgeons between Topeka and Denver. I am an officer in the District of Women's Club as well as President of our Town Organization.

We have four children. . . . We have a large house so you see when doing practically all my own work, my duties are many and my activities most varied, yet I enjoy my labors and do not feel that I entirely neglect to get pleasure out of life. . . . The house is lighted by electricity. I cook on a **Westinghouse** electric range, wash dishes in an electric dish washer. An electric fan even helps to distribute the heat over part of the house. . . . I wash clothes in an electric machine and iron on an electric **mangle** and with an electric iron. I clean house with electric cleaners. I rest, take an electric massage and curl my hair on an electric iron. Dress in a gown sewed on a machine run by a motor. Then start the **Victrola** and either study Spanish for a while or listen to **Kreisler** and **Gluck** and **Galli**. . . . The Doctor comes home, tired with a days work wherein electricity has played almost as much part as it has at home, to find a wife . . . who is now rested and ready to serve the tired man and discuss affairs of the day. . . .

Possibly he brings in a guest without warning but electricity and a pressure cooker save the day for the hostess. Indeed, I've entertained the Governor of our State and a dozen of our . . . citizens at a little more than an hours notice. . . .

Please accept the thanks Mr. Edison of one most truly appreciative woman. I know I am only one of many under the same debt of gratitude to you. . . .

Sincerely,
MRS. W.C. LATHROP

Source: Excerpt from Mrs. W. C. Lathrop's letter to Thomas Edison, March 5, 1921.

WORD BANK

Westinghouse–an electric company founded in 1886
mangle–a machine for pressing or smoothing clothes
Victrola–a brand of record player
Kreisler–famous violinist in the early 1900s
Gluck and **Galli**–famous singers in the early 1900s

Source 5.2: Appliance Ownership in Philadelphia (Modified)

Note: In 1920, 35% of American homes had electricity. Of these, the majority were urban and suburban homes. This survey of homes with electricity in Philadelphia shows the kinds of appliances different people owned there.

Appliance ownership in 1,300 electrified homes, Philadelphia, 1921

	Poor homes	**Average homes**	**Modern homes** (10–12 years old)	**Better class**
Iron	64%	60%	87%	90%
Vacuum cleaner	33%	40%	83%	84%
Washing machine	11%	5%	28%	32%
Fan	2%	6%	10%	36%
Percolator	1%	4%	6%	19%
Range	–	–	–	3.4%
Refrigerator	–	–	–	–
Radio	–	–	–	–

Source: C. J. Russell, "Philadelphia Survey." Proceedings, NELA Convention, 1921. Copy in the Consolidated Edison Library, New York City. Cited in David Nye, *Electrifying America: Social Meanings of a New Technology, 1880–1940* (Cambridge, MA: MIT Press, 1990), 303.

WORD BANK

modern homes–refers to homes that were newly built
better class–refers to homes of the more affluent or wealthy
percolator–a kind of coffee maker

Source 5.3: Electricity in Rural America (Modified)

Note: Here is one historian's explanation of the low availability and high cost of electricity in rural areas in the 1920s and 1930s.

The federal census of 1920 . . . reported that of the 6,000,000 farms in the United States, only 452,620 had electric lights and 643,899 had some form of running water. . . . Most of the farm homes with electricity were concentrated in New England and the far West where the number of serviced farms ranged from 15 to 45 percent respectively. The Midwest and South ranked lowest, ranging from 10 percent to less than 1 percent. . . .

Until the creation of the Rural Electrification Administration (REA) in 1935, power companies had the **prerogative** to serve farmers, but they were slow or unwilling to do so because of the high cost involved. . . .

Cost was the real stumbling block to service. Rural lines cost $2,000 or more per mile, and since there were usually only two to five dwellings per mile in the country, utilities anticipated low **revenue** to **amortize** investments. They preferred the urban market. Companies expected farmers, therefore, to bear the burden of the initial investment charging them with the cost of the line, or a $500 to $1,000 deposit. Rural rates were also high, about 9 to 10 cents per kilowatt-hour for the minimum usage. No such **adverse** conditions applied to city dwellers who paid 4 to 5 cents per kilowatt-hour and were under no obligation to pay for the cost of the line.

Few rural homeowners could afford to pay for the lines or make the deposit, nor could they at first afford enough appliances to use the amount of electricity necessary to achieve the advantage of lower rates. The effect was an endless cycle of expense for both parties–recipients of service used little power because of high rates, and the utilities charged such rates because of low usage.

Source: Excerpts from D. Clayton Brown, *Electricity for Rural America: The Fight for the REA* (Westport, CT: Greenwood Press, 1980). xv–xvi and 3–5.

WORD BANK

prerogative–an exclusive right
revenue–earned income
amortize–to gradually pay off
adverse–against one's interest

Source 5.4: Affluent Women's Work in the 1920s (Modified)

Note: Here is one historian's explanation of the limited effect new technologies had on the household work of **affluent** women in the 1920s.

The average comfortable housewife of this generation learned to organize the work in her household without the assistance of servants or with far fewer hours of assistance than her mother had had. Where a servant had been replaced by a vacuum cleaner, the comfortable housewife was spending more time than her mother had spent getting the floors and the rugs into shape; where a laundress had been replaced by a washing machine . . . a housewife was spending time on chores that, in her mother's day, had been performed by other people. . . . Every decision to "do it myself" was a decision to increase the time that the housewife would spend at her work. In households that were prosperous, the labor saved by labor-saving devices was that not of the housewife but of her helpers. This is the most salient reason that every time-study of affluent housewives during these years . . . revealed that no matter how many appliances they owned, or how many conveniences were at their command, they were still spending roughly the same number of hours per week at housework as their mothers had.

Source: Excerpt from Ruth Schwartz Cowan, *More Work for Mother: The Ironies of Household Technology from the Open Hearth to the Microwave* (New York: Basic Books, 1983), 178.

WORD BANK

affluent–wealthy

SOURCE 5.5: POOR, RURAL WOMEN'S WORK IN THE 1920S (MODIFIED)

Note: Here is one historian's explanation of the long process of washing clothes used by rural women without the benefit of electric appliances.

Without electricity, even boiling water was work. Without electricity to work a pump, there was only one way to **obtain** water: by hand. A federal study of nearly half a million farm families would show that, on the average, a person living on a farm used 40 gallons of water every day. Since the average farm family was five persons, the family used 200 gallons . . . of water each day–73,000 gallons in a year. The study showed that . . . the well was located 253 feet from the house–and that to pump by hand and carry to the house 73,000 gallons of water a year would require someone to put in during that year 63 eight-hour days, and walk 1,750 miles.

Every week, every week all year long–every week without fail–there was washday. The wash was done outside. A huge vat of boiling water would be suspended over a larger, roaring fire and near it three large "Number Three" zinc washtubs. . . . The clothes would be scrubbed in the first of the zinc tubs, scrubbed on a washboard by a woman bending over the tub. . . .

Then the farm wife would wring out each piece of clothing to remove from it as much as possible of the dirty water, and put it in the big vat of boiling water. . . . She would try to get the rest [of the dirt] out by "punching" the clothes in the vat–standing over the boiling water and using a wooden paddle or, more often, a broomstick, to stir the clothes and swish them through the water and press them against the bottom or sides, moving the broom handle up and down and around as hard as she could for ten or fifteen minutes. . . .

The next step was to transfer the clothes from the boiling water to the second of the three zinc washtubs: the "rinse tub." . . . When the clothes were in the rinse tub, the woman bent over the tub and rinsed them, by swishing each individual item through the water. Then she wrung out the clothes, to get as much of the dirty water out as possible, and placed the clothes in the third tub, which contained **bluing**, and swished them around in *it*–this time to get the bluing all through the garment and make it white–and then repeated the same movements in the dishpan, which was filled with **starch**.

At this point, one load of wash would be done. A week's wash took at least four loads. . . . For each load, moreover, the water in each of the three washtubs would have to be changed. A washtub held about eight gallons. . . . She did the filling with a bucket which held three or four gallons–twenty-five or thirty pounds.

. . . Hauling the water, scrubbing, punching, rinsing: a Hill Country farm wife did this for hours on end–while a city wife did it by pressing the button on her electric washing machine.

Source: Excerpt from Robert Caro, *The Years of Lyndon Johnson: The Path to Power* (New York: Alfred A. Knopf, 1982), 504–509.

WORD BANK

obtain–to receive or take possession of
bluing–a substance used to whiten clothes
starch–a substance used in laundering to stiffen fabrics

Tool 5.1: Putting Sources into Context

Directions: To better understand Mrs. Lathrop's view of the world, try to imagine the time and place in which she wrote this letter. Read Source 5.1 and answer the following questions.

1. Where was this written?

2. Go to http://maps.google.com/ and search for Mrs. Lathrop's town and state.
   a. In what region of the United States is this town located?

   b. In what part of the state is this town?

   c. How far is it to the closest major cities of that time period–Topeka and Denver?

3. Go to the Historical Census Browser at the University of Virginia's library (http://mapserver.lib.virginia.edu).
   a. Click on the 1920 Census data.
   b. Search for two variables: total population and population per square mile.
   c. Note the figures for Kansas in the table below.
   d. Compare the population per square mile for Kansas to other states–go to the bottom of the page and sort the data by population per square mile in descending order. Click "submit." Count from the top to see where Kansas ranked in terms of population density.
   e. Specifying Kansas, note the figures for Norton County in the table below.
   f. Compare the population per square mile for Norton County with other counties in Kansas–go to the bottom of the page and sort the data by population per square mile in descending order. Click "submit." Count from the top to see where Norton County ranked in terms of population density.

	Total population	**Population per square mile**	**Population per square mile rank**
Kansas			
Norton County			

Tool 5.1: Putting Sources into Context (continued)

4. Would you characterize Mrs. Lathrop's town as rural, urban, or suburban? Why?

5. When was this source written?

6. What else was happening at the time this was written? List 3 events or issues of the day, and explain why they might be important to understanding this source.

7. According to her letter, what material goods does Mrs. Lathrop own? List them.

8. List details from Mrs. Lathrop's letter that might indicate her social status.

9. How representative of women in Kansas in the 1920s do you think Mrs. Lathrop was? Use details from your reading and research to support your answer.

Tool 5.2: Comparing Mrs. Lathrop to Her Contemporaries

1. What percentage of farms in Kansas had electricity in 1920? (Hint: See Source 5.3)

2. Based on Source 5.3, what kind of rural or farm households had electricity in 1920? Explain using evidence from the sources.

3. Why didn't more rural households have electricity?

4. In what part of the country is Philadelphia located? Was Philadelphia an urban or rural area in 1920? How do you know? Use the 1920 Census data to justify your answer.

Tool 5.2: Comparing Mrs. Lathrop to Her Contemporaries (continued)

5. Take the list of material goods and appliances that you made in Tool 5.1 for Mrs. Lathrop. Compare what she owns with poor, average, and better-class homes in Philadelphia in 1921.

Appliances	Mrs. Lathrop	"Poor" in Philadelphia survey	"Average" in Philadelphia survey	"Better class" in Philadelphia survey

6. How does Mrs. Lathrop's household compare with rural, urban, upper-class, and lower-class households?

7. Based on these sources and the 1920 Census, what conclusions can you make about Mrs. Lathrop's social status? Explain the basis for your conclusions using evidence from the sources.

8. How representative was Mrs. Lathrop of women in 1921? Cite evidence from the sources to support your ideas.

Tool 5.3: The 1920s Woman: The Effects of Electricity in the 1920s

1. What does Mrs. Lathrop do during the day that she describes to Mr. Edison? Using Source 5.1, list her activities.

2. How do you think Mrs. Lathrop's daily life compares to that of the majority of rural housewives?

3. Using Sources 5.4 and 5.5, compare the process of doing laundry in the 1920s for the rural poor and "comfortable," or upper-class, housewives.

Doing laundry

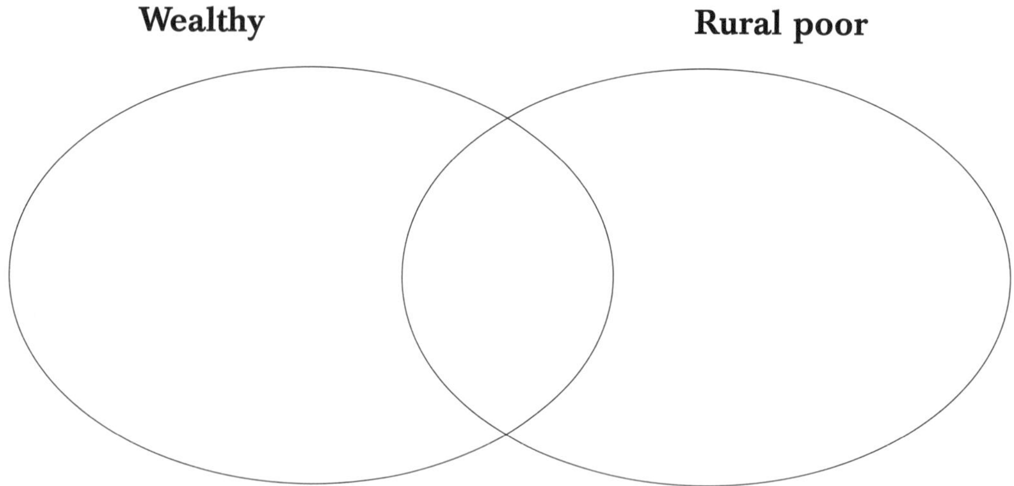

4. Reexamine Source 5.1. List some words and phrases that indicate how Mrs. Lathrop feels about her life.

Tool 5.3: The 1920s Woman: The Effects of Electricity in the 1920s (continued)

5. Why do you think Mrs. Lathrop did not say anything negative about electricity in her letter?

6. How do you think Mrs. Lathrop's peers in rural areas that lacked electricity would describe their lives?

7. According to Cowan, how did electricity and new technology change Mrs. Lathrop's life? (Hint: Compare Mrs. Lathrop with her mother. Use the Venn diagram below to get a sense of these changes.)

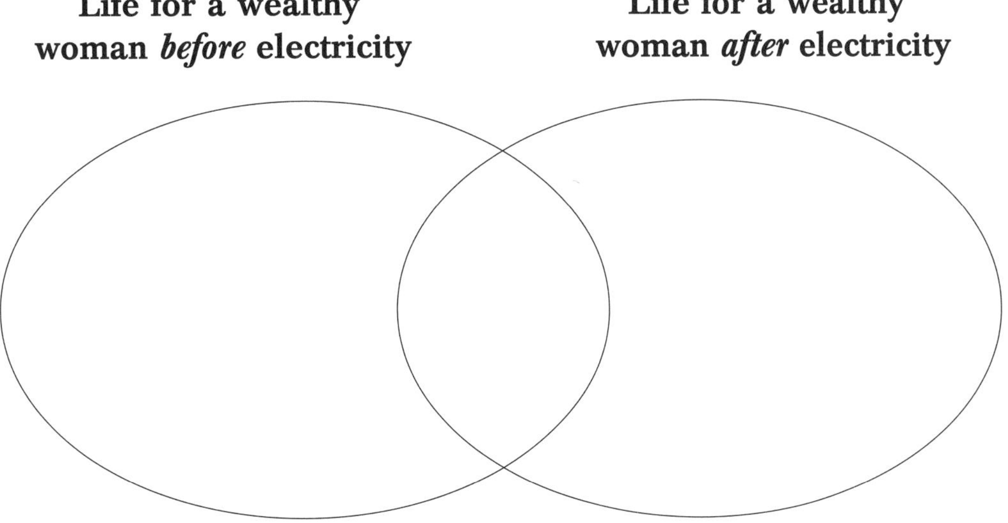

8. Whose lives were changed by electricity in 1921? Were these changes positive? Explain why or why not, using the evidence before you.

Tool 5.4: Assessing Students' Understanding of Perspective, Representativeness, and Corroboration

Directions: Using the sources provided, create a schedule for a day in the life of four different women living in 1921. Cite the sources that helped you construct these women's schedules.

POOR URBAN WOMAN	POOR RURAL WOMAN
7 am	7 am
8 am	8 am
9 am	9 am
10 am	10 am
11 am	11 am
12 pm	12 pm
1 pm	1 pm
2 pm	2 pm
3 pm	3 pm
4 pm	4 pm
5 pm	5 pm
6 pm	6 pm
7 pm	7 pm
Sources that helped me create this schedule:	*Sources that helped me create this schedule:*
WEALTHY URBAN WOMAN	**WEALTHY RURAL WOMAN**
7 am	7 am
8 am	8 am
9 am	9 am
10 am	10 am
11 am	11 am
12 pm	12 pm
1 pm	1 pm
2 pm	2 pm
3 pm	3 pm
4 pm	4 pm
5 pm	5 pm
6 pm	6 pm
7 pm	7 pm
Sources that helped me create this schedule:	*Sources that helped me create this schedule:*

Which schedule seems most like Mrs. Lathrop's? How do you know?

How does Mrs. Lathrop's schedule compare to the other schedules?

Suggested Resources

http://www.fordham.edu/halsall/women/womensbook.html
This page, run by Paul Halsall at Fordham University, is one of several Internet History Sourcebooks. This particular page features links to documents and websites that focus on women's history both in North America and around the world.

http://www.womenshistorymonth.gov/
This page, produced by the Library of Congress, has a rich and varied collection of primary documents related to women's history in the United States. There is a long list of exhibits and collections that include photographs, advertisements, propaganda posters, and text-based documents.

http://ocp.hul.harvard.edu/ww/
Run by Harvard University, this site focuses on women's work in the United States from 1800 to 1930. The collection includes images and text-based documents.

http://www.nwhm.org/education-resources/
This page, run by the National Women's History Museum, includes several cyber exhibits of different aspects of women's history in America.

http://www.ourdocuments.gov/doc.php?flash=old&doc=46#
See Thomas Edison's patent application for the electric light bulb at this site, run by the Our Documents.Gov website (a cooperative effort by National History Day, National Archives and Records Administration, USA Freedom Corps, Siemens, *U.S. News & World Report*, and The History Channel).

http://edsitement.neh.gov/view_lesson_plan.asp?id=408#LESSON1
This page, run by the National Endowment for the Humanities, offers a series of lessons to help students understand life before and after new technologies were introduced in the late 1800s and early 1900s.

http://www1.assumption.edu/WHW/
This page is the product of a grant by the National Endowment of the Humanities and is run by Assumption College, the American Antiquarian Society, the Alliance for Education, and the Worcester Women's History Project. It includes a rich collection of primary documents as well as teacher resources with ideas for integrating women's history into the curriculum.

CHAPTER 6

"Dust to Eat, and Dust to Breathe, and Dust to Drink"

Arthur Rothstein, Sand piled up in front of outhouse on farm. Cimarron County, Oklahoma. April 1936. Farm Security Administration–Office of War Information Photograph Collection. Available at http://www.loc.gov/pictures/item/fsa1998018977/PP/

"Men and women huddled in their houses, and they tied handkerchiefs over their noses when they went out, and wore goggles to protect their eyes." The opening pages of John Steinbeck's Pulitzer Prize–winning novel *The Grapes of Wrath* describe the grim realities of living in Oklahoma in the mid-1930s. Life as people knew it disappeared, blown away by the dust, and many, like Steinbeck's Joad family, fled their homes to make a new life. The Joads' trip on Route 66 and their struggles to find sustainable work in California are the subject of Steinbeck's tale, one that has captivated readers since its appearance in 1939. Not only is it an engaging story, Steinbeck's novel was a political and social critique that exposed the exploitation and mistreatment of California's farm workers.

The story of those who left the afflicted region during the 1930s Dust Bowl is familiar to many. Okies, Dorothea Lange's photos, Woody Guthrie's songs, and the Joads–these particulars are lodged in our collective memory. But what about the people who didn't leave the Plains during what seemed an interminable 8 years of drought? What about the stories of the intrepid farmers who stayed behind even as the land drifted and disappeared beneath them–as dust crept into their homes through unprotected cracks or, more ominously, descended in a black cloud that smothered all it touched? Such stories don't trigger the same recognition or touchstone quality that those of the migrants do. Yet they are just as much a part of our past as those more easily recounted.

History is full of stories. Stories are how we share what happened in bygone days and how we make sense of that past. Often, they are what initially piques our interest to explore the past and its specifics and significance. And these stories require making innumerable choices: Whose story will we tell? What events will we focus on? What are the critical specifics for weaving an accurate story about that past? Unlike Steinbeck's stunning piece of fiction, historical stories must stick to the documentary record and be supported by evidence.[1] In this chapter, we examine various stories about the Dust Bowl, first the stories of those left behind, then stories of explanation–how did the Dust Bowl happen? Historians move beyond descriptive stories to tell explanatory stories, and the ways that they have explained this environmental and human disaster have changed over time. All of these aspects are integral to understanding the Dust Bowl and the stories we tell about it.

Whose Story Do We Tell?

Caroline Henderson was a schoolteacher who moved to the Oklahoma Panhandle in 1907, the year the Indian and Oklahoma territories joined to become a state. Caroline would spend almost 60 years there, meeting her husband, building a homestead, raising a daughter, earning her master's degree in literature, and writing for magazines and journals. Her articles, filled with clear and compelling descriptions, helped to bring national attention to the plight of the Dust Bowl residents during its darkest days.

The "Dust Bowl" refers to the region of the Great Plains that suffered the erosion and dust storms in the 1930s most acutely. This region, encompassing parts of Oklahoma, Texas, Kansas, Colorado, and smaller areas of New Mexico and Nebraska, extended approximately 100 million acres, or over one-third of the Great Plains. Within that region, the "blow area" shifted in size and location, prompting historian Donald Worster to call the Dust Bowl "an event as well as a locality."[2] The hardest-hit areas were the Texas and Oklahoma Panhandles and the southwestern corner of Kansas. Between the worst years of the storms, 1935–1937, this shifting blow area covered approximately 50 million acres of the southern plains.

This area was one of the last regions in the continental United States to be settled. With few trees, little rainfall, and high temperatures, it had been called both the Great American Desert and No Man's Land.[3] Settlers from the verdant, water-rich South, Midwest, and East weren't anxious to try farming in this semi-arid climate. And the railroads that facilitated westward settlement didn't reach the Oklahoma Panhandle until 1916, adding to the region's isolation.

Caroline Henderson was part of the early-20th-century settlement of this region. She would be there during its prosperous years, when normal (if still sparse) rainfall, wartime demand for grain, and the railroad helped create economic good times. But she would suffer more hard times than good. And those hard times became almost unbearable during 1932–1940, the years of the Dust Bowl.[4]

On April 14, 1935, a huge dust storm hit the region. J. H. Ward, in the southeastern county of Baca, Colorado, saw the ominous, thick cloud rolling over the hill toward him; he took photos of what must have been a terrifying sight as the cloud approached, swallowing everything in its path (Source 6.1). Folksinger Woody Guthrie would write a song that day, with the eerie title "So Long, It's Been Good to Know Yuh." Guthrie wrote about leaving his home on "the west Texas plains," as he had "to be driftin' along," and more ominously that the dust storm "hit like thunder" and seemed like "the end of the world," capturing the fear of his neighbors. That April day would come to be known as Black Sunday and was likely the worst dust storm that hit the Plains during the 1930s. The very next day, the term "Dust Bowl" was coined by Associated Press reporter Robert E. Geiger.[5]

Dust storms known as "rollers" and "black blizzards" were relatively frequent in the "dirty '30s." In 1932, at least 14 storms hit the region, and from 1933 to 1938, there were more than 300.[6] Mostly occurring in the winter and spring, these storms blackened the sky, sweeping over and through the landscape, infiltrating homes, eyes, and lungs–once the dust descended, there was no escape. People of all ages suffered from "dust pneumonia." Buildings and crops were covered and destroyed, schools and towns shut down, transportation stopped, and people wondered whether Armageddon had hit and what they had done to deserve it.

The storms wreaked havoc on the Dust Bowl region and extended beyond. Giant clouds of dust advanced across the continent to both Eastern and Southern coasts. In May 1934, headlines in the *New York Times* proclaimed, "Huge Dust Cloud, Blown 1,500 Miles, Dims City 5 Hours." That cloud was estimated to be 1,800 miles wide, weigh 300 million tons, and increase the dust particles in the air in New York City by 2.7 times.[7] Three hundred miles off the Atlantic Coast, ships reported dust on their decks, while later storms left a residue along the Gulf Coast.[8]

But the Black Sunday storm was what one Kansas resident called "the darkest day of all."[9] Residents who had suffered ferocious storms in prior weeks welcomed the fine weather that morning. Yet what started as a beautiful Sunday with temperatures in the 80s and a clear view of the horizon quickly descended into a storm so terrible that Pauline Winkler Grey later remembered thinking "it was the end of the world."[10] Moving from North Dakota southerly and westerly into Kansas and Colorado, the storm was reported to be 200 miles wide and moving at 65 miles an hour. Temperatures dropped quickly; echoing other eyewitnesses, Ward's photograph shows the contrast between the clear sky and the tons of topsoil barreling toward him. "It was as though the sky was divided into two opposite worlds . . . blue sky, golden sunlight and tranquility; . . . [and] a menacing curtain of boiling black dust."[11] One boy, playing with a friend in Hays, Kansas, ran for home but couldn't outpace the storm–the next day he was found smothered to death by dust. Little wonder that many fled the Dust Bowl. The storms were an implacable enemy that attacked residents' economic livelihood, health, and safety, and threatened daily life.

Yet some stayed. Caroline Henderson was one of the approximately 7 of 10 people who continued to live in the region during its blackest days.[12] In April 1935, she penned a letter entitled "Dust to Eat" and sent it to Franklin Delano Roosevelt's Secretary of Agriculture, Henry Wallace (Source 6.2). In the lengthy letter, one sees why Henderson was credited with informing her contemporaries about the Dust Bowl residents' experiences and courage. Henderson wrote of the "marvelous" changes that had occurred in her 27 years as a homesteader, where "unbroken buffalo grass sod has given way to cultivated fields," and dreams of a Jeffersonian yeoman farmer's life seemed within reach. But when drought and dust came, the "daily physical torture, confusion of mind, [and] gradual wearing down of courage" threatened to destroy that dream. Henderson claimed the "bitter reality . . . and violent discomfort" of the storms were too great to describe, but she goes on to write vividly of their daily details.

Henderson wrote of the hope and effort it took to transform the Plains into farms, described the disaster wrought by the Dust Bowl and the government response to that disaster, and ended with hope–a hope that, combined with her memories, held her on her farm. She applauded the federal government's aid to the region, and credited it with preventing even more abandoned homesteads and farms, a claim later supported by historians.[13]

Lawrence Svobida left behind his own account of surviving the Dust Bowl (Sources 6.3 and 6.4). In 1929, Svobida settled in Meade County in the southwest corner of Kansas (not far from Henderson). He would stay just long enough to experience the worst of the disaster. His 1940 book, *Farming the Dust Bowl: A First-Hand Account from Kansas*, also described the disaster and the damage it wrought. The "gales . . . chopped off the plants . . . then proceeded to take the roots out. . . . They blew away the topsoil," and left behind a ground that was "almost as hard as concrete. . . . [It was] a destroying force beyond my wildest imaginings." Svobida focused on the destruction of the land that was the farmer's lifeblood. His account reiterated what others said, that green plant life was wiped out and the region was reverting to what earlier Americans had called it: the Great American Desert.

So what was it like to endure the Dust Bowl? Although not as well known as those of the migrants, the stories of those who stayed give us a dramatic view into a past we would otherwise miss. In his 2006 book, subtitled "Those Who Survived the Great American Dust Bowl," journalist Timothy Egan called their story *The Worst Hard Time*. The book received three awards, testifying to the power of these overlooked stories.

What Caused the Dust Bowl? What Story Do We Tell?

Yet there are other stories to be told about this event. Historians tell stories that explain why events happen. Primary sources are one major source of evidence for those explanations, and both the Henderson and Svobida excerpts provide glimpses into the causes of the Dust Bowl.

Henderson celebrated the changes she saw in the Plains, where cultivated fields had defeated grass sod, and new machinery "revolutionized methods of farm work." Svobida, on the other hand, viewed the same changes differently. He agreed on the important impact of "power farming," but called it "the death knell of the Plains" rather than a boon. His memoir recounts seven failed crops, whereas Henderson wrote 4 years earlier, following success in farming her land. These factors may have helped to shape their differing views of the transformation, but both stories recognized that massive changes had occurred to the Great Plains, and that farming methods were largely responsible.

This conclusion was shared by a contemporary report into the causes of the Dust Bowl (Sources 6.5, 6.6, and 6.7). When President Franklin Delano Roosevelt took office in March 1933, the Dust Bowl was in full swing. In July 1936, the president asked for a report on the causes of the crisis so that steps could be taken to prevent another. The Great Plains Drought Area Committee conducted a "preliminary study" that included consulting available records and taking a 2-week trip through the most severely affected areas from Amarillo in the Texas Panhandle to Rapid City, North Dakota. The Committee included leaders of the Works Progress Administration and government agencies in charge of land use, agriculture, and soil conservation. It was an impressive group, chaired by Morris Cooke, Administrator of the Rural Electrification Administration, and included Rexford G. Tugwell, Administrator of the Resettlement Agency, and Henry A. Wallace, Secretary of Agriculture. Such an esteemed delegation indicated that Roosevelt saw the Dust Bowl as an important national problem–as did the millions of dollars spent on conservation of physical assets and aid to the region following his inauguration.

At the end of August 1936, the committee issued their "personal and confidential" report to the president. It included important conclusions. The 4 years of drought were not the real culprit for the Dust Bowl disaster. "Over cropping, over grazing, and improper farm methods" were to blame. "Mistaken public policies" were largely responsible, including the country's homesteading policy and the encouragement of a misguided system of agriculture. (Two maps, early in the report, showed the Great Plains as a region of "predominantly low rainfall" and "high wind velocity." They made the point that it wasn't the weather that had changed, but rather the patterns of settlement and farming.) The president's committee found that preventing future disasters–indeed, ensuring the future of the region–would depend "on the degree to which farming practices conform to natural conditions," and that these had been badly misaligned for decades. The report was clear: The Dust Bowl was not a natural disaster. It was a man-made one.

The report included "lines of action" that centered on identifying land use regions, something that would require government involvement and oversight. Was an area more suited to farming or cattle grazing? Which land would need to be reclaimed as grassland? What kinds of grasses would best conserve the soil? Water rights needed to be reconsidered, and local, state, and Federal governments would have to reclaim private lands in order to plan and control their use. Farmers needed to engage in soil conservation and communities needed to work together to build more sustainable land use regions. Relief programs would help promote these advancements, along with government involvement and regulation. The report called for a "coordinated program of cooperation" and stated, "The fundamental purpose of any worthwhile program must be not to depopulate the region but to make it permanently habitable. Any other outcome would be a national failure which would have its effects, tangible and intangible, far beyond the affected area."

Explanations for the Dust Bowl that focused on the vagaries of weather held little sway for these investigators. The committee's report made a compelling case for a man-made disaster, wrought not only by individual settlers, but also by government policies ill-suited to the region. Even so, the report did not necessarily change everyone's views of the catastrophe. For many people, rain alone could spell a return of good times to the Plains. Caroline Henderson's lament that the "one satisfactory solution" to the problem of drought "is beyond all human control" was a common sentiment. Residents prayed for rain to turn their fortunes around. (At least one community took matters into their hands when residents of Dalhart, Texas, tried dynamiting the clouds in order to force rain from them.)[14]

With its "lines of action" and call for government at all levels to cooperate on the "reorganization of farming practices," the report suggested that solutions to the crisis existed beyond waiting for rain. In that respect, it can be read as a hopeful document, just as Caroline Henderson held onto hope through the darkest storms. The Plains could be farmed more wisely and made permanently habitable through reclamation, soil conservation, and coordinated efforts. Anything less would be a "national failure."

Indeed, the Dust Bowl had not only attracted investigation by the federal government. National funds and programs were set up to ease the hardship of residents and support wise use of the land. The first government program applied to the region was a feed-and-seed loan fund initiated by Congress and reluctantly approved by President Herbert Hoover after the Red Cross had proven inadequate to the task. Plains voters, who knew that more help was needed, uncharacteristically voted Democrat in 1932, helping to elect Roosevelt. Besieged by crises, Roosevelt passed a flurry of New Deal programs in his first 100 days. While none of them directly targeted the Dust Bowl region, they established agencies–most notably the Agricultural Adjustment Administration (AAA)–that would oversee later efforts. When drought conditions worsened dramatically and the huge dust storm of May 24, 1934, hit the East Coast, national efforts accelerated.

In June 1934, Roosevelt got a $525 million drought relief package passed that included aid to farmers and cattlemen in the form of emergency loans, income supplements, job programs, and government purchase of cattle. Farmers and cattlemen were also paid for reducing production. Included were monies to acquire lands and return them to grass, relocate residents, and create a shelterbelt of trees. Such aid would continue throughout the decade, with the notable exception of payments for production reduction, which were deemed unconstitutional by the Supreme Court in 1936. (Subsequent efforts shifted to support for planting soil-conserving plants and eliminating soil-depleting crops.)

Farmers received aid to conserve their soil for future crops. As Svobida described, strip listing–plowing deep furrows perpendicular to the winds to minimize blowing–was a core strategy for doing this. Federal monies to support strip listing passed through local institutions into farmers' hands. This meant that farmers had work even during the worst drought years.

Federal aid to the Plains area persisted throughout the 1930s. Generally, the Federal programs had two main purposes: restoring the area to former levels of production and prosperity, and conserving and protecting the land. In combination, such aid meant that Plains residents received as much or more per capita than any group in the country during the Great Depression.

People Acted on Nature. Was the Dust Bowl a natural disaster, the result of severe climate conditions? Or did people's actions cause this tragedy? Was the government's 1936 report right in its characterization of causes? What role did government policies and actions play in making and managing the "dirty '30s"?

Historians agree on some of these matters, but debate persists on others. The first question is likely the easiest. In a 1986 article titled "Dust Bowl Historiography," Harry C. McDean identified a consensus among modern historians "that the Dust Bowl was not a natural disaster; it was a disaster caused by what people did to nature."[15]

What exactly did people do to nature? Historian Donald Worster told a compelling story of these events in his award-winning 1979 book, *Dust Bowl: The Southern Plains in the 1930s* (Source 6.9). Part Two of Worster's book is entitled "Prelude to Dust" and includes the two chapters "What Holds the Earth Together" and "Sodbusting." These titles serve as shorthand for the story of how a land dependent on grass was destroyed by overgrazing and extensive farming. Worster wrote, "An old and unique ecological complex has been destroyed by man, leaving him with no buffer against the elements, leaving the land free to blow away. It was not the first time some large part of the natural vegetation had died, but it was the only time that it had happened because of a deliberate strategy carried out by human beings."[16]

Worster's "once upon a time" began with geologic history, then discussed soil development, climate patterns, and the flora and fauna of the southern Plains. He mentioned prehistoric man and the Plains Indian culture, which accepted "in every way the primacy of the grass" and "showed a pattern of ecological restraint."[17] Worster contrasted this with the attitudes of settlers who arrived after the Indians had largely been pushed onto reservations.

The southern Plains were not settled until after the Civil War. Until the 1880s, the settlers who came were mostly involved with raising cattle. Fortunes changed quickly: In 1880 cattlemen earned high slaughterhouse prices, but the harsh winter of 1886 decimated the herds, and 85% perished.[18] Worster called this reversal of fortune a harbinger of things to come. The end of the Plains Indian Wars and above-average rainfall in the early 1880s brought more farmers to the southern Plains, and with them, the region's large-scale if uneven transformation to a farming economy.

Those who arrived struggled to make a living, given the vicissitudes of farming, exacerbated by the difficult soils, periodic pest infestations, and hostile climate. Many turned to cash crops, especially wheat, breaking more sod to plant more crops in hopes of turning a profit. Between 1890 and 1910, the number of farms and amount of land under cultivation soared. In 1890, 5,762 farms and ranches in a 22-county area in Kansas, Colorado, and Texas had an average size of 256 acres. By 1910, the number of farms and their relative sizes had doubled. Farms continued to grow and in 1920 averaged 771 acres: by 1930, the average size reached 813 acres.[19] More and more sod was busted as more and more acres were cultivated. During good times, farmers planted additional crops to make more profit. During the bad, they planted more acres to make up their losses.

These tremendous changes are captured by two images from the Great Plains Report (Sources 6.5 and 6.6). The first shows the Plains' original groundcover, dominated by grasses with trees along the western border and occasionally in the southeastern area. Trees and lumber were scarce in the region, and settlers necessarily built homes from the sod itself.[20] The second visual shows the rapidly expanding acres dedicated to farming, spanning the years 1879–1929, starting just before large-scale agricultural settlement of the Plains and ending on the cusp of the disastrous Dust Bowl years. The later 30 years saw cultivation increase more than twofold for an absolute total increase of more than 60 million acres!

Innovative farm machinery made breaking the sod and planting crops more efficient, and accelerated the radical remaking of land from grassland to farm. The Industrial Revolution of the late 19th century happened not only in manufacturing, but in agriculture as well. Farms became larger and more factorylike, while machines replaced human effort. Steel plows broke the tough sod more easily, tractors replaced horses for tilling, and machines like combines could do several things at once (harvest and thresh the wheat). Such farming equipment meant that farmers could break and farm the land more quickly and with much less elbow grease.

More crops meant more profit. Some have called the 1910s and 1920s the "Great Plow-up." When World War I shut down Russian wheat production and increased international demand for grain, farmers expanded their fields to meet demand that persisted beyond the Great War. Wheat prices stayed mostly stable throughout the 1920s, and the tractors kept plowing new fields. Between 1925 and 1930, farmers "tore up the native vegetation on 5,260,000 acres in the southern plains–an area nearly seven times as large as the state of Rhode Island."[21] Even with all this farming, prosperity wasn't assured: Farmers faced the cost of new machinery, slim margins for error, and the return of European competition as the 1920s roared on.

Glory times spawned a new kind of opportunist who depended on machines that could plow acres in a day and farm hundreds of acres at a time. Known as "suitcase farmers," these opportunists would plant a crop and then leave, relying on chance as to whether the crop flourished or withered. These were not the traditional American farmers, working a homestead where their family lived and upon which their livelihood depended. Such tenant and absentee farmers were less likely to care about sustaining the land's productivity or using soil conservation methods than more permanent residents. In the worst cases, suitcase farmers would simply cut their losses and abandon their tilled fields, applying no conservation methods whatsoever. But, in fact, practices like plowing under crop residue, rotating fields, and leaving bare stalks to stabilize the soil–all of which conserved the topsoil–were not common for many southern Plains farmers.

Historians Disagree. Historians agreed on many causes of the dust storms, including sod-busting, overfarming, farm mechanization, and lack of soil conservation. But what causes people to engage in these practices in the first place? Donald Worster argued that it was the American culture of capitalism that ultimately caused the Dust Bowl (Source 6.8). "The attitude of capitalism–industrial and pre-industrial–toward the earth was imperial and commercial; none of its ruling values taught environmental humility, reverence, or restraint. This was the cultural impetus that drove Americans into the grassland and determined the way they would use it."[22]

Donald Worster told a compelling story, richly detailed with vivid descriptions and forceful arguments. It is a historical story, one that explains the Dust Bowl using varied kinds of evidence. And it stands in contrast to other accounts of the Dust Bowl by attributing cause to capitalism's unbridled appetite for profit.

Published 2 years after Worster's book, R. Douglas Hurt's *The Dust Bowl* agreed that "man's inhabitation . . . and . . . adoption of a new agricultural technology" contributed to the dust storms (Source 6.9).[23] However, Hurt did not identify capitalism as the prime cause. Instead, he told a story of interrelated factors, balancing natural and man-made elements, like the drought that wiped out crops that would have helped stabilize the soil, with humans' "technological abuse of the land."

Such is the nature of stories in history. Historians can examine the same evidence and find different meanings in it, just as they can ask different questions about the same event to illuminate varied characters' experiences. Because of the work of historians like Worster and Hurt, how we understand the meaning of the Dust Bowl has changed. Before, the Dust Bowl was mostly characterized as a natural disaster, a story of brave farmers who persisted in the face of natural disaster and saved the Plains for all of us.[24] Others saw the hostile environment as a catalyst for human innovation and ingenuity.[25] But Worster and Hurt helped change the lens on this event. Rather than casting nature as the primary agent that acted upon the brave settlers, it was those same settlers and their culture who acted upon nature. According to this view, human arrogance, not Mother Nature's fickleness, caused the suffering we associate with the Dust Bowl.

Was the Dust Bowl a story of nature's violence unleashed, or one of intrepid settlers who persevered through nature's hard times? Was it a story of humans exploiting the land, industrialization run amok, and the use of farm machines without regard to sustainability? Or was it the story of how government policies can accelerate exploitation, regulate it, or remedy it? Perhaps the Dust Bowl is the story of the particularity of this one event, how it became a perfect storm of many factors that came together in this particular place at this particular time.[26]

There are many stories to be told about the Dust Bowl, some better than others. Some are simply wrong, as they don't have evidence to support them and are inconsistent with what scientists and historians know about the event. Others alight on the very same evidence and largely agree on the facts of this event, but come to completely different conclusions about what "caused" these facts. Historians, William Cronon wrote, "configure the events of the past into causal sequences–stories–that order and simplify those events to give them new meanings."[27] Stories of explanation require a coherent and unified plot that demands that the teller make choices about what matters and what should be included.

In the case of the Dust Bowl, the story includes how people and nature acted upon one another and are inextricably connected. Focusing solely on the drought of the early 1930s, on the one hand, or on the human response to that drought on the other, gives an inaccurate picture of these precarious times on the Plains and why they occurred. The interdependence between humans and the planet they live on raises questions about what we value and how we should behave in the face of a limited, fragile ecosystem. Given our present challenges–climate change, increasing population, and the ongoing crush for natural resources–the Dust Bowl is very much a story for our times. It reminds us that our actions affect the natural world and can determine whether that world will sustain our growing population or fall victim to it.

Why Teach About the Dust Bowl?

Multiple Stories and Making Sense of Them. Stories captivate. They are an enduring and central piece of the human experience. We tell stories not only to share knowledge, but also to teach the difference between right and wrong, inspire our children, and create community. Engaging and irresistible, stories permeate our lives.

And they are central to history. We use stories to make sense of the past, and it is a rare day in history class when a story is not shared. But how often do we ask students to consider the *multiple* stories embedded in a particular historical event? No single story can capture all that is true about a historic event, person, or era. Human experience is too varied and complex. People experience events differently and motivations can be hidden and multiple.

Studying the Dust Bowl offers concrete opportunities to consider multiple stories and how they work. Many students know stories about the Okies, but few have considered the stories of those who stayed behind. A straightforward question like "What stories are we missing when we focus on the Okies?" helps students recognize that history includes a variety of perspectives and experiences.

History as Explanation and Framing. Why did the Dust Bowl happen? Explaining the past is central to the historian's work, but this is not necessarily obvious to our students. Historians like Donald Worster and R. Douglas Hurt write stories that explain the interrelated causes of the event they investigated. In the past, the Dust Bowl was often depicted as a natural disaster, one that would have happened regardless of the way people settled and farmed the region. However, as historians have looked more closely at the grazing and farming practices of the settlers, at climatic records, government policies and legislation, and common beliefs and values, that story has been overturned. Students can learn that histories explain, rather than merely describe, events.

They can also learn about subfields in American history and how historians use distinctive analytic frames to study the past. Explaining the Dust Bowl requires looking closely at interactions between people and their natural world–the focus of environmental historians like Donald Worster. Subfields in American history (e.g., environmental, military, and women's history) influence the questions historians ask and the stories they tell.

Cross-Curricular Connections with Science and English Language Arts. Exploring the Dust Bowl is an opportunity to integrate different subjects and make cross-curricular connections in lessons. Students can read *The Grapes of Wrath* in English language arts, while studying the stories of those who stayed in their history class. Differences between fiction and history can be highlighted, such as the necessity of evidentiary warrants for historical narratives and claims. History's focus on explanation can be contrasted with Steinbeck's use of story for social critique.

This topic is also ripe for scientific study. Scientists and scientific investigation become allies in figuring out the causes of the Dust Bowl and the methods of preventing another. Wind, climate, and soil patterns all matter in explaining the Dust Bowl. Geographical variations, agricultural science, and farming techniques influenced the extent and ferocity of the dust storms. Soil conservation methods can be examined and the science behind them uncovered and investigated. Students can gain a fuller picture of the event while learning more about different academic disciplines.

Prompting Further Research into Contemporary Issues. We are in the midst of a "Green Revolution," a change in consciousness about our relation to the Earth. To get elected, politicians must take stands on local and international environmental questions, while school districts adapt energy-saving measures and look for ways to go green. Many students are captivated by environmental issues and stories and eager to learn more. This topic and the materials associated with it capitalize on such interest. As a severe environmental disaster of the 1930s, the Dust Bowl allows students to contemplate the interaction between people and the environment from a distance, where reduced passions can lead to heightened analysis and tolerance for complexity. Was such a disaster avoidable? What kinds of causal agents should be considered? What lessons can we learn from this event?

These materials can also prompt students to investigate more contemporary desertification problems. Case studies outside the United States, such as deforestation in Brazil or efforts sponsored by the United Nations Convention to Combat Desertification, help students see that environmental issues are international concerns, and that environmental tragedies do not respect political boundaries.

How Might You Use These Materials?

Scenario 1 (1 Hour Lesson). What story is told? In an "Opening Up the Textbook" lesson,[28] use these documents to deepen students' understanding of the Dust Bowl and help them to recognize the limits of the textbook account.

Assign homework to prepare for the lesson. After reading the textbook passage that addresses the Dust Bowl, students should consider: What story does the textbook tell of this event?

Begin the lesson with this question and ask students to use specifics to illustrate and detail the story the textbook tells (Tool 6.1). Many textbooks focus on the Okies and others who left the region because of the terrible conditions. Some textbooks represent the Dust Bowl as a purely natural disaster caused by drought. Use the appropriate documents to "open up" these stories. For example, students can read and analyze Sources 6.2, 6.3, and 6.4 to find out more about the experiences of those who stayed. Regarding causes, students can read and analyze some of the documents that address the human impact on the region (select from Sources 6.5, 6.6, 6.7, 6.8 and 6.9). In either case, students should be guided by the question(s): What do these sources add to the textbook account? How do they support or contest the textbook story? What story do they tell that is not told by the textbook? Lead a whole-class discussion that explores these questions, prompting students to back up assertions with evidence from the sources. Finally, emphasize the role of evidence in history as the enduring constant in historical investigation.

To close the lesson, **have students evaluate the statement, "There are multiple stories and perspectives in history." Direct them to use information and accounts from the day's lesson to strengthen their written evaluations.**

> **Targeted list of skills in this scenario**
>
> - Identifying story and argument in historical accounts
> - Complicating accepted stories by examining historical evidence
> - Considering multiple stories of historical events

Scenario 2 (1–3 Hour Lesson). What caused the Dust Bowl? Use the sources to engage students in investigating the causes of this event.

Start the lesson by projecting the photo (Source 6.1) and asking students to notice its date, content, how they might have felt seeing the cloud roll toward them, and what they know about the Dust Bowl. Consider playing for students Woody Guthrie's song, "So Long, It's Been Good to Know Yuh." (You can find it on YouTube, but be sure to select the Dust Bowl rather than the World War II version.) Then introduce the lesson's central inquiry question: What caused the Dust Bowl?

As students generate causes, list their answers on the blackboard. In three successive rounds, pairs of students then work with document sets and accompanying worksheets (Tool 6.2) to help them craft an accurate list of causes. After each round of documents, lead a whole-class discussion where you revisit the guiding question and prompt students to defend their answers with evidence from the documents. Use questions that students have generated from working with the documents to highlight how historical digging can lead to more questions.

In the first round, students work with the Henderson and Svobida accounts (Sources 6.2, 6.3, and 6.4). In the second, they use excerpts from the 1936 *Report of the Great Plains Drought Area Committee* (Sources 6.5, 6.6, and 6.7). In the third round students consider the interpretive secondary accounts (Sources 6.8 and 6.9). Finally, **students write an answer to the question, "What caused the Dust Bowl?" Their responses should include evidence, especially direct quotes and specifics from the documents, to support their argument.**

Targeted list of skills in this scenario

- Identifying causes of a historical event
- Recognizing the concept of multiple causation in history
- Evidence-based thinking and argumentation
- Synthesizing multiple accounts

Scenario 3 (2 Hour Lesson). Whose story is told? Use the materials to integrate English language arts and history curricula and teach students important differences between the two. (This scenario is best executed in collaboration with an English language arts colleague.)

Before the lesson, have students read John Steinbeck's novel *The Grapes of Wrath*, up to at least Chapter 10 where the Joads leave their farm. Start the lesson with the question: Whose story is being told in Steinbeck's tale? Then pass out the Svobida and Henderson documents (Sources 6.2, 6.3, and 6.4), written by people who stayed on their homesteads during the 1930s. Ask students whose story is told by these accounts. What do these accounts add to your understanding of the Dust Bowl?

Identify Sources 6.2, 6.3, and 6.4 as primary sources for studying the Dust Bowl. Make the point that historians analyze primary sources to tell stories about the past. Share with them one of the historian accounts (Source 6.8 or 6.9). Ask them to identify the argument and story in the excerpt. Ask: What did this historian use in order to write a historical story? After they identify evidence and sources as necessary, ask whether Steinbeck needed these things to write his story of the Dust Bowl. Use this example to distinguish between fiction and history. You may also consider Steinbeck's novel as a primary source that offers insight into the events and the context of the time, but reiterate the point that fiction and history do not follow the same rules.

Assess students by asking them to write 1–3 paragraphs agreeing or disagreeing with the following statement: "Using both fictional and nonfictional sources can help us understand the past." Students should take a stance and then explain it using at least two specific supporting examples.

Targeted list of skills in this scenario

- Identifying story and argument in historical accounts
- Distinguishing between history and fiction

Scenario 4 (2 Hour Lesson). Springboard to independent research: Use these materials to propel students toward using guided research to elaborate a story (see Tool 6.3).

Use one of the previous scenarios to introduce the idea of multiple stories. After students recognize at least two alternative stories, have them choose one to learn more about. First, have students write a paragraph telling the story as they know it and identifying what they would like to learn more about. Then direct them to resources and Web-based archives where they can learn more about these topics (in order to get started, see the Suggested Resources section).

Ask students to find at least three sources that add to the story they are investigating. Students should analyze each source and identify when, where, and why it was produced; whether it is a secondary or primary source; and how it supports, contests, or extends other sources they have read.[29] Students should record where they found each source and any questions that arise from their analyses. Finally, **have them retell the story in several paragraphs using information, quotes, and data uncovered during their investigation and citing the sources for that specific supporting evidence.**

Targeted list of skills in this scenario

- Identifying multiple stories about the same historical event
- Locating historic sources
- Analyzing and corroborating sources
- Synthesizing multiple accounts
- Building a narrative of a past event based on sources

Sources and Tools

Source 6.1: Photograph taken by J. H. Ward, April 14, 1935, in Baca County, Colorado

Source: J. H. Ward, Dust storm. Colorado. Photograph. 1935. From Library of Congress, *America from the Great Depression to World War II: Photographs from the FSA-OWI, 1935–1945*, http://hdl.loc.gov/loc.pnp/fsa.8b26995

SOURCE 6.2: HENDERSON LETTER (MODIFIED)

Note: Teacher Caroline Henderson began homesteading in the Oklahoma Panhandle in 1907, where she met her husband. Caroline was a published writer who wrote for *The Practical Farmer, Ladies' World*, and *The Atlantic Monthly* magazines. At age 58, she wrote to Secretary of Agriculture Henry A. Wallace, who later credited her with helping America to understand farmers' problems and courage.

[Changes in the Plains]

For twenty-seven years this little spot on the vast **expanses** of the great plains has been the center of all our thought and hope and effort. And **marvelous** are the changes that we have seen and in which we have participated.

The almost unbroken buffalo grass sod has given way to cultivated fields. The small rude huts or dugouts of the early days have been replaced by reasonably comfortable homes. The old trails have become wide graded highways. Railways have been built, reducing our journey to market from thirty miles . . . to two and a half. Little towns have sprung up with attractive homes, trees, flowers, schools, churches, and hospitals. Automobiles and trucks, tractors and combines have revolutionized methods of farm work and manner of living. The wonderful crop of 1926 when our country alone produced 10,000,000 bushels of wheat–more, it was said, than any other equal area in the world–revealed the possibilities of our productive soil under modern methods of farming. It seemed as if at last our dreams were coming true. . . .

[Dust to Eat]

Yet now our daily physical torture, confusion of mind, gradual wearing down of courage, seem to make that long continued hope look like a vanishing dream. For we are in the worst of the dust storm area where "dust to eat" is not merely a figure of speech, but the phrasing of a bitter reality, increasing in seriousness with each passing day. Any attempt to suggest the violent discomfort of these storms is likely to be vain except to those who have already experienced them.

This wind-driven dust, fine as the finest flour, **penetrates** wherever air can go. "Dust to eat," and dust to breathe and dust to drink. Dust in the beds and in the flour bin, on dishes and walls and windows, in hair and eyes and ears and teeth and throats, to say nothing of the heaped up **accumulation** on floors and window sills after one of the bad days.

Pastures have changed to **barren** wastes and dooryards around humble little homes have become scenes of dusty **desolation**. . . .

Source 6.2: Henderson Letter (Modified) (continued)

[Government Help]

In this time of severe stress, next to the **enduring** character of our people credit must be given to the various activities of the federal government. Without some such aid as has been furnished, it seems certain that large sections must have been virtually abandoned. . . .

Yet common sense suggests that the regions which are no longer entirely self-supporting cannot rely **indefinitely** upon government aid. So the problem remains and the one satisfactory solution is beyond all human control. Some of our neighbors with small children, fearing the effects upon their health, have left temporarily "until it rains." Others have left permanently, thinking doubtless that nothing could be worse. Thus far we and most of our friends seem held–for better or for worse–by memory and hope.

Source: Excerpts from Caroline Henderson's letter to U.S. Secretary of Agriculture, Henry A. Wallace, sent July 26, 1935, from the Oklahoma Panhandle. In Alvin O. Turner (Ed.), *Letters from the Dust Bowl* (Norman: University of Oklahoma Press, 2001), 140–142; 146–147.

WORD BANK

expanses–areas
marvelous–wonderful, great
penetrates–enters, breaks in
accumulation–collection
barren–unproductive, empty
desolation–misery, sadness, despair
enduring–stable, continuing
indefinitely–forever

Source 6.3: Svobida Account (Modified)

Note: Lawrence Svobida was a young farmer who came to Oklahoma in 1929 and farmed there until 1939. He suffered seven crop failures in 8 years. When he left, he wrote what he called a "true inside account" of his struggles. He wanted to share the story of the "average farmer" without sugar-coating it, as he claimed others had.

The **gales** chopped off the plants even with the ground, then proceeded to take the roots out. They did not stop there. They blew away the rich topsoil, leaving the subsoil exposed: and then kept sweeping away at the "hard-pan," which is almost as hard as concrete.

This was something new and different from anything I had ever experienced before–a destroying force beyond my wildest imaginings. When some of my own fields started blowing, I was utterly **bewildered**.

I took counsel with some of my neighbors who had had greater experience, but received little in the way of encouragement. According to their information, there was little hope of saving a crop once the land had started blowing; and the only known method of checking the movement of the soil was the practice of strip listing. This meant running deep parallel **furrows** twenty or thirty feet apart, in an east and west direction, across the path of the **prevailing** winds. This tends to check the force of the wind along the ground, and allows the fine siltlike dust to fall into the open furrows.

Everyone in the region grasped at this slim chance to save a crop.

Source: Excerpt from Lawrence Svobida, *Farming the Dust Bowl: A First-Hand Account from Kansas,* first published in 1940 (Lawrence: University Press of Kansas, 1986), 59.

WORD BANK

gales–strong winds, windstorms
bewildered–confused
furrows–trenches, grooves
prevailing–usual, main

Source 6.4: Svobida on Nature (Modified)

Here had been **overgrazing** before the coming of the settlers and the invasion of barbed wire, but the **death knell** of the Plains was sounded and the birth of the Great American Desert was **inaugurated** with the introduction and rapid improvement of power farming. Tractors and combines made of the Great Plains regions a new wheat empire, but in doing so they disturbed nature's balance, and nature is taking revenge.

Source: Excerpt from Lawrence Svobida, *Farming the Dust Bowl: A First-Hand Account from Kansas,* first published in 1940 (Lawrence: University Press of Kansas, 1986), 36.

WORD BANK

overgrazing–too much grass eaten by cattle
death knell–bell or signal that announces death
inaugurated–begun

Source 6.5: Map

Note: President Roosevelt asked for a report on the causes of the Dust Bowl in 1933. This map was part of that report.

Source: *Report of the Great Plains Drought Area Committee*, sent to President Roosevelt on August 27, 1936, signed by leaders of eight Federal agencies, including the Department of Agriculture and Soil Conservation Service. Morris Cooke et al., *Report of the Great Plains Drought Area Committee* (Hyde Park, NY: Franklin D. Roosevelt Library, 1936). Available at http://newdeal.feri.org/hopkins/hop27.htm

Source 6.6: Graph

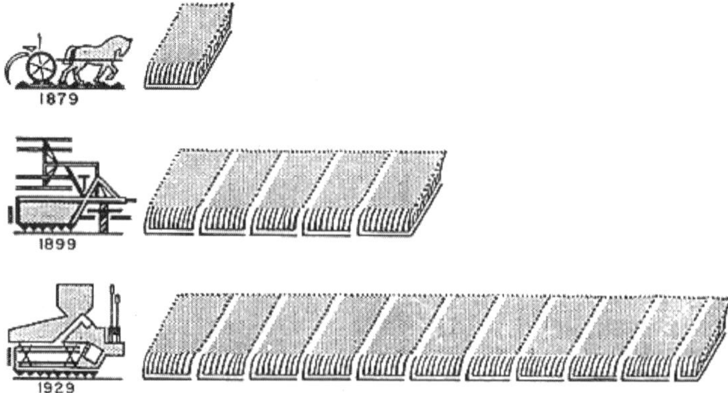

Source: *Report of the Great Plains Drought Area Committee*, sent to President Roosevelt on August 27, 1936, signed by leaders of eight Federal agencies, including the Department of Agriculture and Soil Conservation Service. Morris Cooke et al., *Report of the Great Plains Drought Area Committee* (Hyde Park, NY: Franklin D. Roosevelt Library, 1936). Available at http://newdeal.feri.org/hopkins/hop27.htm

Source 6.7: Committee Report (Modified)

Note: In 1933, President Franklin Roosevelt asked for a report analyzing the causes of the Dust Bowl so that steps could be taken to prevent another. Below is an excerpt from that report.

Dear Mr. President:

. . . The Committee has made a **preliminary** study of drought conditions in the Great Plains area with the hope of outlining a long term program which would **render** future **droughts** less disastrous. . . .

The agricultural economy of the Great Plains will become increasingly unstable and unsafe, in view of the impossibility of permanent increase in the amount of rainfall, unless *over cropping, over grazing and improper farm methods* are prevented. There is no reason to believe that the primary factors of climate temperature, **precipitation** and winds in the Great Plains region have undergone any fundamental change. The future of the region must depend, therefore, on the degree to which farming practices conform to natural conditions. Because the situation has now passed out of the individual farmer's control, the reorganization of farming practices demands the cooperation of many agencies, including the local, State and Federal governments.

. . . *Mistaken public policies* have been largely responsible for the situation now existing. That responsibility must be **liquidated** by new policies. The Federal Government must do its full share in **remedying** the damage caused *by a mistaken homesteading policy, by the* ***stimulation*** *of war time demands which led to over cropping and over grazing, and by encouragement of a system of agriculture* which could not be both permanent and **prosperous**.

Source: Excerpts from *Report of the Great Plains Drought Area Committee*, sent to President Roosevelt on August 27, 1936, signed by leaders of eight Federal agencies, including the Department of Agriculture and Soil Conservation Service (italics added). Morris Cooke et al., *Report of the Great Plains Drought Area Committee* (Hyde Park, NY: Franklin D. Roosevelt Library, 1936). Available at http://newdeal.feri.org/hopkins/hop27.htm

WORD BANK

preliminary–first, introductory
render–make
droughts–periods of dry weather
precipitation–rain
liquidated–settled, cleared up
remedying–making right
stimulation–encouragement
prosperous–financially successful

Source 6.8: Historian Explanation A (Modified)

The Dust Bowl was the darkest moment in the twentieth-century life of the southern plains. The name suggests a place–a region whose borders are as inexact and shifting as a sand dune. But it was also an event of national, even planetary significance. A widely respected authority on world food problems, . . . ranked the creation of the Dust Bowl as *one of the three worst* ***ecological blunders*** *in history.* . . . The Dust Bowl took only 50 years to accomplish. . . . It came about because the culture was operating in precisely the way it was supposed to. Americans blazed their way across a richly **endowed** continent with a **ruthless**, devastating **efficiency** unmatched by any people anywhere. When the white men came to the plains, they talked expansively of "busting" and "breaking" the land. And that is exactly what they did. Some environmental **catastrophes** are nature's work, others are the slowly accumulating effects of ignorance or poverty. The Dust Bowl, in contrast, was the **inevitable** outcome of a culture that deliberately, self-consciously, set itself that task of dominating and exploiting the land for all it was worth. . . .

The Dust Bowl . . . came about because the **expansionary** energy of the United States had finally encountered a **volatile**, marginal land, destroying the delicate ecological balance that had evolved there. We speak of farmers and plows on the plains and the damage they did, but the language is inadequate. What brought them to the region was a social system, a set of values, an economic order. . . . **Capitalism**, it is my contention, had been the decisive factor in this nation's use of nature.

Source: Donald Worster (1979), *Dust Bowl: The Southern Plain in the 1930s*. New York: Oxford University Press, 4–5 (italics added).

WORD BANK

ecological–environmental
blunders–mistakes, errors
endowed–gifted, resourced
ruthless–cruel
efficiency–effectiveness
catastrophes–disasters, tragedies
inevitable–unavoidable, necessary
expansionary–spreading out
volatile–unstable, unpredictable
capitalism–an economic system based, among other things, on private ownership of capital

Source 6.9: Historian Explanation B (Modified)

Dust storms in the southern Great Plains, and indeed, in the Plains as a whole, were not unique to the 1930s. ***Drought**, lack of vegetation, and wind* have caused the dust to move since the formation of the Plains. The elimination of any one causal element, though will significantly reduce or eliminate dust storms. When all three elements are present, however, the dust blows. During the early nineteenth century and before, when buffalo were the primary occupants of the Plains, drought and prairie fires destroyed the native grass and exposed the soil to wind erosion. Later in the nineteenth and early twentieth centuries, however, other factors contributed to dust storms–notably man's ***inhabitation** of the southern Plains and the adoption of a new agricultural technology.* . . .

Many factors contributed to the creation of the Dust Bowl–soils subject to wind erosion, drought which killed the soil-holding vegetation, the **incessant** wind, and technological improvements which facilitated the rapid breaking of the native sod. The nature of southern Plains soils and periodic influence of drought could not be changed, but the technological abuse of the land could have been stopped. This is not to say that mechanized agriculture **irreparably** damaged the land–it did not. New and improved **implements** such as tractors, one-way disk plows, grain drills, and combines reduced plowing, planting, and harvesting costs and increased agricultural productivity. However, the new technology also had negative effects. Increased productivity caused prices to fall, and farmers **compensated** by breaking more sod for wheat. At the same time, farmers gave little thought to using their new technology in ways that would conserve the soil.

Source: R. Douglas Hurt (1981), *The Dust Bowl: An Agricultural and Social History* (Chicago: Nelson-Hall), 15, 30 (italics added).

WORD BANK

drought–period of dry weather
inhabitation–moving in, occupying
incessant–nonstop, constant
irreparably–permanently
implements–equipment, tools
compensated–adjusted, made do

Tool 6.1: Opening Up the Textbook

What story is told about the Dust Bowl?

Account	What story does this account tell?	What specifics are included?
Your Textbook		
Source #___		
Source #___		
Source #___		

1. How is the textbook's story similar to and different from one of the other sources you read?

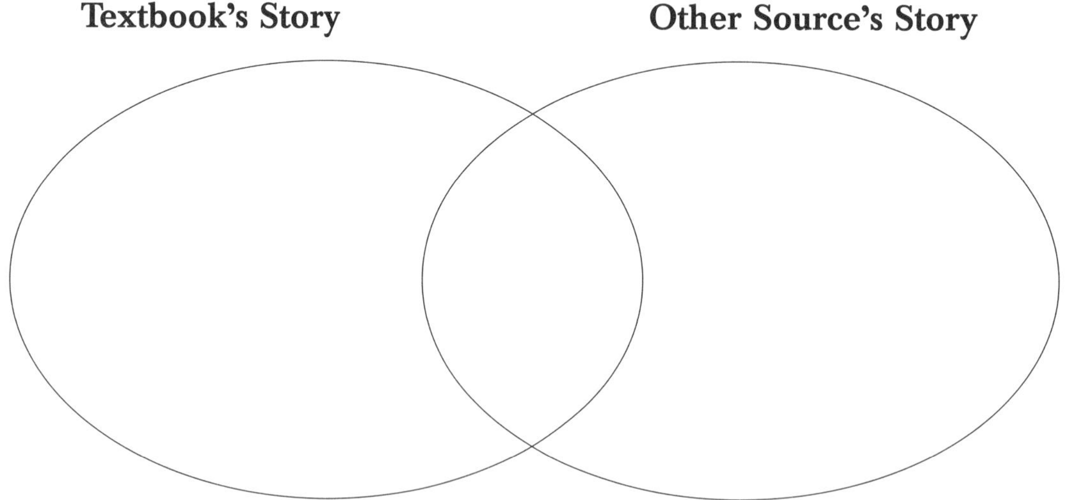

2. In a paragraph, evaluate the following statement using evidence from what you have read today: "There are multiple stories and perspectives in history."

Tool 6.2: What Caused the Dust Bowl?

Hypothesis:

Source	Author/ Date	What causes does this document suggest?	How do you know? Write a quotation that suggests this cause.
6.2			
6.3			
6.4			
Hypothesis:			
6.5			
6.6			
6.7			
Hypothesis:			
6.8			
6.9			

Tool 6.3: Springboard to Research

1. List different stories about the Dust Bowl that you have read.

2. a. Pick one story you would like to know more about and list it here.

   b. Write a short paragraph summarizing this story.

   c. Write 2–3 questions that you have about this story. (Think about what else you want to know and what you don't understand.)

TOOL 6.3: SPRINGBOARD TO RESEARCH (continued)

3. Find three sources (documents, photos, video) that help you learn more about the story. Fill out the following chart for each.

IDENTIFY YOUR SOURCE			
What is the source's title?			
Where and when was it created?			
Is it a secondary or primary source?			
URL where you found it?			
ANALYZING & CORROBORATING SOURCES			
Does this source support, contest, or extend what you know?			
Explain what information this source supports, contests, or extends.			
Share a quotation that led to this conclusion.			
Record any questions you have.			

4. Retell the story in 1–3 paragraphs.
   a. Include information, quotes, and data that you found in your investigations.
   b. Cite your sources for that information/data/quotes. Include the author and date of the source in parentheses at the end of the sentence so that it looks like this: (author, date).

Suggested Resources

http://memory.loc.gov/fsowhome.html
America from the Great Depression to World War II: Photographs from the FSA-OWI, 1935–1945 is an extensive collection of photos from the Farm Security Administration–Office of War Information. The collection is part of the Library of Congress's American Memory site and can be searched by subject, creator, and location.

http://memory.loc.gov/ammem/award97/ndfahtml/hult_sod.html
Use this site to help students understand how life in a sod house differs from their own. Part of the Fred Hulstrand: History in Pictures collection that documents the settling of the northern Plains, this resource is a fine introduction to sod houses and includes photographs and descriptions.

http://www.kansashistory.us/dustbowl.html
Dust Bowl History includes a well-chosen collection of primary and secondary sources, including photographs, data charts, and songs. These can be used for background knowledge or for further investigation.

http://www.pbs.org/wgbh/americanexperience/features/introduction/dustbowl-introduction/
Created by the PBS series *American Experience*, this site includes a short video about the Dust Bowl and a helpful timeline, lesson plan, and essays and interviews (including one with Donald Worster).

http://www.williamcronon.net/researching/index.htm
A web-based primer on historical research compiled and produced by historian William Cronon and his students. Includes ways to read sources particularly important for doing environmental history, including landscapes. Also see Cronon's home page for more resources regarding environmental history.

http://www.livinghistoryfarm.org/farminginthe20s/machines_01.htm
Helpful for the farming-ignorant, this site includes brief explanations of different farm machines and how they changed over time in 1920s Nebraska. Explanations are easy to follow and accompanied by photographs and primary accounts.

http://worldhistoryforusall.sdsu.edu/units/eight/landscape/08_landscape7.pdf
This teaching unit explores issues of environmental change in the first half of the 20th century. Produced by the World History for Us All website, a project of San Diego State University and the National Center for History in the Schools, it provides materials and background knowledge for bringing an international perspective to these changes, and includes sources that address population growth, migration, and the growing use of tractors and fossil fuel.

http://www.howstuffworks.com/framed.htm?parent=dust-bowl-cause.htm&url=http://www.ciesin.org/docs/002-193/002-193.html
This article, written in 1986, offers a contemporary and international lens on desertification.[30] It includes definitions, a historical overview, and data on the degradation and disappearance of ground cover for regions around the world.

http://newdeal.feri.org/
The New Deal Network, sponsored by the Franklin and Eleanor Roosevelt Institute, offers a good collection of historical sources and other teaching resources to help flesh out lessons on the Great Depression and New Deal. Here you can find a more complete version of the 1936 *Report of the Great Plains Drought Area Committee.*

CHAPTER 7

Rosa Parks and the Montgomery Bus Boycott

Rosa Parks's booking photo, Feb. 26, 1956, Available at http://search.creativecommons.org/?q=rosa%20parks

It's a story that's been retold countless times: An ordinary working woman, a seamstress, fatigued after a long day on her feet, waits for the bus on a sweltering summer afternoon. When she boards, she plops down in the front seat in the forbidden "White Section." The bus driver menacingly barks: "Move y'all, I want those seats."[1] Rosa Parks, a 42-year-old African American woman, does not move.

In this singular act of courage, Rosa Parks stared down the institution of segregation, and in so doing, as writer Janet Stevenson described the precise moment, "the whole shaky edifice of Jim Crow began to totter."[2] Like Paul Revere setting out from Boston on his midnight ride, or Patrick Henry shaking his fist at the House of Burgesses, Rosa Parks's iconic act is indelibly etched in American memory. But there's a crucial difference between Parks and these other figures: She was not part of the nation's landed gentry, neither a New England craftsman nor a Virginia planter. She was an ordinary Black woman, the daughter of a carpenter and a schoolteacher. An ordinary woman who committed an extraordinary act. A simple yet daring act.

Today's students have heard this story dozens of times, and many can visualize Mrs. Parks sitting with dignity in the front seat of a Montgomery bus. In 2008 2,000 students from all 50 states were asked to name "the most famous woman in American history, not including wives of presidents." Rosa Parks's name was at the top of that list.[3] In the last 30 years, more biographies have been written about her than practically any woman in the school curriculum.[4]

In an age when young people are accused of not knowing basic historical facts, the story of Rosa Parks is a foundation teachers can depend on. Most students know the story by heart. Even if they can't remember the name of the protagonist, they know her unmistakably as "the lady on the bus."

There's only one problem: Much of what they know about Rosa Parks has become so distorted by myth and legend that it's tough getting to the real truth.

The confusion starts right at the beginning, with the setting of that fateful day. Ask students to close their eyes and imagine Mrs. Parks waiting for the bus. Many will describe a beating Alabama sun that frayed everyone's nerves, especially Mrs. Parks's, whose legs ached from 8 hours on her feet. The problem is that the day in question was actually the first of December, and Montgomery was experiencing an unseasonable cold spell, with intermittent rain and temperatures dipping into the mid-40s.[5] As for those aching feet, Rosa Parks declared over and over that she was no more fatigued on this day than any other.[6] Despite such denials, textbooks harp on the notion that Mrs. Parks's "neck and back hurt" or that "she didn't feel well."[7] If she experienced fatigue, notes civil rights historian Alden D. Morris, it was a moral and spiritual fatigue from a system that had denied her basic rights and dignity.[8] As Mrs. Parks put it, "My resistance to being mistreated on the buses and anywhere else was just a regular thing with me and not just that day."[9]

The narrative becomes more tangled when you ask students where Mrs. Parks sat on the bus. Montgomery buses had 36 seats, not counting the first, reserved for the driver (see Tool 7.1). The 10 seats behind the driver were considered the front of the bus, the next 16 the middle, and the last 10 the back. So where exactly did Rosa Parks sit?

If your students are like the hundreds we've queried, you will get all three answers: front, middle, and back. Establishing such a simple fact should be a cinch, but when students consult "authorities," trusted standbys like encyclopedias and textbooks, they are led deeper into a mystifying thicket.

Let's start with the following passage from the *World Book Encyclopedia*:

> Parks, a seamstress, was arrested for violating a city law requiring blacks to sit in the rear of public buses. She had taken a seat in the front of the bus and disobeyed the driver's order to move so a white person could sit down.[10]

World Book Encyclopedia seats Parks in the front of the bus. *The Americans,* a major U.S. history textbook, moves her to a different place: "On December 1, 1955, Rosa Parks . . . took a seat in the front row of the 'colored' section of a Montgomery bus," placing her somewhere in the middle of the bus.[11] A different textbook states that on boarding, Mrs. Parks "found an empty seat in the section reserved for whites," implying she sat in one of the "sacred ten" seats at the front, which were reserved for White riders even when no White person was on board.[12] And an earlier edition of *The Americans* links Parks' alleged fatigue with her choice of seats: "Tired after a long day's work, she sat down in the front section, which was reserved for whites."[13]

What's the truth? Since secondary sources cannot agree, perhaps consulting a primary source–the original police report (Source 7.1)–will put the issue to rest.

No such luck. The "white section" described in the police report is ambiguous, since the city code gave drivers the authority to adjust the number of white seats to correspond to the changing racial composition of the bus. Other than the 10 seats immediately behind the driver, always reserved for Whites no matter what, the designation of the middle seats could shift depending on the number of Black and White riders on the bus at any particular moment. Thus, the report does not solve the question of where exactly Mrs. Parks sat.[14] Furthermore, when examining the police report, some astute students will question its reliability: Can we take the word of two White police officers in Montgomery, Alabama, in describing the crime of violating Jim Crow laws in 1955?

In fact, the police account was initiated by James F. Blake, the driver of the Cleveland Avenue bus who reported the infraction. Would Blake have any motivation to exaggerate the offense? Rosa Parks claimed she "had history" with Mr. Blake. Years before, in 1943, he had kicked her off his bus when she refused to exit and reboard through the back entrance after having paid her fare, a practice sanctioned by the Montgomery City Code but applied irregularly by drivers.[15] Mrs. Parks avoided riding his bus for 12 years following the incident. Did Blake remember her on that December day in 1955, just as she seemed to remember him? Did the memory of her stubbornness influence Blake's perception of the day's events?

Blake's account was recorded by two policemen, F. B. Day and D. W. Mixon. Did these officers want to make sure the official record justified Parks's arrest? Curiously, the handwritten portion of their report, presumably written at the time of the arrest, simply states that Parks was "refusing to obey orders of bus driver" (Source 7.2). The typed report, however, clarifies that she was "sitting in the white section of the bus," while the officers add that they "also saw her."

Facts elude. As students compare the versions in the textbook and encyclopedia entry with the separate statements in the police report, they'll see how the most straightforward historical question turns into a jumbled puzzle, one not always solved by going back to primary sources.

What about Parks's decision to remain seated despite the driver's orders? Was that a spontaneous act, or had it been carefully orchestrated by civil rights leaders? After all, Mrs. Parks was secretary for Montgomery's National Association for the Advancement of Colored People (NAACP) and had spent a summer at Myles Horton's Highlander Folk School learning the philosophy and tactics of civil disobedience.[16] Seen in that light, was her refusal a spur-of-the-moment decision or a calculated act of defiance?

Some students will claim that it would settle everything if they could just ask Mrs. Parks. Sources of information always contain errors, but the person at the center of the event–a national heroine, the first woman to lie in honor in the Capitol Rotunda–would surely be reliable, and would put unresolved questions to rest.

Such an assumption disappoints as well.

During her life, Rosa Parks told her story myriad times–in newspaper and radio interviews, on TV, and in autobiographies written for schoolchildren. An examination of these accounts reveals even more contradictions and inconsistencies, not surprising to anyone familiar with the frailty of human memory or even their own difficulty recalling details about events in the distant past.[17] In the autobiography written with Jim Haskins in 1992, Mrs. Parks states that upon boarding the bus, she "saw a vacant seat in the middle section of the bus and took it."[18] Five years later, in a book about her life written for elementary schoolchildren, she reports that on the day of her arrest she "was sitting in one of the seats in the back section."[19] Thus, even an appeal to Rosa Parks herself will not supply definitive answers.

For students just getting started on historical thinking, the question of "where did Rosa Parks sit?" has a special appeal. The question is concrete. Students do not have to engage with arcane language and abstract issues to understand the issue. And despite its many versions and the clouds of misinformation perpetuated by textbooks, the answer is not in dispute. Parks's arrest on December 1, 1955, was appealed and made its way to the

Alabama Court of Appeals on March 28, 1956. A statement of agreed-upon facts, signed by both prosecution and defense, included a diagram of the bus with all 36 seats numbered. The diagram places Mrs. Parks in seat number 12, immediately behind the "sacred ten" seats permanently reserved for White riders (Source 7.3).

Case closed.

Yet, as so often happens in history, solving one question opens up another: Did Rosa Parks actually break the law when she refused to give up seat 12? As she told Sidney Rogers in a 1956 radio interview, Parks did not think so.[20]

According to the Montgomery City Code, Chapter 6, Section 10–11, a driver could order a Black passenger to relinquish a seat only if vacant seats were available in the rear section (see Tool 7.2).[21] The Code states:

> It shall be unlawful for any passenger to refuse to take a seat among those assigned to the race to which he belongs, at the request of any such employee in charge, if there is such a seat vacant.[22]

The crucial issue for Black riders was whether there were vacant seats on the bus, excluding the "sacred" first 10. In other words, the driver could legally order Blacks to move out of the middle section to an available seat at the back. But if there were no vacant seats, the Black riders were not obliged to relinquish their seats.

Unlike the city code, the Jim Crow laws of Alabama's State Code contained no such caveat (see Tool 7.2). It simply stated that:

> The conductor or agent of the motor transportation company in charge of any vehicle is authorized and required to assign each passenger to the division of the vehicle designated for the race to which the passenger belongs.[23]

Unlike the city code, the state law gave the bus driver the authority to remove Black riders from their seats to make room for Whites, whether that meant the passenger would have to stand for the remainder of the trip or not. In other words, there was a discrepancy between state and local laws.

The issue is further complicated by the question of whether additional seats were available to Mrs. Parks that afternoon. If there were none, then driver Blake was, at the very least, in violation of Montgomery's City Code. The statement of stipulated facts in the brief before the Alabama Court of Appeals notes that "the evidence is in dispute as to whether or not there were vacant seats in the negro section."[24] Mrs. Parks stated she did not believe she was violating the law when she refused to give up her seat.[25] And if there were no vacant seats in the back section, she would have been correct–at least according to city law.

What about the question of whether this was a spontaneous act, or one carefully planned? In the 1956 interview Mrs. Parks stated that her refusal to move was unplanned and unscripted. In fact, her belief that she was not breaking the law seems to corroborate this.

> *Sidney Rogers*: What made you decide in the first part of the month of December 1955 that you had had enough?
> *Rosa Parks*: The time had just come when I had been pushed as far as I could stand to be pushed, I suppose.
> *Sidney Rogers*: Well, Mrs. Parks, had you planned this?
> *Rosa Parks*: No I hadn't.
> *Sidney Rogers*: It just happened.
> *Rosa Parks*: Yes it did.[26]

Had she planned to be arrested, it's likely that Rosa Parks would have chosen an act that more clearly violated the segregation laws she opposed. In later interviews, including a 1992 interview on National Public Radio, she reiterated that she had not planned on being arrested and that she had no premonition of the events that would follow.[27]

The Montgomery Bus Boycott in Context

Questions do not end there. Rosa Parks was arrested on a Thursday evening. How was it that in the short period between Thursday and Monday, 42,000 Black citizens of Montgomery were able to organize a boycott of public transportation, each finding alternative routes to and from work? How did a boycott that seemed to catch fire at a moment's notice command such widespread support and commitment? Can one accurately claim that Rosa Parks's actions "sparked" or "initiated" or "set into motion" the boycott that lasted for over a year?

When it began, no one knew for sure whether the bus boycott would succeed. African Americans made up the majority of riders on the Montgomery City Lines. Yet, 3 days after Parks's arrest, not a single Black person boarded a bus. Thousands somehow made it to their jobs and found ways to pick up their children from school, purchase groceries they needed for dinner, and make their way home. The key to understanding the power and effectiveness of a social movement of this magnitude, one that depends on but rises above the efforts of any one individual, lies in unlocking the word "somehow."

Montgomery had a long history of Black activism and was the source of important experience in community-wide mobilization. In 1900, four years after *Plessy v. Ferguson* gave legal sanction to Jim Crow's "separate but equal" rule, the City of Montgomery mandated separate seating on the new electric trolley lines, the first system of its kind in the South.[28] Trolley owners disliked the idea, believing that it would be impracticable and hurt profits.

It was too late. Montgomery was caught in a wave that swept through 27 Southern cities, among them Norfolk, Nashville, New Orleans, Mobile, Augusta, Atlanta, and Houston, requiring separate seating on public transportation. There were attempts by Blacks to boycott public transport, most of them sporadic and uneven. Only four could be called successful–Pensacola, Jacksonville, Mobile, and Montgomery. In fact, Montgomery's 1900 streetcar boycott was so successful that 10 days into it, the *Atlanta Constitution* reported that "there has been a decided falling off in the travel of the negroes and the boycott is on."[29] Three months later, the paper reported that trolley company profits had fallen 25%, and that Black riders had complied with the boycott with "surprising persistency."[30] The trolley boycott lasted for 2 years. While it did not defeat Montgomery's Jim Crow laws–separate accommodations would become part of Southern life well into midcentury–it led to a compromise that was enacted into Montgomery's City Code: A driver could order a Black rider to move only if there were vacant seats at the back. Hence, the source of the discrepancy between the Montgomery City Code and Alabama State Code.

By 1955 Montgomery was the site of political and social activism in the Black community. In this one city alone there were 68 organizations dedicated to advancing the rights of African American citizens.[31] One of these, the Women's Political Council (WPC), founded by Professor Mary Fair Burks of Alabama State University, was comprised of educated Black women: Alabama State faculty members, nurses, public schoolteachers, social workers, and other professionals. In 1955 the WPC responded to over 30 complaints about indignities faced by Black riders on city buses, including the case of 15-year-old Claudette Colvin. On March 2, nearly 8 months before Rosa Parks came to public attention, Claudette, an "A" student at Booker T. Washington High School, refused to give up her seat to a White rider and was forcibly removed from the bus. In doing so, Claudette Colvin followed in the wake of Black women–Geneva Johnson, Viola White, Katie Wingfield, Espie Worthy–similarly ill-treated, sometimes beaten, for standing up to the power of Montgomery City Lines.

Just as Rosa Parks was not the first to deny her seat to a White rider, neither was the idea for a boycott spontaneously hatched on December 1, 1955. Discussions of a boycott had been floating in the air for years. In May 1954, Jo Ann Gibson Robinson, WPC president and professor of English at Alabama State University, sent a letter to Montgomery's mayor threatening a boycott if conditions did not improve. "Even now," Robinson wrote, "plans are being made to ride less, or not at all, on our buses" (Source 7.5). Robinson wrote her letter more than 18 months before Rosa Parks was arrested.

News of Mrs. Parks's arrest on December 1 spread quickly throughout Montgomery's Black community. Hearing about it that evening, Jo Ann Robinson called Fred D. Gray, one of two Black lawyers in Montgomery. When she suggested that the time was ripe to initiate a boycott, Gray asked, "Are you ready?" Robinson's actions communicated just how ready she was. By the middle of that night and into the early hours of the next morning, she typed up a leaflet announcing the action. With the help of Alabama State's mimeograph machine, she used 35 reams of paper to run off 17,500 duplicates, which, when cut into thirds, produced 52,500 leaflets: enough and then some for every member of Montgomery's Black community. Between four and seven o'clock the next morning, Robinson and her colleagues mapped distribution routes. By midafternoon, Montgomery was abuzz with news of the planned boycott. Leaflets were distributed to Montgomery's Black churches so that the action could be announced during Sunday morning services. Robinson and other members of the WPC spent the weekend charting assembly points for Monday pickups, organizing phone banks, subsidizing rates with Black taxi drivers, and organizing 200 cars and trucks for use as alternative transport.

Despite intense opposition, the boycott continued for over a year. Members of the WPC and the Montgomery Improvement Association (MIA), an organization of Black leaders formed to coordinate the effort, worked tirelessly to keep the boycott afloat. On June 4, 1956, the U.S. District Court ruled on *Browder v. Gayle*, another case challenging the constitutionality of Jim Crow. On November 13, the Supreme Court upheld *Browder v. Gayle*, effectively declaring that local and state bus segregation laws were unconstitutional.[32] With that ruling on December 20, 1956, the 381-day bus boycott came to a halt.

The Montgomery Bus Boycott is a story of community organization and mass protest in the face of often violent opposition. From the very beginning, the efforts of Jo Ann Robinson and other members of the WPC helped to create widespread support for the boycott. On the evening of Monday, December 5, 1955, leaders held a mass meeting to make further plans for protest. One local newspaper estimated that over 7,000 Black citizens of Montgomery participated in the meeting.[33]

While Rosa Parks was certainly present, the meeting was not simply about her arrest. Rather, Rosa Parks became a symbol of the discontent and repression that had long been simmering beneath the surface. Regarding her role in the boycott and the importance of her presence at the meeting, Reverend Ralph Abernathy, one of the leaders of the MIA, noted that Rosa Parks was presented to the crowd because "we wanted her to become symbolic of our protest movement"[34] (Source 7.6). Not only was she a symbol of the protest, she was a *strategically* selected symbol. Dr. Martin Luther King, Jr., the charismatic 28-year-old pastor of Dexter Street Church, described Mrs. Parks as "one of the finest citizens of Montgomery—not one of the finest Negro citizens, but one of the finest citizens of Montgomery."[35]

Movements need symbols, and Rosa Parks was ideally suited to become a symbol of protest against segregation on Montgomery buses. The leaders of the protest acknowledged this. But the Montgomery Bus Boycott is a more complex story than that of a lone woman who refused to be unseated. It is the story of a community that mobilized with the help of dozens of organizations; each had its own agenda and philosophy, but put aside their differences and acted as a unified force. As history shows us, whether it's Montgomery in 1955, the Gdansk shipyards in 1980, or Berlin in 1989, nothing is more powerful than the variegated human collective emerging as a single force.

At the same time, a "mass movement" is an abstraction, and abstractions are notoriously difficult to narrate. The human desire for concreteness makes us pull individuals from the crowd, and sometimes allows these figures to overshadow less vivid, but equally important stories. The human mind can easily visualize a dignified woman steadfastly refusing to give up her seat despite threats by the agents of an unjust system. What is less easy to visualize, and certainly less compelling to narrate, is groups of citizens coming together week after week in church basements, plotting strategy over stale coffee, filing minutes, and scheduling further meetings.

We forget that the crowning of heroes is sometimes arbitrary. No doubt Rosa Parks was a woman of incredible courage and moral strength. But the same could be said for Jo Ann Robinson, whose keen political skill and powers of community organization were a linchpin of the boycott's success. Your students will know the story of Mrs. Parks, but it is unlikely that any one of them ever heard of Jo Ann Robinson. Yet Jo Ann Robinson was no less a hero than Rosa Parks. The fact that we sanctify Parks and ignore Robinson teaches us about the fickle nature of historical memory, and raises questions about what we consider significant from the past.

Challenges for Students

What happens when we try to expand the view that the "whole shaky edifice of Jim Crow began to totter" with Rosa Parks's arrest, or that this one act "quietly set off a social revolution"?[36] In our work with high school classes, we have found that the story of Rosa Parks is so deeply ingrained that even after being confronted with evidence that expands it, many students hold tight to the traditional story. Consider the following excerpt by Ryan, an 11th-grader responding to the prompt: *Why did the boycott of Montgomery's buses succeed?* Before writing his essay, this student and his classmates examined a variety of primary sources, including Jo Ann Robinson's letter and Ralph Abernathy's statement. Rather than changing his understanding in light of new information, this student squeezes the new information to fit his preexisting ideas (see Figure 7.1).

Ryan reproduces the familiar romanticized account of Rosa Parks, describing her as "quaint," an adjective that appears nowhere in the documents he reviewed. He casts the relationship between Parks's arrest and the bus boycott as one of cause and effect. When he draws on information from the documents, rather than disrupting the story he knows, it is (incorrectly) added to it. Ryan's quotation from Jo Ann Robinson's letter violates the basic rule of chronology; he uses it to support the claim that Black citizens "bonded" with one another *after* Parks's arrest, even though the letter was actually written 18 months *before* the incident took place.

Shawna, a student in the same class, responded differently. For her, the encounter with documentary evidence changed the entire picture of what happened in Montgomery (see Figure 7.2).

Shawna places Rosa Parks's arrest in the context of an ongoing effort by Montgomery's Black community to put an end to the demeaning practices of Jim Crow. While Parks's arrest is given its due (Shawna describes it as "the crowning incident"), it is placed in a chain of events, part of a longer struggle that began before Parks's arrest and continued well after.

How is it that these two students, both good readers and writers, members of the same class and exposed to the same materials, could produce such divergent accounts? Ryan addressed the essay question head-on, and even integrated source material into his final essay. But instead of using these sources to refashion his understanding, Ryan fell into a trap that snares many: Rather than reading the documents carefully, Ryan *raided* them in search of quotations to prop up an already formed hypothesis. Shawna, on the other hand, allowed an encounter with source material to rehabilitate a preconceived notion of the bus boycott and Parks's role in it. By attending to the date of the Jo Ann Robinson document and placing events in temporal sequence, Shawna realized that Parks's actions had important predecessors, and that what began on Monday, December 1, 1955, had been percolating for months, if not years.

These two essays are in no way unusual. Anyone with classroom experience has seen the light bulb of new understanding go off for some students, while others hold tenaciously to prior beliefs, even when faced with evidence to the contrary. At the same time, these essays remind us of an important principle: *While sources can*

Figure 7.1. Ryan's Essay

A quaint African-American woman seated herself on a Montgomery public bus one winter day in 1955. When she refused to abdicate her seat to a white citizen, Rosa Parks unknowingly initiated one of history's largest and longest public boycotts. Ms. Parks was incarcerated for not subjecting her seat. This created community-wide rage through the African-Americans. The solution the oppressed people developed was public boycott of all Montgomery city buses until the abiding laws were changed to suit people of either race.

This strike took much strategy, and coordination throughout the African-American populace. Coordinating the boycott presented a task within itself. Different methods were mapped out for people to use to attend work, school or other outings. The whole of the population bonded with their neighbors to find a way to rise above the issue at hand. "More and more of our people are arranging with neighbors and friends to ride to keep from being insulted and humiliated by bus drivers." (Letter from Robinson to Mayor).[37]

A quaint African-American woman seated herself on a Montgomery public bus one winter day in 1988. When she refused to abdicate her seat to a white citizen, Rosa Parks unknowingly initiated one of history's largest and longes boycotts. Ms. Parks was incarcerated for not sujecting her seat. This created community-wide rage through the African-Americans. The solution the oppressed people developed was public boycott of all Montgomery city buses until the abiding laws were changed to suit people of either race.

This strike took much strategy, and cordination throughout the African-American populace. Coordinating the boycott presented a task within itself. Different methods were mapped out for people to use to attend work, school, or other outings. The whole of the population bonded with their neighbors to find a way to rise above the issue at hand. "More and more of our people are arranging with neighbors and friends to ride to keep from being insulted and humiliated by bus drivers." (Letter from Robinson to Mayor)

Figure 7.2. Shawna's Essay

It is very common to hear that the incident, where Rosa Parks refused to give up her seat to a white man, is what started the Montgomery Bus Boycott. However, this is not the case. Though Rosa Parks' arrest was the crowning incident in the history of civil rights and may have been what got the boycott started, the plans for a bus boycott had been talked about months earlier. This event was a highly organized and determined effort and planned through very carefully.

A year before the boycott, discussions of changing the bus laws were proposed to the Montgomery City Council. These propositions were addressed, but only some of the laws were slightly changed. "Busses have begun stopping on more corners where negroes live than previously. However, the same practices in seating and boarding continue." (letter from Jo Ann Robinson, President of the Women's Political Council).

It is very common to hear that the incident, where Rosa Parks refused to give up her seat to a white man, is what started the Montgomery Bus Boycott. However, this is not the case. Though Rosa Parks' arrest was the crowning incident in the history of civil rights and may have been what got the boycott started, the plans for a bus boycott had been talked about months earlier. this event was a highltiy organized and determined effort and planned through very carefully.

A year before the boycott, discussions of changing the bus laws were proposed to the Montgomery City Council. these propositions were addressed, but only some of the laws were slightly changed. "Busses have begun stopping on more corners where negroes live than previously. However, the same practices in seating and boarding continue." (letter from Jo Ann Robinson, President of the Women's Political Council).

enliven instruction by restoring the voices of original actors, they provide no magic formula for success. An encounter with primary evidence that directly challenges students' beliefs may still leave some unaffected. Just as we sometimes refashion our beliefs in the face of new data, we also alter new data by twisting it to fit preconceived patterns. Sometimes we simply ignore new evidence altogether. In either case, the result is the same: We grasp tightly to our prior beliefs.

The story of the Montgomery Bus Boycott has become synonymous in collective memory with Rosa Parks's arrest. This notion is reinforced by postage stamps, posters on buses, children's biographies, and elementary school assemblies commemorating Black History Month. One of the biggest challenges to new learning is the belief that we have little to learn. History leads to open-mindedness only when we pay attention to detail, when we pause long enough to place information in temporal sequence, when we allow new data to inform and challenge our understanding. The story of the Montgomery Bus Boycott provides a test case for helping students realize that what they "know" about this event is, in many respects, less than what they originally thought.

Why Teach About Rosa Parks and the Montgomery Bus Boycott?

A Familiar Story with Unfamiliar Twists. Unlike new topics in the curriculum, the story of Rosa Parks is one that students have heard since elementary school. Some will bring vivid narratives to class, certain that everything they know is true, while others will scratch their heads, wondering why they are studying the story for the umpteenth time. It is this very familiarity that provides entry into the question of how we determine truth about a myth-strewn past. Of the many questions we can ask about the Montgomery Bus Boycott, "Where did Rosa Parks sit?" is the most concrete. It is a straightforward factual question without any of the nuances of meaning, multiple causality, and inference that can trip students up.

Determining the basic facts of an event is central not only to historical understanding but our entire legal system: Every day thousands of fates rest on determining the basic facts of a case. Factual detective work is complicated, especially when trusted sources such as encyclopedias and textbooks contradict one another. The police report, which should have shed light on where Rosa Parks sat, offered further challenges; it turns out there was not one report, but two, and the question remains whether Officers Day and Mixon skewed their records in a particular direction. Nor does Mrs. Parks resolve the problem, as she remembered different things at different times in her life.

This deceptively simple question–"Where did Rosa Parks sit?"–offers students an opportunity to think hard about different sources and different kinds of evidence: autobiographical accounts; textbook narratives; primary documents; and ultimately, the source that puts the question to rest, a court document signed by both parties in a joint statement of facts.

Whom Does History Remember and Forget? The question of who history chooses to remember and forget cannot be answered by a single document. Instead, it forces us to examine how we pluck figures from the past's cast of characters, elevating some as heroes while sentencing others to obscurity. Is refusing to give up a seat inherently more significant than engaging in political organizing and choosing the right moment to spring into action by composing a leaflet and distributing it to 42,000 members of a community? Why is one action considered heroic and worthy of commemoration on postage stamps and the other not? Rosa Parks and Jo Ann Gibson Robinson were contemporaries, and both worked for social change. By considering them in tandem, students have the chance to examine one of the core issues of historical understanding: What makes a person, an act, or an event worthy of being remembered?

Teaching About Social Movements. It is much easier for students to pin the success of the Montgomery Bus Boycott on the heroic actions of a few individuals than to understand how entire communities could put aside differences and come together in unison. The bus boycott succeeded because ordinary citizens committed innumerable ordinary acts. They left the house 45 minutes earlier. They organized phone trees to make sure that everyone knew where to catch one of the ad hoc taxis. They pooled their financial resources to provide transportation in case of emergencies. They suffered the inconvenience of waiting for rides whenever the alternative transport system broke down. These small acts were committed day after day, month after month, for 381 days, until the back of the Montgomery City Lines was nearly broken. Understanding mass collective action unlocks the door to understanding Jim Crow's demise. By understanding the dynamics of social action, students will be able to address other mass movements in American history–abolition, women's suffrage, unionization, and the antiwar protests of the 1960s.

How Might You Use These Materials?

Scenario 1 (1 Hour Lesson). Where did Rosa Parks sit? This scenario revolves around a concrete question and puts students in the role of historical detective.

Begin by asking students to retell the story of Rosa Parks, and then ask them to mark where among the 36 seats on the blank bus diagram (Tool 7.1, Part One) Mrs. Parks sat. You will get a variety of answers. Ask students how they determined which of these answers was true. Then, arrange students in groups and have them consider Source 7.1 and Source 7.2 along with the graphic organizer in Tool 7.1, Part Two. Have them fill out the graphic organizer as they analyze documents and then return to the blank bus diagram. **Ask them to decide as a group where to place Mrs. Parks on the bus diagram. Allow each group to make an oral argument justifying their choice.**

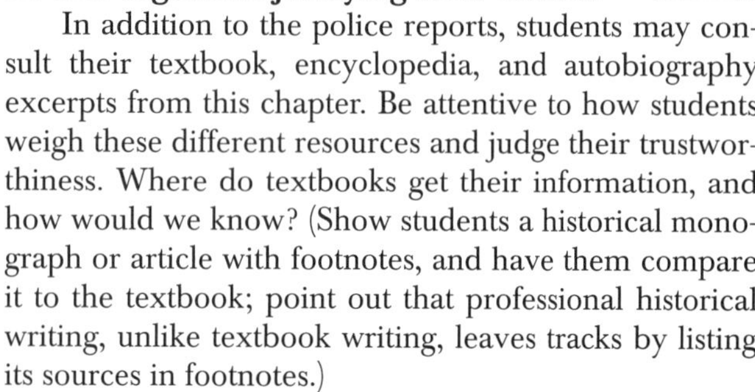

In addition to the police reports, students may consult their textbook, encyclopedia, and autobiography excerpts from this chapter. Be attentive to how students weigh these different resources and judge their trustworthiness. Where do textbooks get their information, and how would we know? (Show students a historical monograph or article with footnotes, and have them compare it to the textbook; point out that professional historical writing, unlike textbook writing, leaves tracks by listing its sources in footnotes.)

Consider why such differences might exist. Given these sources, is there a way to know for sure where Mrs. Parks sat? Many students will say no, an answer that raises the question of how we can know *anything* for sure. If we can't even establish basic facts about where a person has sat (an act for which she was arrested, which made its way to the Alabama Court of Appeals), how can we establish the facts of *any* issue?

At this point you should let students know that you have withheld one crucial document: the diagram from the court case (Source 7.3) signed by the prosecution and the defense. While many questions in history are unanswerable, in this case the basic facts are not in dispute. This raises the obvious question of why so many secondary sources get it wrong.

Targeted list of skills in this scenario

- Evidence-based thinking and argumentation
- Determining reliability of sources
- Corroborating/cross-checking sources

Scenario 2 (1 Hour Lesson). Did Rosa Parks break the law when she refused to give up her seat? This lesson can accompany the previous one or stand on its own. It pivots on teaching students to read closely, and carefully examines two texts: the Montgomery City Code and the Alabama State Code.

The issues here are complex, and many students will be challenged by the technicalities of the legal code. Moreover, they will be unfamiliar with the peculiarities of Jim Crow–the notion of the 10 "sacred seats" behind the driver that could never be occupied by Blacks even when aisles were packed and not a single White was in sight. Once you've established the contours of riding the bus during the Jim Crow era, slow down the reading process and help students wend their way through these two difficult texts (Tool 7.2).

Targeted list of skills in this scenario

- Analyzing legal codes
- Close reading

Scenario 3 (1.5–3 Hour Lesson). What led to the success of the Montgomery Bus Boycott? This scenario gets at the larger question of the Montgomery Bus Boycott as a whole and challenges students to go beyond how a single woman's action could topple the whole edifice of Jim Crow.

You can begin with students' background knowledge about the story. Expose them to educator Herbert Kohl's version of the stereotypical way the story is told in children's books and ask if anyone would emend it (Source 7.4). In groups, have students create a timeline that includes the boycott, Jo Ann Robinson's letter to Mayor Gayle, and Ralph Abernathy's statement (Tool 7.3, Sources 7.5 and 7.6). On a timeline, have them plot events related to the boycott. **Then ask them to identify what led to the success of the Montgomery Bus Boycott; have them select quotations that highlight each author's positions. Have students do the same with the two high school students' essays; ask your students which essay best reflects the evidence they have just reviewed. In either case, students could share their ideas in discussion or in an essay or paragraph.**

Alternately, ask students to write an essay in response to the question "How should we remember Rosa Parks and Jo Ann Robinson?" Students should explain how each figure is typically remembered and then how they think Parks and Robinson *should* be remembered.

Targeted list of skills in this scenario

- Questioning narrative accounts
- Distinguishing between myth and history
- Evidence-based thinking and argumentation

Sources and Tools

Source 7.1: Police Report (Typed)

Misc.

POLICE DEPARTMENT
CITY OF MONTGOMERY

Date 12-1-55 19

Complainant J.F. Blake (wm)

Address 27 No. Lewis St. Phone No.

Offense Misc. Reported By Same as above

Address Phone No.

Date and Time Offense Committed 12-1-55 6:06 pm

Place of Occurrence In Front of Empire Theatre (On Montgomery Street)

Person or Property Attacked

How Attacked

Person Wanted

Value of Property Stolen Value Recovered

Details of Complaint (list, describe and give value of property stolen)

We received a call upon arrival the bus operator said he had a colored female sitting in the white section of the bus, and would not move back.

We (Day & Mixon) also saw her.

The bus operator signed a warrant for her. Rosa Parks,(cf) 634 Cleveland Court.

Rosa Parks (cf) was charged with chapter 6 section 11 of the Montgomery City Code.

Warrant #14254

THIS OFFENSE IS DECLARED:
UNFOUNDED ☐
CLEARED BY ARREST ☐
EXCEPTIONALLY CLEARED ☐
INACTIVE (NOT CLEARED) ☐

Officers F. B. Day
D. W. Mixon

Division Patrol Time 7:00 pm
12-1-55

Source: Typed police report submitted by Officers Day and Mixon, who arrested Rosa Parks, on December 1, 1955 (original can be found at http://www.archives.gov/education/lessons/rosa-parks/#document).

Source 7.2: Police Report (Handwritten)

POLICE DEPARTMENT — MONTGOMERY, ALABAMA

Date of Arrest 12-1-55.
Charges Refusing to obey order of bus driver. Chapter 6 Sec. 11 of City code
Disposition $10 + cost (app)
Nationality Negro
Age 42 Height 5 Feet 3 Inches
Complexion Black
Build Med.
Scars and Marks None
Employed by Montgomery Fair.
Relatives Husband, R. A. Parks. 634 Cleveland court.
Remarks:
Case No. 4464

Arrested by Day + Mixon
Residence 634 Cleveland court Montgomery.
Place of Birth Tuskegee ala.
Date of Birth Feb. 4 1913.
Weight 140 Eyes Brown.
Hair Black.
Occupation alteration shop.

Source: Handwritten police report submitted by Officers Day and Mixon, who arrested Rosa Parks on December 1, 1955 (http://www.archives.gov/education/lessons/rosa-parks/#documents).

Source 7.3: Signed Bus Diagram

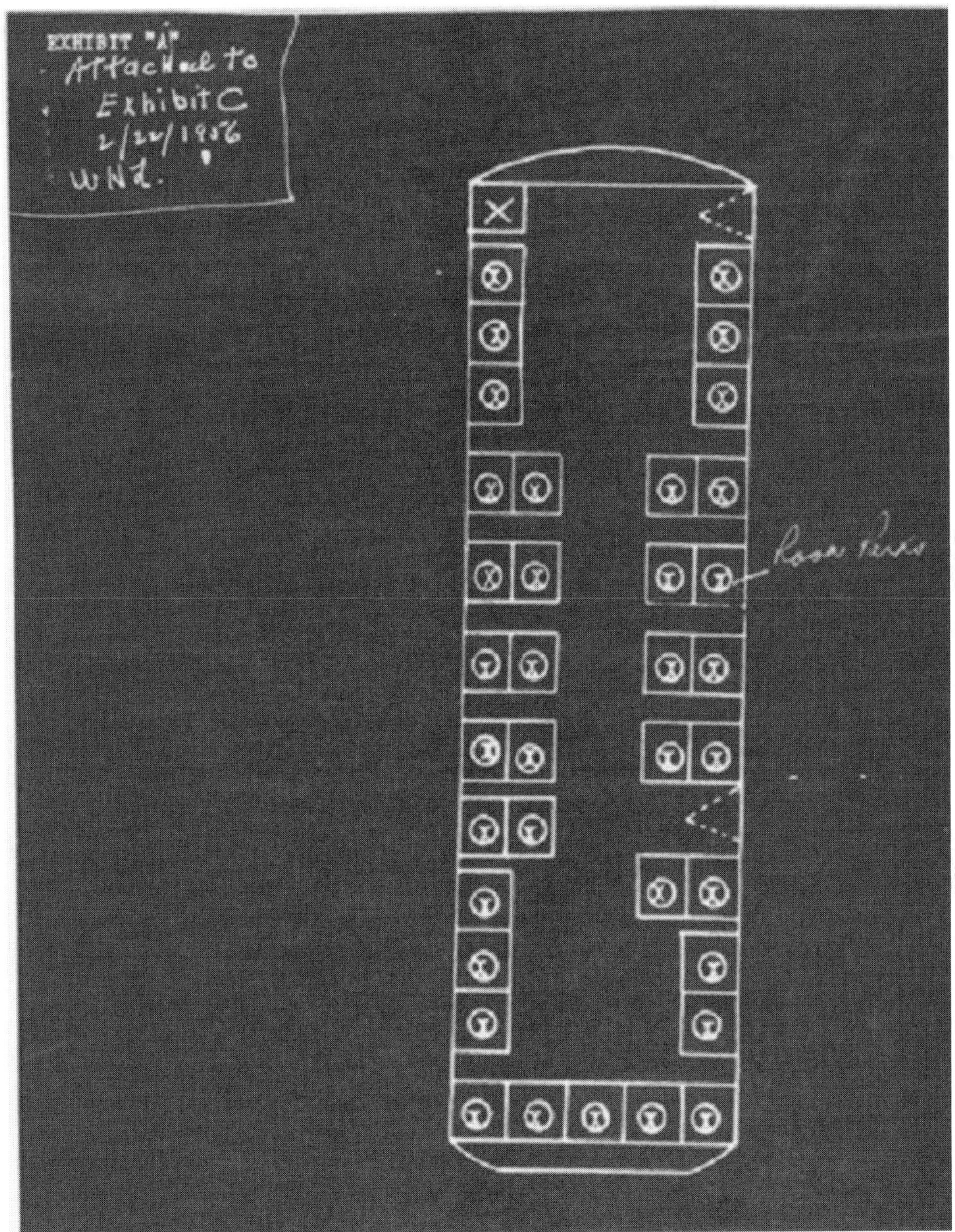

Source: Bus diagram agreed to by the prosecution and defense in the case of Rosa Parks, submitted February 22, 1956 (http://www.archives.gov/education/lessons/rosa-parks/#documents).

Source 7.4: Textbook Version

Note: Author and educator Herbert Kohl surveyed how more than 20 history textbooks told the story of Rosa Parks's refusal to give up her seat on December 1, 1955. Here he presents the standard story as told by these textbooks.

"Rosa was tired: The story of the Montgomery bus boycott"

Rosa Parks was a poor seamstress. She lived in Montgomery, Alabama, during the 1950s. [In] those days there was still segregation in parts of the United States. That meant that African Americans and European Americans were not allowed to use the same public facilities such as restaurants or swimming pools. It also meant that whenever it was crowded on the city buses African Americans had to give up seats in front to European Americans and move to the back of the bus.

One day on her way home from work Rosa was tired and sat down in the front of the bus. As the bus got crowded she was asked to give up her seat to a European American man, and she refused. The bus driver told her she had to go to the back of the bus, and she still refused to move. It was a hot day, and she was tired and angry, and became very stubborn.

The driver called a policeman, who arrested Rosa.

When other African Americans in Montgomery heard this they became angry too. So they decided to refuse to ride the buses until everyone was allowed to ride together. They boycotted the buses.

The boycott, which was led by Martin Luther King, Jr., succeeded. Now African Americans and European Americans can ride the buses together in Montgomery.

Rosa Parks was a very brave person.

Source: Herbert Kohl, *She Would Not Be Moved* (New York: The New Press, 2005), 7–8.

Source 7.5: Robinson Letter to the Mayor

Note: In this letter, Jo Ann Robinson writes the mayor of Montgomery asking for fair treatment on the buses.

Honorable Mayor W. A. Gayle
City Hall
Montgomery, Alabama

Dear Sir:

The Women's Political Council is very grateful to you and the City Commissioners for the hearing you allowed our representative during the month of March, 1954, when the "city-bus-fare-increase case" was being reviewed. There were several things the Council asked for:

1. A city law that would make it possible for Negroes to sit from back toward front, and whites from front toward back until all the seats are taken.
2. That Negroes not be asked or forced to pay fare at front and go to the rear of the bus to enter.
3. That busses stop at every corner in residential sections occupied by Negroes as they do in communities where whites reside.

We are happy to report that busses have begun stopping at more corners now in some sections where Negroes live than previously. However, the same practices in seating and boarding the bus continue. Mayor Gayle, three-fourths of the riders of these public conveyances are Negroes. If Negroes did not patronize them, they could not possibly operate.

More and more of our people are already arranging with neighbors and friends to ride to keep from being insulted and humiliated by bus drivers. There has been talk from twenty-five or more local organizations of planning a city-wide boycott of busses.

We, sir, do not feel that forceful measures are necessary in bargaining for a convenience which is right for all bus passengers. . . . Please consider this plea, and if possible, act favorably upon it, for even now plans are being made to ride less, or not at all, on our busses. We do not want this.

Respectfully yours,
The Women's Political Council
Jo Ann Robinson, President

Source: Excerpt from a letter written by Jo Ann Robinson, May 21, 1954, Montgomery, Alabama. Reprinted in Jo Ann Gibson Robinson, *The Montgomery Bus Boycott and the Women Who Started It*, ed. David J. Garrow (Knoxville: University of Tennessee Press, 1987).

Source 7.6: Abernathy Remembers

Note: In the following excerpt, Reverend Ralph Abernathy remembers the first mass meeting of the Montgomery Improvement Association (MIA) at a local Baptist church on the first day of the boycott. After this, the MIA held regular weekly meetings until the boycott ended.

We, M. L. King and I, went to the meeting together. It was drizzling; I had been working up until the last minute on the resolutions. I was given instructions: one, to call off the protest, or two, if indicated, to continue the protest until the grievances were granted. We had had a successful "one-day protest," but we feared that if we extended it beyond the first day, we might fail; it might be better after all to call the protest off, and then we could hold this "one-day boycott" as a threat for future negotiations. However, we were to determine whether to continue the protest by the size of the crowds. . . .

When we got about twenty blocks from the church we saw cars parked solid. . . . As we got closer to the church we saw a great mass of people. The *Montgomery Advertiser* estimated the crowd at approximately 7,000 persons all trying to get in a church that will accommodate less than 1,000. It took us about fifteen minutes to work our way through the crowd by pleading: "Please let us through–we are Reverend King and Reverend Abernathy. Please permit us to get through." . . . Those inside applauded for at least ten minutes.

It was apparent that the people were with us. It was then that all of the ministers who had previously refused to take part in the program came up to Reverend King and me to offer their services. This expression of togetherness on the part of the masses was obviously an inspiration to the leadership and helped to rid it of the cowardly, submissive, over timidity.

We began the meeting by singing *Onward Christian Soldiers, Marching as to War*. . . . Mrs. Rosa Parks was presented to the mass meeting because we wanted her to become symbolic of our protest movement. Following her we presented Mr. Daniels, who happily for our meeting had been arrested on that day. . . . The appearance of these persons created enthusiasm, thereby giving momentum to the movement. We then heard the resolutions calling for the continuation of the boycott . . . unanimously and enthusiastically adopted by the 7,000 individuals both inside and outside the church. . . .

Source: Excerpt from Ralph Abernathy's master's thesis, "The Natural History of a Social Movement," Atlanta, GA, 1958.

Tool 7.1: Where Did Rosa Parks Sit?

PART ONE: Mark "RP" in the seat where you believe Rosa Parks sat when she was arrested on December 1, 1955 (each box is a seat).

DRV

PART TWO: Complete this chart as you read, discuss, and analyze the two police reports.

Document	**Reasons to trust this source**	**Reasons to doubt this source**	**According to this source, where did Rosa Parks sit?**	**How can you tell? Cite an excerpt from the source.**
Police report (Typed)				
Police report (Hand-written)				

Tool 7.2: Comparing the Montgomery City Code and the Alabama State Code

Directions: Read each law carefully and answer the questions that follow it. Then consider the key question at the end.

> It shall be unlawful for any passenger to refuse to take a seat among those assigned to the race to which he belongs, at the request of any such employee in charge, if there is such a seat vacant.
>
> –Montgomery City Code, Chapter 6, Sections 10–11, 1952

1. What does "unlawful" mean?

2. When does a passenger NOT have the right to refuse to take a seat when asked by someone who works for the bus company?

   A passenger ***cannot*** *refuse to take a seat when . . .*

3. When does a passenger have the right to refuse to take a seat when asked by someone who works for the bus company?

   A passenger ***can*** *refuse to take a seat when . . .*

Tool 7.2: Comparing the Montgomery City Code and the Alabama State Code (continued)

> The conductor or agent of the motor transportation company in charge of any vehicle is authorized and required to assign each passenger to the division of the vehicle designated for the race to which the passenger belongs.
>
> –Title 48, §301(31a, b, c), Code of Alabama of 1940

1. What does "authorized" mean?

2. In which section (or "division") will passengers be assigned seats?

3. What will passengers have in common with other passengers in their section?

Agree or disagree with this statement:

"Rosa Parks broke the law when she refused to give up her seat."

Explain why you agree or disagree, and refer to the sources to support your answer.

Tool 7.3: What Led to the Success of the Montgomery Bus Boycott?

1. Add the dates of the documents and events related to the boycott to this timeline.

R.P. arrest

12/1/1955

2. Complete this chart as you read the different materials for this lesson.

Source	Author's Point of View About What Led to the Success of the Boycott	Evidence Used to Support Author's Point of View (include quotations)
Textbook version by Herbert Kohl		
Jo Ann Robinson		
Ralph Abernathy		
Ryan's Essay		
Shawna's Essay		

Suggested Resources

http://memory.loc.gov/ammem/aaohtml/exhibit/aointro.html
"African American Odyssey," an exhibit run by the Library of Congress, includes images, documents, and overviews of different time periods in the struggle for African American civil rights, from early U.S. history through the civil rights movement of the 20th century.

http://www.pbs.org/wgbh/amex/eyesontheprize/story/02_bus.html
At this site PBS houses the video series *Eyes on the Prize: America's Civil Rights Movement, 1954–1985,* along with a wide range of primary and secondary sources. The site includes original video footage, photographs, and other documents from the era. The Montgomery Bus Boycott is one of the many events highlighted.

http://montgomery.troy.edu/rosaparks/museum/
The Rosa Parks Museum is located at Troy University in downtown Montgomery, Alabama. This site includes information about Rosa Parks's life and the Montgomery Bus Boycott.

http://www.sojournproject.com/
Sojourn to the Past is an organization for middle and high school students that leads field trips through civil rights–era hot spots in the southern United States.

http://historicalthinkingmatters.org/rosaparks/
This site was created by Stanford University's History Education Group and George Mason University's Center for History and New Media. This particular section focuses on the Montgomery Bus Boycott and includes primary documents, historians' analyses of documents, historians' explanations of relevant background, ideas for using historians' think-alouds, web quests, and modified documents.

CHAPTER 8

To Blink or Not to Blink: The Cuban Missile Crisis

Jack Schneider

Central Intelligence Agency. President Kennedy meets in the Oval Office with General Curtis Lemay and reconnaissance pilots who flew the Cuban missions. 1962. Available at http://www.maryferrell.org/wiki/index.php/Photos_-_JFK_Library_-_Cuban_Missile_Crisis_-_p1

"We were eyeball to eyeball, and I think the other fellow just blinked" is how Dean Rusk, President John F. Kennedy's Secretary of State, characterized the outcome of the Cuban Missile Crisis. For 2 weeks in October 1962, Rusk and other members of JFK's Executive Committee (or "Ex Comm") held the fate of the world in their hands. Their actions, as it turned out, would keep the United States and Soviet Union from plunging into a nuclear conflict of apocalyptic proportions.

Rusk's phrase quickly became the banner for Cold War-era policymakers who advocated a continued arms buildup. The "other fellow blinked," as Rusk and others like him argued, only because of America's tactical military strength. Fail to maintain America's arms advantage over the Soviet Union, they cautioned, and the Russians would be camping on our doorsteps. This hawkish stance, grounded in mythic stories about the fearless brinkmanship of the Kennedy Administration, had major consequences for the future of U.S. foreign policy–consequences that included the continued proliferation of exorbitantly expensive nuclear stockpiles and the escalation of the Vietnam War.

Not surprisingly, this version of the Cuban Missile Crisis also became legend among the American public. Conveyed through accounts in the press, popular histories, and of course American history textbooks, it told of a consensus that emerged among the members of Ex Comm favoring "a blockade of Cuba with other military measures, including possibly an air strike and even an invasion, to follow if the missiles were not removed."[1] Textbook accounts appearing shortly after the withdrawal of missiles from Cuba similarly portrayed a hard-line stance taken by the United States. "Khrushchev," the authors of *Story of America* wrote, "had gambled on being able to face the U.S. with a secretly built powerful offensive base on its doorstep"–a move that would have given him "a major victory in the cold war."

> It soon became evident, however, that he was not willing to risk actual war with the United States. Faced with President Kennedy's vigorous counter-measures, solid Organization of American States backing for the United States, and the skillful mediation of Secretary General U Thant of the United Nations, he agreed to remove the offensive weapons. So the crisis passed.[2]

While *Story of America* gave more credit to the Organization of American States and the United Nations than did many American newspapers, the outline of the story stayed the same–Kennedy drew a line in the sand. Khrushchev, seeing that he had no chance against superior American firepower, wisely backed down.

Another textbook from the mid-1960s, *United States History*, covered the nuclear standoff similarly:

> Instead of testing the blockade, the Soviet ships turned back. People everywhere breathed easier, especially after Khrushchev himself backed down. In an exchange of letters with Kennedy, the Soviet leader promised to remove offensive weapons from Cuba and to permit inspection by the United Nations to verify the removal. In return, he asked the United States to lift its blockade and not to invade Cuba. Kennedy agreed.[3]

Providing an even more thorough account than *Story of America*, *United States History* made it clear that although the Soviet premier backed down, he received something in return for withdrawing the Soviet missiles from Cuba.

One final excerpt–this one from *A History of the United States* (1966)–completes the picture:

> Soviet ships carrying jet aircraft and military supplies to Cuba changed course rather than risk an encounter with American ships or planes enforcing the blockade. When America's allies and the Organization of American States

> gave strong support to President Kennedy's stand, Soviet Premier Khrushchev agreed to remove the offensive weapons under UN supervision. In return, he asked that the United States lift its blockade and agree not to invade Cuba. . . . The outcome of the crisis was a clear-cut victory for the United States and the free world. It convinced Khrushchev that President Kennedy was prepared to use force if necessary to block Soviet domination of any country in Latin America. The Soviet leader had therefore decided not to risk touching off a nuclear holocaust by pushing his plans in Cuba.[4]

Picking up where *United States History* and *Story of America* left off, *A History of the United States* editorialized that the victory for the United States and the world was "clear-cut." More importantly, the triumph had unquestionably convinced the Soviets that the Americans were indeed a formidable opponent. The lesson? Only a strong America ready to flex its military muscle could guarantee world peace.

What the Textbooks Missed

While accounts of the Cuban Missile Crisis written shortly after the event vary, their general narrative is largely the same: The Soviets gambled by moving nuclear weapons into Cuba–a risky but calculated move designed to win the upper hand in the Cold War. But the United States never flinched. With the strength of tactical American air and sea power behind him, President Kennedy and his Ex Comm advisors fearlessly stared down the Soviets. In return for removal of Soviet missiles, the Americans promised not to invade Cuba, which, after the Bay of Pigs fiasco, didn't look too promising anyway. The victory was clear. The other guy blinked.

If the story of the Cuban Missile Crisis had stopped unfolding in the mid-1960s, the textbook narratives would have gotten it more or less right, or at least as right as they could have gotten it. But over the next few decades, the story of the nuclear standoff in Cuba would continue to change in subtle but important ways.

Take, for instance, the two negotiation letters that Nikita Khrushchev sent to President Kennedy in 1962. The first letter, dated Friday, October 26, demanded that the United States promise to never invade Cuba, in return for the removal of Soviet missiles from the island. The second letter, dated Saturday, October 27, demanded that the United States remove its intermediate-range Jupiter missiles from Turkey. Many textbook accounts of the crisis leave out all details about the letters. The textbooks that do address them usually explain that Ex Comm advised Kennedy to ignore the second letter and accept the offer in the first, which he did.

The "two-letter" account–Kennedy acting on the first and ignoring the second–is largely corroborated by Robert F. Kennedy's *Thirteen Days* (Source 8.1), the diary kept by the president's brother during the crisis, published a year after RFK's assassination. In his diary, Robert Kennedy described how after Ex Comm met on Saturday, October 27, he phoned Soviet Ambassador Anatoly F. Dobrynin and asked to meet that night at the Department of Justice. The Americans were willing to discuss the possibility of withdrawing missiles in Turkey, but not without conditions. As RFK reported in his diary, he told Dobrynin that "there could be no *quid pro quo* or any arrangement made under this kind of threat."[5] He echoed this message in a top-secret memo to Secretary of State Dean Rusk (Source 8.2). "Per your instructions," the attorney general wrote to Rusk, "I repeated that there could be no deal of any kind and that any steps toward easing tensions in other parts of the world largely depended on the Soviet Union and Mr. Khrushchev taking action in Cuba and taking it immediately."[6]

Here is where the plot thickens. When we turn to the Soviets to tell the story, we get a different impression. Former Soviet Premier Nikita Khrushchev's memoir (Source 8.3), published after his death, not only claims that the Americans took the second letter seriously, but also that they acted on it. According to Khrushchev, Kennedy willingly agreed to the letter's terms–"In exchange for withdrawal of our missiles, [President Kennedy] would remove American missiles from Turkey and Italy"[7]–and that the exchange was indeed a *quid pro quo* (Latin, meaning "one thing for another"), the very thing Robert Kennedy denied.

Did President Kennedy remove missiles aimed at Moscow in return for the withdrawal of Soviet missiles from Cuba? Textbook accounts from the mid- and late-1960s never mention such a deal. But then, how could they? After all, Robert Kennedy's *Thirteen Days* wasn't published until 1969, while Khrushchev's *Khrushchev Remembers: The Last Testament* was published in 1974.

And what about textbooks published after both books came out? Not a word. As the authors of the textbook *America Is*, published in 1995, wrote:

> Although the United States had shown the Soviet Union that it meant what it said, work on the missiles continued. Then, on October 26, President Kennedy heard from Soviet Premier Khrushchev. In a few days, they came to terms on Cuba. The Soviet Union agreed to remove the missiles. As a result, the United States agreed to end the quarantine and not to invade Cuba.[8]

Though more detailed, the story presented in *The American Anthem* (2007) is much the same:

> [Kennedy] received a letter from Khrushchev offering to remove the missiles if the United States pledged never to

> invade Cuba. The next day he received a tougher letter from Khrushchev demanding that the United States remove its missiles from Turkey. The Ex Comm advised Kennedy to ignore the second letter and accept the offer in the first letter. The president did so, and Khrushchev announced he would dismantle the missiles.[9]

While the latter textbook account includes the story of Khrushchev's letters, it rejects outright the possibility that Kennedy agreed to remove Jupiter missiles from Turkey in exchange for a Soviet withdrawal from Cuba.

The question of whether President Kennedy and his advisors agreed to a *quid pro quo* with the Soviets in 1962 is a fascinating historical controversy. In fact, our whole understanding of this incident hinges on it. If there was no deal, then the traditional Cold War narrative remains intact. Brute strength, not back-room deals kept from public view, saved us from World War III. On the other hand, if the Soviet view is right–that resolution came about by brokering a deal–we have to revise our understanding, and accept that war was averted because the superpowers came up with an agreement that both sides could live with.

Students' textbooks often overlook or minimize. But the second letter shows students that while textbooks are a good place to start, even the most massive tomes are incomplete. Sometimes, in fact, they're just plain wrong. Scrutinizing the textbook not only teaches students to take a critical approach to reading, it can show them the need to puzzle through historical sources in order to find out what really happened. This approach, what we refer to as "Opening Up the Textbook," changes the text from an inert authority, always issuing the final word, to one more historical source that must be critically evaluated like any other.[10]

So, What Happened? The question at the heart of the Cuban Missile Crisis is simple: Did the Kennedy Administration agree to remove missiles pointed at Moscow from the Turkish border in exchange for the withdrawal of Soviet missiles from Cuba? In short, is the story of "the other fellow blinking" more myth than history?

While Khrushchev's book makes the case that there was an explicit exchange, evidence in the form of a top-secret American memo contradicts that claim. Robert Kennedy's message to Dean Rusk was clear: "I replied that there could be no *quid pro quo*–no deal of this kind could be made. This was a matter that had to be considered by NATO."[11]

Do we believe RFK just because he was on our side? No. Historical understanding is not the same as rooting for your favorite team. We are obliged to consider all of the evidence, even when it comes from the other side.

Instead of sifting through endless mountains of he said/she said, historians seek corroborating evidence. Corroboration, a practice at the core of historical reasoning, is the act of comparing different accounts in order to piece together an accurate picture of what happened. Rather than simply accepting one version of a story over another, historians work to discover points of overlap and departure. What, they ask, is common to the various accounts? When do they disagree? Where do they diverge? What might explain these discrepancies? How might the accounts be reconciled?

Thus, the question of whether to believe Nikita Khrushchev or Robert Kennedy is not just a Cold War riddle, but a shining example for students of the detective work historians must do. And so, to solve this riddle, we must turn to other documents to help us reconstruct the story.

Case in point: In addition to Robert Kennedy's diary and Nikita Khrushchev's memoir, a secret communiqué addressed the matter of the second letter. Released by Soviet officials 3 decades after the events in question, the document–a coded transmission from Ambassador Dobrynin's Washington office back to Moscow–confirms why historians generally benefit from the passage of time, and the surfacing of new information.

In this secret cable, released following the dissolution of the Soviet Union (Source 8.4), Dobrynin describes his meeting with RFK. Shortly after the Ex Comm received Khrushchev's second letter, the president's brother called Dobrynin to schedule a meeting. Both sources agreed to this. The two sides, according to both Dobrynin and Kennedy, reached agreement on American assurances not to invade Cuba. But where RFK claimed to stand firm on the question of removing Jupiter missiles from Turkey, the Soviet Ambassador tells a different story:

> "And what about Turkey?" I asked R. Kennedy.
>
> "If that is the only obstacle to achieving the regulation I mentioned earlier, then the president doesn't see any unsurmountable difficulties in resolving this issue," replied R. Kennedy. "The greatest difficulty for the president is the public discussion of the issue of Turkey. Formerly the deployment of missile bases in Turkey was done by a special decision of the NATO Council. To announce now a unilateral decision by the president of the USA to withdraw missile bases from Turkey–this would damage the entire structure of NATO and the U.S. position as the leader of NATO. . . . However, President Kennedy is ready to come to agree on that question with N.S. Khrushchev, too. I think that in order to withdraw these bases from Turkey," R. Kennedy said, "we need 4–5 months."[12]

Dobrynin's account seems to settle the matter, corroborating Khrushchev's account and undermining both

Robert Kennedy's story and the "the other guy blinked" theory. According to Dobrynin, the Americans received Khrushchev's second letter and quickly called for a meeting in which the details of the *quid pro quo* were hashed out.

Still, the Soviet ambassador may have had some other motives for writing the cable–something historians must consider when using the document to corroborate Khrushchev's version of the story. Dobrynin, only 43 at the time of the missile crisis, was the youngest person to serve as Soviet Ambassador to the United States, and had only arrived in Washington that year. Perhaps, historians have speculated, the young ambassador was simply telling Khrushchev what he wanted to hear, that is, doing whatever it took to keep his job. How else, they ask, could Dobrynin have survived in that post until 1986, with so many Soviet premiers ousted during that time span? Beyond that, it was in the Soviets' interest to claim that a deal had been brokered. Who wants to admit that they caved in to pressure? Better to save face by claiming a deal had been reached.

Even so, were one tempted to view Dobrynin's account as reliable, there is still the question of Robert Kennedy's diary. Real corroboration, after all, utilizes different vantage points. And the Americans' position regarding the withdrawal of missiles from Turkey–Kennedy's diary, edited into *Thirteen Days* by his friend Ted Sorenson after RFK was assassinated in 1968–indicates that there was no *quid pro quo.*

Or does it?

In search of further corroborating evidence, historical detectives might turn to a 1989 conference in Moscow in which Sorensen dropped what was, at the time, nothing short of a bombshell. Saying that he wanted to make a "confession," Sorensen stunned his audience by announcing: "I was the editor of Robert Kennedy's book. And," he continued, "the diary was very explicit that [the missile agreement] was part of the deal." But because the missile deal was still a secret in 1969, when *Thirteen Days* was published, Sorenson took it upon himself to act as censor and "edit that out of [RFK's] diaries" (Source 8.5). This is a polite way of saying that he took it upon himself to fabricate history.

Let's take stock. Khrushchev's second letter, as the Soviets claimed, and Ted Sorenson now admits, was not "ignored" by the Americans. Nor did President Kennedy simply give his Soviet counterpart the evil eye. Rather, the Americans engaged in diplomatic negotiations and reached a deal with their adversaries.

But if that is the case, it begs the question: Why? Why would Kennedy negotiate with the Soviets if the American Navy could enforce its blockade of Cuba and the American Air Force could, if necessary, destroy the Soviet missiles on the island? The answer, it turns out, is a simple one: The impact of America's tactical military advantage during the Cuban Missile Crisis was overstated. Kennedy's Joint Chiefs of Staff, according to scholar Thomas Blanton, told the President that air strikes could not guarantee the destruction of all Soviet missiles placed in Cuba.[13]

Why all the secrecy? Why did the Kennedy Administration continue to perpetuate stories of unblinking brinkmanship? Why not come clean about an arrangement that prevented World War III, especially if the cost was only what President Kennedy called "some obsolete missiles in Turkey?"[14]

One issue, which Dobrynin mentions in his cable, was Kennedy's fear that publicly announcing the agreement might hurt NATO as well as the United States's position as alliance leader. McGeorge Bundy, another member of Kennedy's Ex Comm, confirmed this concern, noting that "for all its costs, secrecy prevented a serious political division both within the United States and in the Atlantic Alliance."[15]

At stake for the Kennedys was the possibility that if the truth had been revealed at the height of Cold War mania, they would appear soft on Soviet aggression. JFK, in the 1960 presidential race, had criticized then-Vice President Nixon for allowing a Communist regime to seize power 90 miles off the Florida coast. Consequently, as president, Kennedy took great pains to appear proactive toward Cuba, particularly after the Bay of Pigs fiasco and leaks about failed attempts to assassinate Fidel Castro. Attorney General Robert Kennedy had his own presidential ambitions, and as Soviet Ambassador Anatoly Dobrynin recalled in his memoir, RFK feared that "his prospects could be damaged if this secret deal about the missiles in Turkey were to come out."[16] Whether out of concern for national security or their own electoral future, the Kennedy team believed that a story about aggressiveness and strength would play better than one about diplomacy and flexibility.

Did the Movie Get It Right? Movies often get it wrong. And yet, in terms of galvanizing student interest and helping students imagine the world as it once was, film is among the most powerful tools in a teacher's arsenal. One recent motion picture, featuring the factual history behind the Cuban Missile Crisis, takes its title from Robert Kennedy's diary; naturally, teachers will wonder if *Thirteen Days* got it right.[17]

In terms of the diplomatic negotiations between the Americans and the Soviets, the movie is surprisingly accurate, recounting details that most textbook narratives omit. Yes, President Kennedy stares down Soviet ships and Dean Rusk observes that the other guy blinked. But the film also tells the story of the Kennedy brothers flexibly adapting to the threat, working to build consensus among the members of Ex Comm in favor of quarantine rather than air raid or invasion.

The film realistically depicts the leak to columnist Walter Lippmann about a possible missile exchange, the second letter from the Soviets, and the meeting between Robert Kennedy and Ambassador Dobrynin in which promises were made to withdraw American missiles from Turkey in exchange for a Soviet withdrawal from Cuba and to keep the agreement secret.

But, as scholar Philip Brenner notes, the film also invents history in the name of viewer interest.[18] Perhaps the most significant distortion is the apparently pivotal role played by Kennedy aide Kenny O'Donnell in the crisis (played by Kevin Costner, the character makes critical decisions, like instructing Navy pilots to deny being fired on during reconnaissance flights over Cuba). Also questionable is the degree to which a KGB agent stationed in Washington speaks for Premier Khrushchev.

Such inaccuracies, if included for the sake of dramatic narrative, might easily be forgiven. Of greater concern is the overall impression students will get from watching *Thirteen Days*. Recalling a conversation he had with his teenage daughter about why the Soviets put missiles in Cuba, Brenner notes that the conclusion she drew from the film was a simple one: The Soviets were bad. The film rarely portrays the Soviets (or the Cubans, for that matter) as malevolent forces, but because it focuses exclusively on the American response to the crisis, it's hard to resist sympathizing with the United States against a seemingly irrational and belligerent foe. Besides, it's natural to root for the home team.

But the Soviet decision to move missiles into Cuba did not come out of nowhere. During his short time in office, John F. Kennedy had expanded America's arms advantage over the Soviet Union, giving the United States a nearly ten-to-one advantage in long-range bombers and missiles.[19] In an effort to placate hard-liners within the Russian ranks, as well as protect Cuba against another U.S.-backed covert operation, Khrushchev decided to place intermediate-range ballistic missiles on the island. Such a move, states Brenner, was "a cheaper way to provide some deterrent against a feared U.S. attack than to build many new intercontinental ballistic missiles that could be launched from the Soviet Union."[20] While the Russians may have brought the world to the brink of nuclear disaster, they did not do so without cause.

That narrative is omitted from the film. As a consequence, viewers without a broader context (read: your students) may well walk away believing that the United States was the unsullied good guy and the Soviets irrational warmongers. Instead, rather than a story of good and evil, the Cuban Missile Crisis is one of rivals simultaneously displaying weakness and strength, defense and aggression, restraint and belligerence. In the end, it was plain old-fashioned diplomacy–secret deals in which neither side got everything it wanted–that averted World War III.

Why Teach About the Cuban Missile Crisis?

A Story That Gradually Reveals Itself. It's hard for students to grasp that sometimes the more distant we are from an event, the more we understand about it. Yet, in many instances, this is exactly how we come to know the past. Teaching the Cuban Missile Crisis presents a ripe opportunity to show students how our understanding of history changes. As time puts distance between historians and an event, pieces of the puzzle start to fall into place. History, after all, is never completely transparent–if it were, historians wouldn't need to work so hard piecing it together. According to Sergei Khrushchev, the son of the former Soviet premier, "President Kennedy didn't want to leave any traces to go down in history and he was afraid of being accused of catering to the communists. Nothing could be done about that . . . the important thing was that they, the President and Father, understood each other's aspirations and could trust each other."[21] Not surprisingly, putting together the story of the Cuban Missile Crisis has been a challenge for historians. But with declassified documents coming to light, and revelations from participants like Ted Sorenson, the story of the Cuban Missile Crisis is becoming clearer.

Corroborating Sources. Because historical accounts may often contradict one another, historians corroborate sources in an effort to reconcile discrepancies. In this sense, historical reasoning and jurisprudential reasoning have a lot of overlap. Thus, the Cuban Missile Crisis is a great opportunity to introduce students to the type of detective work that historians do. Once one begins to corroborate sources about the events of 1962, the story turns out to be quite different from the traditional narrative. As one scholar has put it, the reality is less that Kennedy won a staredown against Khrushchev, and more that the conflict was ultimately "resolved only because both men were willing to risk humiliation rather than Armageddon."[22] By bringing in new sources, historians determine not only that the Kennedy Administration agreed to withdraw missiles from Turkey, but that they felt it was important to conceal this fact from us, the public at large.

Thinking About the Lessons Drawn from History. The frequently drawn lesson from the Cuban Missile Crisis is that the United States must unflinchingly face down the aggressions of its enemies. The American foreign policy in Vietnam pursued by the Kennedy and Johnson administrations, for instance, was driven by the view that only unyielding military force could meet the Communist threat.

But it appears that the lesson of unblinking brinkmanship is historically inaccurate. Stanford historian Barton Bernstein asks whether a belief in Kennedy's "'victory'" in the missile crisis may have influenced Lyndon Johnson as he "struggled on, even against the counsel of advisors, for his own triumph in Southeast Asia in 1966–1968." Bernstein goes on to suggest that President Johnson might have felt "psychologically, and even politically, more free to change policy if he had known, along with his fellow Americans, the truth of the October 1962 settlement."[23] But he did not. Thus, the story of the Cuban Missile Crisis not only highlights the importance of getting history right, it raises questions about what types of lessons we can draw from the past.

How Might You Use These Materials?

Scenario 1 (2–3 Hour Lesson). Was World War III prevented because the "other guy blinked"? Or was Armageddon cheated because American and Soviet diplomats reached a compromise that allowed both parties to save face? Use these primary sources to engage students in corroborating historical accounts before accepting any version as true. This scenario offers a different take on the "Opening Up the Textbook" strategy from Chapter 6.

Begin this lesson by asking students to read a textbook account of the Cuban Missile Crisis (either one of those listed in this chapter or the one from your textbook). Whether or not the book mentions Khrushchev's second letter, the question remains: How can we know how the Kennedy Administration responded?

Divide students into groups, giving them Robert Kennedy's top-secret memorandum to the Secretary of State (see Source 8.2a for the adapted version, and Source 8.2b for the original "Top Secret" government document), asking them to consider what really happened during his meeting with Soviet Ambassador Dobrynin. Allow the groups time to discuss, then provide them with two additional documents–the excerpts from Kennedy's diary (Source 8.1) and Nikita Khrushchev's memoir (Source 8.3). Students will likely engage in a rudimentary form of corroboration, noting that because the two documents by Robert Kennedy are consistent, his account must be true. Other students will come to the conclusion that it's Kennedy's word against Khrushchev's, our side against theirs.

At this point, give students Dobrynin's declassified cable (Source 8.4), and ask how the story it tells affects their understanding of what happened. Then, provide them with Ted Sorenson's "confession" (Source 8.5).

Finally, have students select an excerpt from the movie *Thirteen Days* and explain how it is accurate or inaccurate based on what they learned from the sources in this lesson. Students must include evidence from the documents or other research that led them to their decision about the film's accuracy.

Targeted list of skills in this scenario

- Questioning narrative accounts in textbooks and film
- Corroborating sources
- Evidence-based thinking and argumentation
- Constructing a narrative based on evidence

Scenario 2 (1–2 Hour Lesson). Why hide the truth? This scenario, which expands on the first, is designed to give students practice in thinking about historical context.

First, lead students through the analysis and discussion rounds described in the previous scenario. For this scenario, ask students to consider *why* the Kennedy Administration wished to conceal their diplomatic negotiations from the American public.

Provide students with transcript excerpts of a 1960 presidential debate between John F. Kennedy and Richard Nixon (Source 8.6) and a 1961 top-secret memo from Richard Goodwin to President Kennedy (Source 8.7). The first document provides evidence that Kennedy had promised to be tough on Cuba when running for president, while the second indicates how problematic the failed Bay of Pigs invasion was for the Kennedy Administration. Next, provide students with the excerpt from Anatoly Dobrynin's memoir (Source 8.8), which indicates that because Robert Kennedy had presidential ambitions, he could not afford to look soft on Cuba or Communism. The graphic organizer (Tool 8.1) will help students keep track of their thinking.

After allowing time to discuss the importance of these documents and what they indicate, ask the students to work individually or in groups. Consider giving students an essay assignment to explain why the Kennedy Administration concealed their negotiations with the Soviets from the American public. Encourage students to include and explain excerpts from the documents that led them to their conclusions.

Targeted list of skills in this scenario

- Contextualizing sources and historical events
- Building an explanation of a past event based on sources

Scenario 3 (1 Hour Lesson). What does the past look like when you're standing in the other guy's shoes? This scenario uses a Soviet textbook to help students understand perspective and also to give them practice in close reading.

Provide students with excerpts from other nations' textbooks and how they describe the Cuban Missile Crisis (Tool 8.2). These excerpts give students practice in close reading and honing their sensitivity to the language of historical narrative. In the first excerpt, from a Cuban textbook, use of the word "mercenary" will alert an attentive reader to the book's stance. Students, however, may not grasp the inference or know what "mercenary" means. Even if they miss this clue, the word "hostile" in the next sentence should tip them off. In the second excerpt, from a Soviet book, the adjective "severe" in the first sentence alerts the reader that this description is not likely from a U.S. textbook. However, this clue alone does not settle the matter until subsequent sentences fall into place: The book explains it was a sequence of American actions that set off the conflict, with seemingly no provocation from the Soviet side.

Targeted list of skills in this scenario

- Perspective recognition
- Close reading

Sources and Tools

Source 8.1: Excerpt from *Thirteen Days* (Modified)

Note: Robert Kennedy was the brother of President John Kennedy and Attorney General of the United States in 1962. In this diary excerpt, he writes about his negotiations with Soviet Ambassador Dobrynin regarding the missiles in Cuba.

I telephoned Ambassador Dobrynin about 7:15 P.M. and asked him to come to the Department of Justice. We met in my office at 7:45. I told him first that we knew that work was continuing on the missile bases in Cuba and that in the last few days it had been **expedited**. . . .

We had to have a commitment by tomorrow that those bases would be removed. I was not giving them an **ultimatum** but a statement of fact. He should understand that if they did not remove those bases, we would remove them. President Kennedy had great respect for the Ambassador's country and the courage of its people. Perhaps his country might feel it necessary to take **retaliatory** action; but before that was over, there would be not only dead Americans but dead Russians as well.

He asked me what offer the United States was making, and I told him of the letter that President Kennedy had just transmitted to Khrushchev. He raised the question of our removing the missiles from Turkey. I said that there could be no **quid pro quo** or any arrangement made under this kind of threat or pressure and that in the last analysis this was a decision that would have to be made by NATO. However, I said, President Kennedy had been anxious to remove those missiles from Italy and Turkey for a long period of time. He had ordered their removal some time ago, and it was our judgment that, within a short time after this crisis was over, those missiles would be gone.

I said President Kennedy wished to have peaceful relations between our two countries. He wished to resolve the problems that confronted us in Europe and Southeast Asia. He wished to move forward on the control of nuclear weapons. However, we could make progress on these matters only when the crisis was behind us. Time was running out. We had only a few more hours–we needed an answer immediately from the Soviet Union. I said we must have it the next day.

Source: Robert F. Kennedy, *Thirteen Days: A Memoir of the Cuban Missile Crisis* (New York: New American Library, 1969), 107–109.

WORD BANK

expedited–speeded up, dealt with quickly
ultimatum–a final demand
retaliatory–designed to hurt someone back
quid pro quo–something done in exchange

Source 8.2a: Excerpt from Robert Kennedy's Memo to Dean Rusk (Modified)

Note: In this official memo, Attorney General Robert Kennedy reports to Secretary of Defense Dean Rusk about his meeting with the Soviet Ambassador.

At the request of Secretary Rusk, I telephoned Ambassador Dobrynin at approximately 7:15 p.m. on Saturday October 27th. I asked him if he would come to the Justice Department at quarter of eight. We met in my office. . . . He asked me . . . what offer we were making. I said a letter had . . . been **transmitted** to the Soviet Embassy which stated . . . that the missile bases should be **dismantled** and all offensive weapons should be removed from Cuba. In return, if Cuba and Castro and the Communists ended their **subversive** activities . . . we would agree to keep peace . . . and not permit an invasion from American soil.

He then asked me about Khrushchev's other proposal dealing with the removal of the missiles from Turkey. I replied that there could be no ***quid pro quo***–no deal of this kind could be made. . . . Per your instructions I repeated that there could be no deal of any kind and that any steps toward easing tensions in other part of the world largely depended on the Soviet Union and Mr. Khrushchev taking action in Cuba and taking it immediately.

Source: Top-secret memo from Robert Kennedy, Attorney General, to Secretary of Defense Dean Rusk, October 30, 1962.

WORD BANK

transmitted–sent
dismantled–taken apart
subversive–intended to hurt or overthrow the government
quid pro quo–something done in exchange

Source 8.2b: Top-Secret Memo from Robert Kennedy to Dean Rusk (Original)

Office of the Attorney General
Washington, D.C.

October 30, 1962

MEMORANDUM FOR THE SECRETARY OF STATE

FROM THE ATTORNEY GENERAL

At the request of Secretary Rusk, I telephoned Ambassador Dobrynin at approximately 7:15 p.m. on Saturday, October 27th. I asked him if he would come to the Justice Department at a quarter of eight.

We met in my office. I told him first that we understood that the work was continuing on the Soviet missile bases in Cuba. Further, I explained to him that in the last two hours we had found that our planes flying over Cuba had been fired upon and that one of our U-2's had been shot down and the pilot killed. I said these men were flying unarmed planes.

I told him that this was an extremely serious turn in events. We would have to make certain decisions within the next 12 or possibly 24 hours. There was a very little time left. If the Cubans were shooting at our planes, then we were going to shoot back. This could not help but bring on further incidents and that he had better understand the full implications of this matter.

~~TOP SECRET~~

Memorandum for
The Secretary of State October 30, 1962

He raised the point that the argument the Cubans were making was that we were violating Cuban air space. I replied that if we had not been violating Cuban air space then we would still be believing what he and Khrushchev had said ~~[illegible]~~ -- that there were no long-range missiles in Cuba. In any case I said that this matter was far more serious than the air space over Cuba and involved peoples all over the world.

I said that he had better understand the situation and he had better communicate that understanding to Mr. Khrushchev. Mr. Khrushchev and he had misled us. The Soviet Union had secretly established missile bases in Cuba while at the same time proclaiming, privately and publicly, that this would never be done. I said those missile bases had to go and they had to go right away. We had to have a commitment by at least tomorrow that those bases would be removed. This was not an ultimatum, I said, but just a statement of fact. He should understand that if they did not remove those bases then we would remove them. His country might take retaliatory action but he should understand that before this was over, while there might be dead Americans there would also be dead Russians.

~~TOP SECRET~~

- 2 -

Source: Available at http://www.gwu.edu/~nsarchiv/nsa/cuba_mis_cri/621030%20Memorandum%20for%20Sec.%20of%20State.pdf

Source 8.2b: Top-Secret Memo from Robert Kennedy to Dean Rusk (Original) (continued)

Memorandum for
The Secretary of State

October 30, 1962

He asked me then what offer we were making. I said a letter had just been transmitted to the Soviet Embassy which stated in substance that the missile bases should be dismantled and all offensive weapons should be removed from Cuba. In return, if Cuba and Castro and the Communists ended their subversive activities in other Central and Latin-American countries, we would agree to keep peace in the Caribbean and not permit an invasion from American soil.

He then asked me about Khrushchev's other proposal dealing with the removal of the missiles from Turkey. I replied that there could be no quid pro quo -- no deal of this kind could be made. This was a matter that had to be considered by NATO and that it was up to NATO to make the decision. I said it was completely impossible for NATO to take such a step under the present threatening position of the Soviet Union. ~~K some time elapsed -- and per your instructions, I mentioned four or five months -- I said I was sure that these matters could be resolved satisfactorily.~~

Per your instructions I repeated that there could be no deal of any kind and that any steps toward easing tensions in other parts of the world largely depended on the Soviet Union and Mr.

~~TOP SECRET~~

Memorandum for
The Secretary of State

October 30, 1962

Khrushchev taking action in Cuba and taking it immediately.

I repeated to him that this matter could not wait and that he had better contact Mr. Khrushchev and have a commitment from him by the next day to withdraw the missile bases under United Nations supervision for otherwise, I said, there would be drastic consequences.

RFK:amn

~~TOP SECRET~~

Source 8.3: Khrushchev Remembers

Note: Nikita Khrushchev was the leader of the Soviet Union during the Cuban Missile Crisis. In his memoir, he recalls what President Kennedy told him during the crisis.

President Kennedy said that in exchange for the withdrawal of our missiles, he would remove American missiles from Turkey and Italy.

Source: Excerpt from *Khrushchev Remembers: The Last Testament.* Introduction, commentary, and notes by Edward Crankshaw, trans. and ed. by Strobe Talbott (Boston: Little, Brown, 1974), 512.

Source 8.4: Dobrynin Cable to Moscow (Modified)

Note: During the Cuban Missile Crisis, Anatoly Dobrynin was the Soviet Ambassador to the United States. Here, he recalls his negotiations with U.S. Attorney General Robert Kennedy.

"And what about Turkey?" I asked R. Kennedy.

"If that is the only obstacle to achieving the regulation I mentioned earlier, then the president doesn't see any **insurmountable** difficulties in resolving this issue," replied R. Kennedy. "The greatest difficulty for the president is the public discussion of the issue of Turkey. . . .

"However, President Kennedy is ready to come to agree on that question with N.S. Khrushchev, too. I think that in order to withdraw these bases from Turkey," R. Kennedy said, "we need 4–5 months. This is the minimal amount of time necessary for the U.S. government to do this, taking into account the procedures that exist within the **NATO** framework. On the whole Turkey issue," R. Kennedy added, "if Premier N.S. Khrushchev agrees with what I've said, we can continue to exchange opinions. . . . However, the president can't say anything public in this regard about Turkey." . . . R. Kennedy then warned that his comments about Turkey are extremely confidential; besides him and his brother, only 2–3 people know about it in Washington.

. . . After meeting with me he immediately went to see the president, with whom, as R. Kennedy said, he spends almost all his time now.

Source: Anatoly Dobrynin, from Russian Foreign Ministry archives, translation from copy provided by NHK, in Richard Ned Lebow and Janice Gross Stein, *We All Lost the Cold War* (Princeton, NJ: Princeton University Press, 1994), Appendix, 523–526, with minor revisions. http://www.gwu.edu/~nsarchiv/nsa/cuba_mis_cri/621027%20Dobrynin%20Cable%20to%20USSR.pdf

WORD BANK

insurmountable–unable to be solved
NATO–North Atlantic Treaty Organization

Source 8.5: Theodore Sorenson (Modified)

Note: Theodore Sorenson was the editor of Robert Kennedy's book *Thirteen Days*. The book made Kennedy's diary of the Cuban Missile Crisis public. Here, Sorenson admits that he took top-secret information out of the diary before it was published.

The president [Kennedy] recognized that, for Chairman Khrushchev to withdraw the missiles from Cuba, it would be undoubtedly helpful to him if he could say at the same time to his colleagues on the **Presidium**, "And we have been assured that the missiles will be coming out of Turkey." And so, after the **ExComm** meeting [on the evening of 27 October 1962], as I'm sure almost all of you know, a small group met in President Kennedy's office, and he instructed Robert Kennedy–at the suggestion of Secretary of State [Dean] Rusk–to deliver the letter to Ambassador Dobrynin for referral to Chairman Khrushchev, but to add orally what was not in the letter: that the missiles would come out of Turkey.

Ambassador Dobrynin felt that Robert Kennedy's book did not adequately express that the "deal" on the Turkish missiles was part of the resolution of the crisis. And here I have a confession to make to my colleagues on the American side, as well as to others who are present. I was the editor of Robert Kennedy's book. It was, in fact, a diary of those thirteen days. And his diary was very **explicit** that this was part of the deal; but at that time it was still a secret even on the American side, except for the six of us who had been present at that meeting. So I took it upon myself to edit that out of his diaries, and that is why the Ambassador is somewhat justified in saying that the diaries are not as explicit as his conversation.

Source: Theodore Sorensen, in *Back to the Brink: Proceedings of the Moscow Conference on the Cuban Missile Crisis*, January 27–28, 1989, eds., Bruce J. Allyn, James G. Blight, and David A. Welch (Lanham, MD: University Press of America, 1992), 92–93.

WORD BANK

Presidium–high-ranking members of the Soviet government
ExComm–President Kennedy's closest advisors
explicit–clearly stated

Source 8.6: Kennedy/Nixon Debates (Modified)

Note: In 1960, John F. Kennedy and Richard Nixon ran for president. Kennedy was a senator and Nixon was Vice President at the time. What follows is an excerpt from a debate prior to the election in which the men discuss the status of Cuba in 1960.

PAUL NIVEN: Mr. Vice President [Nixon], Senator Kennedy said last night that the [Eisenhower/Nixon] Administration must take responsibility for the loss of Cuba [to Communist control]. Would you compare the validity of that statement with the validity of your own statements in previous campaigns that the Truman Administration was responsible for the loss of China to the Communists?

RICHARD NIXON: Senator Kennedy has made some very strong criticisms of my part–or alleged part–in what has happened in Cuba. . . . Now with regard to Cuba, let me make one thing clear. There isn't any question but that we will defend our rights there. There isn't any question but that we will defend **Guantanamo** if it's attacked. There also isn't any question but that the free people of Cuba–the people who want to be free–are going to be supported and that they will **attain** their freedom. No, Cuba is not lost, and I don't think this kind of **defeatist** talk by Senator Kennedy helps the situation one bit.

FRANK McGEE: Senator Kennedy, would you care to comment?

MR. KENNEDY: In the first place I've never suggested that Cuba was lost except for the present. In my speech last night I indicated that I thought that Cuba one day again would be free. Where I've been critical of the Administration's policy [is in] the failure of the Administration to use its great influence to persuade the Cuban government to hold free elections, particularly in 1957 and 1958. I hope some day [Cuba] will rise; but I don't think it will rise if we continue the same policies toward Cuba that we did in recent years.

Source: Transcript of the Second Kennedy-Nixon Presidential Debate, October 7, 1960, available at http://www.debates.org/index.php?page=october-7-1960-debate-transcript

WORD BANK

Guantanamo–American military base in Cuba
attain–to get or to accomplish
defeatist–negative, reflecting defeat

Source 8.7: Memorandum to the President (Modified)

Note: In this top-secret memo to President Kennedy, Richard Goodwin reports on his 1961 meeting with Che Guevara. Guevara played a major role in helping the Communists come to power in Cuba.

TOP SECRET
MEMORANDUM FOR THE PRESIDENT
Subject: Conversation with Commandante Ernesto [Che] Guevara of Cuba

The conversation took place the evening of August 17 at 2 A.M. Several members of the Brazilian and Argentine delegations had made efforts . . . to arrange a meeting between me and Che. This was obviously done with Che's approval, if not his urging. . . .

He then said that they didn't want an understanding with the U.S., because they knew that was impossible. They would like a [temporary agreement]. . . . He thought we should put forth such a formula because we had public opinion to worry about whereas he could accept anything without worrying about public opinion. . . .

He then went on to say that he wanted to thank us very much for the [Bay of Pigs] invasion–that it had been a great political victory for them–enabled them to consolidate–and transformed them from an aggrieved little country to an equal.

Source: Richard Goodwin, "Memorandum for the President," August 22, 1961, http://www.gwu.edu/~nsarchiv/bayofpigs/19610822.pdf

SOURCE 8.8: DOBRYNIN MEMOIR

Note: Here, Anatoly Dobrynin recalls his negotiations with Robert Kennedy during the Cuban Missile Crisis.

The next day, October 30, Robert Kennedy informed me that the president confirmed the accord on closing American missile bases in Turkey, and that while we could be sure that the appropriate steps would be taken, no connection was to be drawn in public between his decision and the events surrounding Cuba. He said that the White House was not prepared to formalize the accord, even by means of strictly confidential letters, and that the American side preferred not to engage in any correspondence on so sensitive an issue. Very privately, Robert Kennedy added that some day–who knows?–he might run for president, and his prospects could be damaged if this secret deal about the missiles in Turkey were to come out.

I relayed the Kennedy reply to Moscow. Two days later, I told Robert Kennedy that Khrushchev agreed to those considerations and had no doubt that the president would keep his word. . . .

Khrushchev's failure to insist on a public pledge by Kennedy cost him dearly. Kennedy was proclaimed the big winner in the crisis because no one knew about the secret deal. Khrushchev had been humiliated into withdrawing our missiles from Cuba with no obvious gain.

Source: Excerpt from Anatoly Dobrynin, *In Confidence: Moscow's Ambassador to America's Six Cold War Presidents (1962–1986)* (New York: Times Books, 1995), 90.

Tool 8.1: Graphic Organizer for Scenario 2

	What does the document say?	What light does it shed on why the U.S. might have wanted to conceal the truth?
Source 8.6: Kennedy/ Nixon debates		
Source 8.7: Goodwin memo to President Kennedy		
Source 8.8: Dobrynin memoir		

Tool 8.2: Textbook Excerpts

Excerpt 1

The defeat of the mercenary Brigade at the Bay of Pigs made the U.S. think that the only way of crashing the Cuban Revolution was through a direct military intervention. The U.S. immediately embarked on its preparation. . . . As part of their hostile plans, the U.S. considered a self-inflicted aggression in connection with the Guantanamo Naval Base that would allow them to blame Cuba and provide a pretext for invading the island. With that aim, constant provocations took place from the U.S. side of the base; Marines shooting toward Cuban territory, sometimes for several hours.

Does this excerpt come from a textbook from

a. Russia
b. Cuba
c. United States
d. Great Britain

What words and phrases give you clues about where this except is from?

Excerpt 2

In 1960 the United States took severe economic sanctions against Cuba, refusing to supply oil to the island, and cutting back on the purchases of sugar, Cuba's largest and most important export. Forced to make a choice, the Cuban government nationalized the oil industry, sugar processing plants, and other American-owned businesses in Cuba in the summer of 1961. In response, the United States set up an economic blockade of Cuba, stopping trade and prohibiting American tourism to the island. In September 1960, Congress passed a law denying American foreign aid to any nation that assisted Cuba economically or militarily. . . . In this dire situation the Soviet Union and other Communist nations stepped in to purchase Cuban sugar and provide the country with oil and other essential goods.

Does this excerpt come from a textbook from

a. Russia
b. Cuba
c. United States
d. Great Britain

What words and phrases give you clues about where this except is from?

Source: Adapted from an activity provided by the National History Education Clearinghouse, a partnership of George Mason University, the Stanford School of Education, and the American Historical Association, and funded by the U.S. Department of Education, http://teachinghistory.org/history-content/quiz/24233, used by permission. Textbook excerpts from Dana Lindaman and Kyle Ward, *History Lessons: How Textbooks from Around the World Portray U.S. History* (New York: The New Press, 2004), 297–306.

Suggested Resources

http://www.gwu.edu/~nsarchiv/nsa/cuba_mis_cri/
Housed by George Washington University, the National Security Archive includes declassified documents, audio clips, photographs, and a chronology of the crisis.

http://avalon.law.yale.edu/subject_menus/msc_cubamenu.asp
Housed by Yale University, the Avalon Project has a collection of legal and diplomatic documents related to the Cuban Missile Crisis. Memoranda from meetings and phone conversations as well as telegrams between government officials are included.

http://www.mtholyoke.edu/acad/intrel/cuba.htm
Housed by Mt. Holyoke College, Professor of International Politics Vincent Ferraro maintains collections of documents pertaining to American foreign policy. One focuses exclusively on the Cuban Missile Crisis and includes documents from a range of perspectives, including Fidel Castro and Che Guevara.

http://www.youtube.com/watch?v=XbfkXu9qEIM
Watch Kennedy's televised speech to the nation on October 22, 1962. Here Kennedy outlines what had been happening to date in Cuba and between the U.S. and the Soviet Union.

http://www.jfklibrary.org/Historical+Resources/JFK+in+History/Cuban+Missile+Crisis.htm
The Kennedy Presidential Library and Museum in Massachusetts also contains a collection of documents and resources devoted to the Cuban Missile Crisis, including television and radio recordings.

Notes

Introduction

1. *The New York Times*, April 4, 1921.

2. See the multiple-choice item relating to Prosser on the NAEP website, http://nces.ed.gov/nationsreportcard/ITMRLS/itemdisplay.asp. The reference to *Gitlow v. State of New York* appears on page 29 of the *United States History Framework for the National Assessment of Educational Progress* (Washington, D.C.: 2006). National Assessment Governing Board, Department of Education.

3. Gina Biancarosa and Catherine E. Snow, *Reading Next: A Vision for Action and Research in Middle and High School Literacy* (New York: Carnegie Corporation, 2004), 12.

4. See Reed Stevens, Sam Wineburg, Leslie Herrenkohl, and Philip Bell, "Comparative Understanding of School Subjects: Past, Present, and Future," *Review of Research in Education* (2005), *75*(2), 125–157.

5. See Diane Ravitch, *The Language Police: How Pressure Groups Restrict What Students Learn* (2003), and Tamim Ansary, "The muddle machine: Confessions of a textbook editor," *Edutopia* (2008), available at http://www.edutopia.org/muddle-machine.

Chapter 1

1. David A. Price, *Love and Hate in Jamestown: John Smith, Pocahontas, and the Heart of a New Nation* (New York: Knopf, 2003).

2. Ibid., 59.

3. Camilla Townsend, *Pocahontas and the Powhatan Dilemma* (New York: Hill and Wang, 2004), 52.

4. John Smith, "A True Relation by Captain John Smith 1608," in *Narratives of Early Virginia, 1606–1625*, ed. Lyon Gardiner Tyler (New York: Charles Scribner's Sons, 1907), 48. Online facsimile edition at www.americanjourneys.org/aj-074/

5. Philip L. Barbour, ed., *The Complete Works of Captain John Smith (1580–1631),* vol. 2 (Chapel Hill: University of North Carolina Press, 1986), 151.

6. "Powhatan" is the name commonly used for both the tribe led by Pocahontas's father and the chief himself. Wahunsunacock may be a more accurate name for the Indian chief.

7. Henry Adams, "Captain John Smith," *The North American Review 104* (214) (January 1867) 1–30. Also available online at http://cdl.library.cornell.edu/cgi-bin/moa/moa-cgi?notisid=ABQ7578-0104&byte=93017179. Adams's article is a review of Charles Deane's editions of Smith's *True Relation* and Edward Maria Wingfield's *A Discourse of Virginia* in which he questioned Smith's truthfulness, but it is Adams who does a full assault on the same.

8. Paul Lewis, *The Great Rogue: A Biography of John Smith* (New York: David McKay Company, 1966).

9. J. A. Leo Lemay, *The American Dream of Captain John Smith* (Charlottesville: University Press of Virginia, 1991). Also see J. A. Leo Lemay, *Did Pocahontas Save Captain John Smith?* (Athens: The University of Georgia Press, 1992).

10. Philip L. Barbour, *Pocahontas and Her World: A Chronicle of America's First Settlement in Which Is Related the Story of the Indians and the Englishmen–Particularly Captain John Smith, Captain Samuel Argall, and Master John Rolfe* (Boston: Houghton Mifflin, 1970).

11. These words were used by George Percy, an Englishman who traveled on the trio of boats to Jamestown in 1607 and eventually succeeded Smith as leader of the colony. In *A Trewe Relacyon of the Pcedeinges and Ocurrentes of Momente wch have hapned in Virginia from the Tyme Sr Thomas GATES was shippwrackte uppon the BERMUDES ano 1609 untill my depture outt of the Country wch was in ano Dñi 1612.* (Called "A True Relation" by George Percy, 1609–1612).

12. See one examination of the origins and uses of these mythic representations during the colonial, federalist, and antebellum periods in Robert S. Tilton, *Pocahontas: The Evolution of an American Narrative* (Cambridge, UK: Cambridge University Press, 1994). For one example of how scholars look at representations of the story in later years, see Frederic W. Gleach, "Pocahontas at the Fair: Crafting Identities at the 1907 Jamestown Exposition," *Ethnohistory 50* (3) (Summer 2003), 419–445.

13. Townsend, *Pocahontas and the Powhatan Dilemma*; Helen Rountree, *Pocahontas, Powhatan, Opechancanough: Three Indian Lives Changed by Jamestown* (Charlottesville: University of Virginia Press, 2005).

14. Townsend, *Pocahontas and the Powhatan Dilemma*, 56.

15. E. Randolph Turner, "Native American Protohistoric Interactions in the Powhatan Core Area," *Powhatan Foreign Relations*, ed. Helen Rountree (Charlottesville: University Press of Virginia, 1993), 76–93.

16. Louise Woodville, "Uncovering Powhatan's Empire," *Humanities: The Magazine of the National Endowment for the Humanities, 28* (1) (January/February 2007), 17–19.

17. Townsend, *Pocahontas and the Powhatan Dilemma*, 14.

18. Barbour, *Pocahontas and Her World*, 4.

19. Helen C. Rountree, "Pocahontas: The Hostage Who Became Famous," *Sifters: Native American Women's Lives*, ed. Theda Perdue (Oxford: Oxford University Press, 2001), 27.

20. David Lowenthal, "Fabricating Heritage," *History and Memory, 10* (1) (Spring, 1998)

Chapter 2

1. Elias Phinney, *History of the Battle at Lexington on the Morning of the 19th of April, 1775* (Boston: Printed by Phelps and Farnham, 1825); Ian M. G. Quimby, "The Doolittle Engravings of the Battle of Lexington and Concord," *Winterthur Portfolio 4* (1968), 83–108.

2. Ezra Ripley, *A History of the Fight at Concord on the 19th of April, 1775* (Concord, MA: Herman Atwill, 1832).

3. Harold Murdock, *The Nineteenth of April 1775* (Boston: Houghton Mifflin, 1925), 362.

4. Murdock, 363.

5. Arthur B. Tourtellot, *Lexington and Concord: The Beginning of the War of the American Revolution* (New York: W.W. Norton & Co., 1959), 135.

6. Deposition of Nathaniel Mulliken et al., in Clement Sawtell, *A Narrative of the Excursion and Ravages of the King's Troops under the Command of General Gage* (New York: *The New York Times* and Arno Press, 1968).

7. John Barker, *The British in Boston: The Diary of Lt. John Barker* (New York: The New York Times & Arno Press, 1969).

8. Samuel Steinberg, *The United States: Story of a Free People* (Boston: Allyn and Bacon, 1963), 92, reprinted in P. S. Bennett, *What Happened at Lexington Green?* (Menlo Park, CA: Addison-Wesley, 1970), 31.

9. Ezra Stiles, *The Literary Diary of Ezra Stiles*, ed., under the Authority of the Corporation of Yale University, by Franklin Bowditch Dexter (New York: Charles Scribner's Sons, 1901).

10. See Sam Wineburg, *Historical Thinking and Other Unnatural Acts: Charting the Future of Teaching the Past* (Philadelphia: Temple University Press, 2001), 63–88; Sam Wineburg, "What Does NCATE Have to Say to Future Teachers of History? Not Much," *Phi Delta Kappan 86:9* (2005), 662.

11. Wineburg, *Historical Thinking and Other Unnatural Acts: Charting the Future of Teaching the Past*, 67.

12. Ibid., 68.

Chapter 3

1. Abraham Lincoln, *Speeches and Writings 1832–1858*, ed. Don E. Fehrenbacher (New York: Library of America, 1989), 512.

2. Lerone Bennett, "Was Abe Lincoln a White Supremacist?" *Ebony* (February 1968), 35–42.

3. Brian R. Dirck, ed., *Lincoln Emancipated: The President and the Politics of Race* (Dekalb: Northern Illinois University Press, 2007).

4. For examples of scholarship focused on Lincoln's views on race and slavery, see Dirck, *Lincoln Emancipated*; *Our Lincoln: New Perspectives on Lincoln and His World*, ed. Eric Foner (New York: W.W. Norton & Co., 2008); and Phillip M. Guerty, ed., "Lincoln, Race, and Slavery," *Organization of American Historians Magazine of History*, October 2007.

5. See Abraham Lincoln, *The Collected Works of Abraham Lincoln* (Ann Arbor: University of Michigan Digital Library Production Services, 2001), available at http://quod.lib.umich.edu/l/lincoln/

6. Douglas L. Wilson, *Lincoln's Sword: The Presidency and the Power of Words* (New York: Vintage Books, 2006), 6.

7. David Herbert Donald, *Lincoln Reconsidered: Essays on the Civil War* (New York: Vintage Books, 2001), 13.

8. Ibid., 30.

9. Don E. Fehrenbacher, "Only His Stepchildren: Lincoln and the Negro," *Civil War History 20* (1974), 293–310, 293, as quoted in Richard Carwardine, *Lincoln: A Life of Purpose and Power* (New York: Alfred A. Knopf, 2006), 33; Richard N. Current, *The Lincoln Nobody Knows* (New York: McGraw-Hill, 1963).

10. Current, *The Lincoln Nobody Knows,* 19–20.

11. The audiences would not be directly electing either man, as until the passage of the 17th amendment in 1913, state legislatures elected U.S. senators.

12. In each of the debates, one candidate opened with a 60-minute speech, his opponent followed with a 90-minute speech, and then the original speaker had 30 minutes to respond and close.

13. James W. Loewen, *Lies My Teacher Told Me* (New York: Free Press, 1995), 153.

14. Eric Foner, *Free Soil, Free Labor, Free Men: The Ideology of the Republican Party Before the Civil War* (New York: Oxford University Press, 1995), 263. Foner wrote: "At times during the 1850's it seemed that the only weapon in the Democrats' political arsenal was the charge that the Republicans were pro-Negro," and noted that Missouri legislator Francis P. Blair described it as the "incessant theme" of Douglas's campaign.

15. Ibid., 261. These states were Iowa, Indiana, Illinois, and Oregon.

16. Garry Wills, "Dishonest Abe," *Time*, October 5, 1992, 41.

17. Doris Kearns Goodwin, *Team of Rivals: The Political Genius of Abraham Lincoln* (New York: Simon and Schuster, 2005), 8.

18. Foner, *Free Soil, Free Labor, Free Men,* 261–262.

19. Phillip Shaw Paludan, "Lincoln and Negro Slavery: I Haven't Got Time for the Pain," *Journal of the Abraham Lincoln Association* (Summer 2006), paragraph 32 (http://www.historycooperative.org/journals/jala/27.2/paludan.html)

20. George M. Fredrickson, *The Black Image in the White Mind: The Debate on Afro-American Character and Destiny, 1817–1914* (Chicago: University of Chicago, 1971), 43.

21. Paludan,"Lincoln and Negro Slavery."

22. Eric Foner, "Lincoln and Colonization," in *Our Lincoln: New Perspectives on Lincoln and His World*, ed. Eric Foner (New York: W.W. Norton & Co., 2008), 144.

23. Lerone Bennett, *Forced into Glory: Abraham Lincoln's White Dream* (Chicago: Johnson Publishing, 2000).

24. For recent examples, see Foner, "Lincoln and Colonization"; Phillip S. Paludan, "Greeley, Colonization, and a "Deputation of Negroes" in *Lincoln Emancipated: The President and the Politics of Race*, eds. Brian R. Dirck and Allen C. Guelzo (DeKalb: Northern Illinois University Press, 2007), 29–46; Kevin R. C. Gutzman, "Abraham Lincoln, Jeffersonian: The Colonization Chimera" in *Lincoln Emancipated: The President and the Politics of Race*, eds. Brian R. Dirck and Allen C. Guelzo (DeKalb: Northern Illinois University Press, 2007), 47–72; Richard Blackett, "Lincoln and Colonization," *OAH Magazine of History 21* (4) (2007), 19–22.

25. Fehrenbacher, "Only His Stepchildren: Lincoln and the Negro," 308.

26. Foner, "Lincoln and Colonization".

27. See *The Collected Works of Abraham Lincoln*, vol. 5, 372, available at http://quod.lib.umich.edu/l/lincoln/. Statements such as "Without the institution of slavery and the colored race as a basis, the war could not have an existence" angered prominent Blacks such as Frederick Douglass.

28. Abraham Lincoln, *The Collected Works of Abraham Lincoln* (Ann Arbor: University of Michigan Digital Library Production Services, 2001) vol. 5, 389, available at http://quod.lib.umich.edu/l/lincoln/

29. James N. Leiker, "The Difficulties of Understanding Abe: Lincoln's Reconciliation of Racial Inequality and Natural Rights," in *Lincoln Emancipated: The President and The Politics of Race*, ed. Brian R. Dirck (Dekalb: Northern Illinois University Press, 2007).

30. Sam Wineburg, "Reading Abraham Lincoln: An Expert/Expert Study in the Interpretation of Historical Texts," *Cognitive Science 22* (1998), 319–346.

31. Samuel S. Wineburg and Janice Fournier, "Contextualized Thinking in History," in *Cognitive and Instructional Processes in History and the Social Sciences*, eds. M. Carretero and J. F. Voss (Hillsdale, NJ: Erlbaum, 1994).

32. See D. W. Johnson and R. T. Johnson, "Critical Thinking Through Controversy," *Educational Leadership*, May 1988, 58–64; National History Education Clearinghouse, *Structured Academic Controversy in the History Classroom*, http://teachinghistory.org/teaching-materials/teaching-guides/21731

33. Daisy Martin and Sam Wineburg, "Seeing Thinking on the Web," *The History Teacher 41:3*. (Long Beach, CA: Society for History Education, 2008). http://www.historycooperative.org/journals/ht/41.3/martin.html

Chapter 4

1. Howard Zinn, *A People's History of the United States* (New York: Harper Perennial, 2005), 4; Kirkpatrick Sale, *Christopher Columbus and the Conquest of Paradise* (New York: Tauris Parke, 2006).

2. Sam Wineburg, "Unnatural and Essential: The Nature of Historical Thinking," *Teaching History 129* (December 2007), 6–11; Sam Wineburg and Jack Schneider, "Inverting Bloom's Taxonomy," *Education Week* (September 2009), 28; Sam Wineburg, "Columbus Day: 1892 not 1492," *Los Angeles Times* (October 10, 2005), 18.

3. Wineburg, "Unnatural and Essential," 6–11.

4. See Matthew Frye Jacobson, *Whiteness of a Different Color: European Immigration and the Alchemy of Race* (Cambridge: Harvard University Press, 1999).

5. Article II of the National Council of the United States of North America, quoted in Carl Fremont Brand, "The History of the Know Nothing Party in Indiana," *Indiana Magazine of History 18* (1922), 73.

6. "Christopher Columbus–Discoverer of the New World," *Connecticut Catholic 25* (May 1878), 4.

7. Christopher J. Kauffman, *Faith and Fraternalism: The History of the Knights of Columbus, 1882–1982* (New York: Harper and Row, 1982), 16.

8. Thomas J. Schlereth, "Columbia, Columbus, and Columbianism," *Journal of American History 79* (December 1992), 937–968.

9. See "The Tweed Ring in Charge," Chapter 9, in Diane Ravitch, *The Great School Wars: New York City 1805–1973* (New York: Basic Books, 1974), 92–99.

Chapter 5

1. For the full letter, go to http://memory.loc.gov/learn/lessons/99/edison/images/mrs2.gif

2. David Nye, *Electrifying America: Social Meanings of a New Technology, 1880–1940* (Cambridge, MA: MIT Press, 1990), 299.

3. D. Clayton Brown, *Electricity for Rural America: The Fight for the REA* (Westport, CT: Greenwood Press, 1980), xv.

4. Brown, *Electricity for Rural America*, xvi.

5. For more on this, see Ruth Schwartz Cowen's notion of a "work process" in *More Work for Mother: The Ironies of Household Technology from the Open Hearth to the Microwave* (New York: Basic Books, 1983), 11–12.

6. Susan Strasser, *Never Done: A History of American Housework* (New York: Henry Holt, 1982), 105.

7. Brown, *Electricity for Rural America*, xiii.

8. Ibid., xiv.

9. Robert Caro, *The Years of Lyndon Johnson: The Path to Power* (New York: Alfred A. Knopf, 1982), 504–509.

10. Nye, *Electrifying America*, 303.

11. Ibid., 287.

12. Brown, *Electricity for Rural America*, 75.

13. Ibid., 112.

14. Strasser, *Never Done*, 81.

15. Cowen, *More Work for Mother*, 173.

16. Nye, *Electrifying America*, 267.

17. Ibid., 24.

18. In another example, Strasser (*Never Done*, 279) claims that "almost half" of American households had a dishwasher by 1980–59 years after Mrs. Lathrop wrote about hers!

19. Cowen, *More Work for Mother*, 159.

20. Ibid.

21. Italics added. For the full letter, go to http://memory.loc.gov/learn/lessons/99/edison/images/mrs2.gif

22. Cowen, *More Work for Mother*, 174.

23. Ibid., 178.

24. Patricia Albjerg Graham, "Expansion and Exclusion: A History of Women in American Higher Education," in *History of Women in the United States: Education*, ed. Nancy Cott, (New York: K. G. Saur, 1992), 219.

25. Ibid.

26. Ibid.

27. Ibid., 223.

28. Ibid., 225. For another article on these statistics, see Pamela Roby, "Women and American Higher Education," *Annals of the American Academy of Political and Social Science 404* (127) (November 1972), 118–139.

29. Barbara Miller Solomon, *In the Company of Educated Women: A History of Women and Higher Education in America* (New Haven, CT: Yale University Press, 1985), 121.

30. W. Elliot Brownlee, "Household Values, Women's Work, and Economic Growth, 1800–1930," *History of Women in the United States: Domestic Ideology and Domestic Work, Part I*, ed. Nancy Cott, (New York: K. G. Saur, 1992), 205.

31. Brown, *Electricity for Rural America*, 9.

32. Ibid., 116–117.

33. Strasser, *Never Done*, 268.

34. For more on this, see Cowen, *More Work for Mother*.

35. Cowen, *More Work for Mother*, 99.

36. Ibid., 174.

37. Ibid., 178.

38. Ibid.

39. See Cowen, *More Work for Mother*, Chapter 3 for her argument about "the invention of housework."

Chapter 6

1. An argument can be made that Steinbeck's novel is a work of truth, but the point is that the "rules" of fictional stories and historical narratives differ. This is not to argue that in fiction, there isn't truth, but rather that fiction allows invented characters, and straying from the evidence to tell that truth. Or, as Davidson and Lytle state, "Unlike a historian, he [Steinbeck] was not bound by strict rules of evidence and explanation, only by the true expression of the human condition." See James W.

Davidson & Mark H. Lytle, *After the Fact: The Art of Historical Detection* (Boston: McGraw-Hill Higher Education, 1999), 260.

2. Donald Worster, *Dust Bowl: The Southern Plains in the 1930s* (New York: Oxford University Press, 1979), 29.

3. Alvin O. Turner, ed., *Letters from the Dust Bowl* (author Caroline Henderson) (Norman: University of Oklahoma Press, 2001), 10. In 1819, explorer Stephen Long would call it the former and after the Civil War, maps would identify the Oklahoma Panhandle as the latter.

4. Historians differ on exactly what years they call the beginning and the end of the Dust Bowl. But they agree that the storms worsened after 1933 and that 1935–1937 were the worst years.

5. R. Douglas Hurt, *The Dust Bowl: An Agricultural and Social History* (Chicago: Nelson-Hall, 1981), 3.

6. Turner, *Letters from the Dust Bowl,* 19; Worster, *Dust Bowl,* 15.

7. "Huge Dust Cloud, Blown 1,500 Miles, Dims City 5 Hours," *New York Times,* May 12, 1934, 1.

8. Worster, *Dust Bowl,* 14.

9. Pauline W. Grey, "The Black Sunday of April 14, 1935," *Pioneer Stories of Meade County,* 1950, 25, www.kansasmemory.org/item/211072

10. Ibid., 27. Accompanying this was Grey's "satisfying peace" that her efforts earlier that day to patch up all the cracks in her house were holding, so she could have "died happily!"

11. Ibid., 26.

12. See Worster, *Dust Bowl,* Chapter 3, "Okies and Exodusters," for a detailed rendering of migration rates and patterns.

13. Hurt, *The Dust Bowl,* 91–92. For a discussion of how previous histories differed on this point, see Harry C. McDean, "Dust Bowl Historiography," in *Americans View Their Dust Bowl Experience,* eds. J. R. Wunder, F. Kaye, and V. Carstensen (Boulder: University Press of Colorado, 1999), 366–384.

14. Timothy Egan, *The Worst Hard Time: The Untold Story of Those Who Survived The Great American Dust Bowl* (Boston: Houghton Mifflin Company, 2006), 192; Hurt, *The Dust Bowl,* 53–54.

15. McDean, "Dust Bowl Historiography," 369.

16. Worster, *Dust Bowl,* 66.

17. Ibid., 77.

18. Ibid., 83.

19. Ibid., 88; Hurt, *The Dust Bowl,* 21.

20. See the Library of Congress collection at http://memory.loc.gov/ammem/award97/ndfahtml/hult_sod.html for pictures of these almost extinct sod houses.

21. Worster, *Dust Bowl,* 94.

22. Ibid., 97.

23. Hurt, *The Dust Bowl,* 15.

24. See Paul Bonnifield, *The Dust Bowl: Men, Dirt, and Depression* (Albuquerque: University of New Mexico Press, 1979).

25. See James C. Malin, *The Grassland of North America: Prolegomena to Its History* (Lawrence, KS: Author, 1961).

26. McDean, "Dust Bowl Historiography."

27. William Cronon, "A Place for Stories: Nature, History, and Narrative," *The Journal of American History 78*(4) (1992) 1347–1376.

28. For more on the "Opening Up the Textbook" approach and how to work with textbooks, see Chapter 8 on the Cuban Missile Crisis. Also see the following: Sam Wineburg, "Opening Up the Textbook and Offering Students a Second Voice," *Education Week,* June 5, 2007, 36–37; Daisy Martin, "From Lecture to Lesson Through 'Opening Up the Textbook,'" *Organization of American Historians Newsletter,* November 2008, 9; Daisy Martin and Chauncey Monte-Sano, "Inquiry, Controversy, and Ambiguous Texts: Learning to Teach for Historical Thinking," in *History Education 101: The Past, Present, and Future of Teacher Preparation,* eds. W. Warren & D. Cantu (Charlotte, NC: Information Age Publishing, 2007), 167–186. See as well the many resources at http://sheg.stanford.edu

29. The language of "support, contest or extend" comes from Robert B. Bain, "'They Thought the World Was Flat?' Applying the Principles of *How People Learn* in Teaching High School History," in *How Students Learn History, Mathematics, and Science in the Classroom,* eds. M. Suzanne Donovan and John Branford (Washington, D.C.: National Academy Press, 2005), 179–213.

30. H. E. Dregne, "Desertification of Arid Lands," in *Physics of Desertification,* eds. F. El-Baz and M. H. A. Hassan (Dordrecht, The Netherlands: Martinus Nijhoff), 4–34.

Chapter 7

1. Douglas Brinkley, *Rosa Parks: A Life* (New York: Penguin Books, 2000), 106. There are a variety of accounts of what the driver actually said, ranging from "Let me have those front seats. . . . Y'all better make it light on yourselves and let me have those seats" to "Niggers move back." *My Story* by Rosa Parks with Jim Haskins (New York: Puffin Books, 1992) in Janet Stevenson, "Rosa Parks Wouldn't Budge," *American Heritage XXIII* (2) (February 1972).

2. Stevenson, "Rosa Parks Wouldn't Budge."

3. Sam Wineburg, "Goodbye, Columbus," *Smithsonian Magazine 39*(2) (2008), 98–104.

4. Sam Wineburg and Chauncey Monte-Sano, "Famous Americans: The Changing Pantheon of American Heroes," *Journal of American History 93*(2) (2008), 1186–1202.

5. U.S. Department of Commerce Weather Bureau, *Local Climatological Data, with Comparative Data, Montgomery, Alabama,* 1955 (available through NOAA Satellite and Information Service, http://www.nesdis.noaa.gov/).

6. Rosa Parks, interview by Sidney Rogers, *Rosa Parks: Beginning the Bus Boycott,* Pacific Radio Service Interview, Summer 1956.

7. See, for example, Joy Hakim's otherwise excellent chapter in *A History of US: All the People 1945–2001* (New York: Oxford University Press, 1993), 78: "But on the evening of the first day of December in 1955, Mrs. Parks was mostly just plain tired. She had put in a full day at her job. She didn't feel well, and her neck and back hurt. She got on a bus and headed home."

8. Rosa Parks, cited in Alden D. Morris, *The Origins of the Civil Rights Movement: Black Communities Organizing for Change* (New York: Free Press, 1984), 51.

9. Ibid.

10. "Parks, Rosa Lee," *The World Book Encyclopedia* (Chicago: World Book Inc., 1989).

11. Gerald Danzer, J. Jorge Klor de Alva, Larry S. Krieger, Louis Wilson, and Nancy Woloch, *The Americans* (Evanston, IL: McDougal Littell, 2003), 910.

12. Joyce Appleby, Alan Brinkley, and James McPherson, *The American Journey* (Chicago: Glencoe/McGraw-Hill, 2003), 841.

13. Winthrop D. Jordan, Miriam Greenblatt, and John S. Bowes, *The Americans: History of a Free People* (Evanston, IL: McDougal Littell, 1985), 721.

14. Montgomery City Code, Chapter 6, Sections 10–11.

15. Brinkley, *Rosa Parks: A Life,* 58, 106.

16. Ibid., 94–97.

17. See Elizabeth Loftus and Katherine Ketcham, *Witness for the Defense: The Accused, the Eyewitness and the Expert Who Puts Memory on Trial* (New York: St. Martin's Griffin, 1992).

18. Rosa Parks with Jim Haskins, *Rosa Parks: My Story* (New York: Dial Books, 1992), 113.

19. Rosa Parks with Jim Haskins, *I Am Rosa Parks* (New York: Dial Books, 1997), 8.

20. Rogers, *Rosa Parks: Beginning the Bus Boycott.*

21. Montgomery City Code, Chapter 6, Sections 10–11.

22. Montgomery City Code, downloaded from http://www.blackpast.org/?q=primary/browder-v-gayle-1956

23. Title 48, § 301(31a, b, c), Code of Alabama of 1940, as amended, at http://faculty.washington.edu/qtaylor/documents_us/browder_v_gayle.htm

24. *Rosa Parks v. City of Montgomery*, appellate court brief, filed March 28, 1956, Alabama Court of Appeals.

25. Rogers, *Rosa Parks: Beginning the Bus Boycott.*

26. Ibid., 4:00–4:33.

27. Rosa Parks, interviewed by Lynn Neary, *Civil Rights Icon Rosa Parks Dies*, National Public Radio, at http://www.npr.org/templates/story/story.php?storyId=4973548

28. Stewart Burns, *Daybreak of Freedom: The Montgomery Bus Boycott* (Chapel Hill: University of North Carolina Press, 1997), 34.

29. *Atlanta Constitution*, August 16, 1900, cited in Burns, 34, n. 15.

30. *Atlanta Constitution*, September 20, 1900, cited in August Meier and Elliot Rudwick, "The Boycott Movement Against Jim Crow Streetcars in the South, 1900–1906," *Journal of American History* (March 1969), 756–775.

31. Jo Ann Gibson Robinson, *The Montgomery Bus Boycott and the Women Who Started It: The Memoir of Jo Ann Gibson Robinson* (Knoxville: University of Tennessee Press, 1987).

32. E. R. Shipp, "Rosa Parks, 92, Founding Symbol of Civil Rights Movement, Dies," *The New York Times*, October 25, 2005, at http://www.nytimes.com/2005/10/25/national/25parks.html?adxnnl=1&pagewanted=2

33. Ralph Abernathy, "The Natural History of a Social Movement" (Master's thesis, Atlanta, Georgia, 1958), at http://historicalthinkingmatters.org/rosaparks/1/sources/22/

34. Ibid.

35. Shipp, "Rosa Parks, 92, Founding Symbol of Civil Rights Movement, Dies.

36. See Note 2, "Social Revolution," from *Teaching with Documents: An Act of Courage, the Arrest Records of Rosa Parks*, the National Archives website, "Educators and Students," at http://www.archives.gov/education/lessons/rosa-parks/

37. *Historical Thinking Matters*, Resources for Teachers, sample student work (Student B) at http://historicalthinkingmatters.org/rosaparks/1/studentwork/paper2/

Chapter 8

1. George Tames, "Men and Policy," *The New York Times*, December 10, 1962, 11.

2. Ralph Volney Harlow and Hermon N. Noyes, *Story of America* (New York: Holt, Rinehart and Winston, 1964), 793.

3. Richard N. Current, Alexander DeConde, and Harris L. Dante, *United States History* (Atlanta: Scott, Foresman and Co., 1967), 751.

4. Richard C. Wade, Howard B. Wilder, and Louise C. Wade, *A History of the United States* (Boston: Houghton Mifflin Company, 1966), 827.

5. Robert F. Kennedy, *Thirteen Days: A Memoir of the Cuban Missile Crisis* (New York: New American Library, 1969), 107–109.

6. Robert Kennedy, "Memorandum for the Secretary of State from the Attorney General," Office of the Attorney General, Washington, D.C., October 30, 1962.

7. Nikita Khrushchev, *Khrushchev Remembers: The Last Testament*, trans., ed. Strobe Talbott (Boston: Little, Brown, 1974), 512.

8. Henry N. Drewry and Thomas H. O'Connor, *America Is* (New York: Glencoe, 1995), 648.

9. Edward L. Ayers et al., *The American Anthem* (Austin, TX: Holt, Rinehart and Winston, 2007), 885.

10. Sam Wineburg, "Opening Up the Textbook and Offering Students a Second Voice," *Education Week*, June 5, 2007, 3, 37; Daisy Martin, "From Lecture to Lesson Through 'Opening Up the Textbook,'" *Organization of American Historians Newsletter*, November 2008, 9; Daisy Martin and Chauncey Monte-Sano, "Inquiry, Controversy, and Ambiguous Texts: Learning to Teach for Historical Thinking," in *History Education 101: The Past, Present, and Future of Teacher Preparation,* ed. W. Warren and D. Cantu (Charlotte, NC: Information Age Publishing, 2007), 167–186.

11. Kennedy, "Memorandum for the Secretary of State from the Attorney General."

12. Anatoly Dobrynin, from Russian Foreign Ministry archives, translation from copy provided by NHK [Japanese TV station], in Richard Ned Lebow and Janice Gross Stein, *We All Lost the Cold War* (Princeton, NJ: Princeton University Press, 1994), Appendix, 523–526, with minor revisions. http://www.gwu.edu/~nsarchiv/nsa/cuba_mis_cri/621027%20Dobrynin%20Cable%20to%20USSR.pdf

13. Thomas Blanton, "Annals of Brinkmanship," *The Wilson Quarterly*, Summer 1997, 90–93.

14. Ibid., 91.

15. McGeorge Bundy, *Danger and Survival: Choices About the Bomb in the First Fifty Years* (New York: Random House, 1987), 432–436.

16. Anatoly Dobrynin, *In Confidence: Moscow's Ambassador to America's Six Cold War Presidents (1962–1986)* (New York: Times Books, 1995), 90.

17. David Self [Screenwriter], *Thirteen Days.* DVD. Directed by Roger Donaldson. New Line Cinema, 2001.

18. Philip Brenner, "Turning History on Its Head," the National Security Archive, George Washington University, at http://www.gwu.edu/~nsarchiv/nsa/cuba_mis_cri/brenner.htm#2

19. See, for instance, Graham Allison and Philip Zelikow, *Essence of Decision*, 2nd ed. (New York: Longman, 1999); James G. Blight and David A. Welch, *On the Brink: Americans and Soviets Reexamine the Cuban Missile Crisis* (New York: Hill and Wang, 1989).

20. Brenner, "Turning History on Its Head."

21. Sergei N. Khrushchev, *Nikita Khrushchev and the Creation of a Superpower* (University Park: Pennsylvania State University Press, 2000), 641.

22. Blanton, "Annals of Brinkmanship," 93.

23. Barton Bernstein, "Reconsidering the Missile Crisis," in *The Cuban Missile Crisis Revisited,* ed. J. A. Nathan (New York: St. Martin's, 1992), 106.

Index

About the Authors

Sam Wineburg is the Margaret Jacks Professor of Education and (by courtesy) of History at Stanford University. Wineburg directs the Stanford History Education Group, a research and development effort aimed at improving history instruction (http://sheg.stanford.edu). His interdisciplinary scholarship sits at the crossroads of three fields: history, cognitive science, and education, and has been featured on C-SPAN, NPR, and WBUR-Boston, as well as in newspapers across the nation, including the *New York Times*, the *Washington Post,* and *USA TODAY.* Educated at Brown and Berkeley, he taught at the high school and middle school levels before completing his Ph.D. at Stanford in Psychological Studies in Education. His 2002 book, *Historical Thinking and Other Unnatural Acts: Charting the Future of Teaching the Past,* won the Frederic W. Ness Award from the Association of American Colleges and Universities for work that makes the most important contribution to the "improvement of Liberal Education and understanding the Liberal Arts."

Daisy Martin is the Director of History Education for the National History Education Clearinghouse (teachinghistory.org), a federally funded project produced by the Center for History and New Media at George Mason University. A former high school history and civics teacher, she teaches preservice teachers at the University of California at Santa Cruz and Stanford University and works with veteran teachers in a variety of venues, including workshops funded by the Teaching American History grant program, the National Parks Service, and the National Endowment for the Humanities. Martin holds degrees from the University of Michigan, UC Berkeley, and Stanford University, and as a founding member of the Stanford History Education Group she served as its co-director for 2 years. Her current projects include working with teachers to create history performance assessments and investigating states' history/social studies standards and assessment systems.

Chauncey Monte-Sano is Assistant Professor of History and Social Studies Education in the Department of Curriculum & Instruction, University of Maryland. A former high school teacher and National Board Certified teacher, she currently prepares novice teachers for the history classroom and works with veteran history teachers in local school districts through a variety of professional development programs. She has won research grants from the Institute of Education Sciences and the Spencer Foundation and research awards from the National Council for the Social Studies and the American Educational Research Association. As a graduate student at Stanford, she was a founding member of the Stanford History Education Group with Wineburg and Martin. Her current research focuses on understanding and developing students' evidence-based historical writing. Her scholarship has appeared in the *American Educational Research Journal, Theory and Research in Social Education,* the *Journal of the Learning Sciences, Curriculum Inquiry*, and the *Journal of Teacher Education.*